The Rise of the
Shame Society

The Rise of the Shame Society

America's Change from a Guilt Culture into a Shame Culture

Marcel H. Van Herpen

LEXINGTON BOOKS
Lanham • Boulder • New York • London

Published by Lexington Books
An imprint of The Rowman & Littlefield Publishing Group, Inc.
4501 Forbes Boulevard, Suite 200, Lanham, Maryland 20706
www.rowman.com

86-90 Paul Street, London EC2A 4NE

British Library Cataloguing in Publication Information Available

Library of Congress Cataloging-in-Publication Data Available

ISBN 978-1-66692-020-8 (cloth)
ISBN 978-1-66691-469-6 (electronic)

To Ernst Wolff (1949–2021)—Anti-Fascist and Friend

Contents

Acknowledgments

In writing this book I owe a lot to the discussions with members of the Board of the Cicero Foundation, in particular Albert van Driel, Peter Verwey, and Ernst Wolff. Unfortunately Ernst Wolff, a good friend and invaluable discussion partner, passed away in 2021. To him this book is dedicated. I also want to thank Rona Heald, who had a critical look at the English text, the anonymous peer reviewer, and the editorial staff of Lexington Books—especially acquisition editor Courtney Morales and assistant editor Emma Ebert, who, with great professionalism, shepherded the book through the editorial process. Finally I want to thank my wife, Valérie, and my sons, Michiel and Cyrille, who provided continuous and indispensable personal support during the years of research and writing. The responsibility for the book's flaws and limitations is, of course, entirely mine.

Introduction

The Rise of the Modern Shame Society

HOW SOCIALIZATION PATTERNS ARE
CHANGING AND WHAT IT MEANS

Our Western societies are often characterized as "guilt cultures," opposed to non-Western societies, which are considered to be examples of "shame cultures."[1] But is this distinction still valid today? Are we not witnessing the demise of the old Western guilt culture and its gradual replacement by a different model of society: a shame culture? In other words: isn't shame invading our lives together with its twin emotion: humiliation? What are the causes of this change and what does it mean? And how does it impact our daily lives? Is a guilt culture preferable to a shame culture? And if so, why? And if not, why not? This book tries to give answers to these pressing questions. But let us first try to sketch the problem. A good starting point is a book, written by Ruth Benedict during the Second World War, titled *The Chrysanthemum and the Sword*. Ruth Benedict was a special adviser at the US Office of War Information which was dealing with the problem of how to handle the peoples of the occupied countries when the war was over. In her book, published in 1946, she was trying to explain Japan to an American audience. Japan, she argued, was different from America because it had a "shame culture."

True shame cultures rely on external sanctions for good behavior, not, as true guilt cultures do, on an internalized conviction of sin. Shame is a reaction to other people's criticism. A man is shamed either by being openly ridiculed and rejected or by fantasying to himself that he has been made ridiculous. In either case it is a potent sanction. But it requires an audience or at least a man's fantasy of an audience. Guilt does not. In a nation where honor means living up to one's own picture of oneself, a man may suffer from guilt though no man knows of his misdeed and a man's feeling of guilt may actually be relieved by confessing his sin.[2]

Ruth Benedict was convinced of the superiority of guilt over shame as a guarantor of moral behavior, because it is evoked by the individual's conscience and doesn't need the presence or imagined presence of others. Therefore she regretted that "shame is an increasingly heavy burden in the United States and guilt is less extremely felt than in earlier generations. In the United States this is interpreted as a relaxation of morals. There is much truth in this, but that is because we do not expect shame to do the heavy work of morality. . . . "[3]

Benedict's remark that "shame is an increasingly heavy burden in the United States," was a prophetic remark, as was her assessment that shame would be incapable of doing "the heavy work of morality." Her first remark was a sign of great foresight, because in 1946 it was not evident that the United States (and, eventually, other Western societies) would gravitate more and more toward a situation in which shame would become the more dominant way of socialization. However, seventy-five years later there are many indications that her prediction has come true. "Our society *is* a shame-based culture," writes Gershen Kaufman, "but here, shame is *hidden*. There is shame about shame and so it remains under strict taboo. Other cultures, for example, Oriental and Mediterranean, are organized more openly around shame and its counterpart, honor."[4] Another author, Peter Stearns, observed that a Google Ngram search revealed that "references to shame in written texts—in decline in the United States since the mid-nineteenth century—have, in recent decades, increased far more than in other English-speaking countries."[5] Stearns mentions three reasons for this change:

First, a number of conservative judges in the 1960s ruled that shaming was an appropriate punishment for certain crimes like drunken driving or petty theft. The stocks haven't been reintroduced and many higher courts have disputed the new enthusiasm, but many criminals have been required to put shaming signs in their cars or to stand in a mall with a sign proclaiming their wrongdoing. Second, the notorious culture wars in the United States have produced partisan camps eager to shame their opponents. Even liberals, probably hostile to shaming in principle, join the parade, as in the ubiquitous (and so far abortive) efforts to shame our current president [Trump, MHVH] and his supporters. Third, social media have unleashed a torrent of hatred, with fat-shaming and accusations of sexual impropriety, hypocrisy and racism flooding social networks. The efforts can hound victims out of their jobs, force them to relocate—even drive some to suicide.[6]

Stearns and Kaufman are not alone. Other observers come to the same conclusion. One author wrote:

> The way political commentators and other public figures now use "shameful" is not guilt culture in action. It is a throwback to our older shame culture—or, more likely, the vanguard of a new era of shame. "Shameful" in this usage usually is not a careless synonym for "guilty." It is "shameful" in its true sense, deliberately chosen to communicate something about the nature of the person targeted.[7]

Another author, Andy Crouch, pointed to the practice of *doxxing*:

> Typically carried out by anonymous online users with axes to grind and little to lose, doxxing involves making someone's private information public. That includes home addresses, phone numbers, financial histories, medical records—anything that can be found in the endless databases available to canny hackers. Doxxing can be a drive-by prank on most anyone who draws attention. But more often its targets are singled out for humiliation. In a series of events last year that came to be called GamerGate, certain active video gamers targeted journalists, mostly women, who had criticized the outright misogyny found in popular video games. The backlash began with the bilious insults that have become astonishingly common online. But it quickly escalated to "revenge blogs" purporting to reveal those journalists' past indiscretions, and doxxing attacks.[8]

Crouch's article was taken up by *New York Times* commentator David Brooks, who agreed with Crouch's analysis that the United States was moving toward a new kind of shame culture, warning that "the modern shame culture allegedly values inclusion and tolerance, but it can be strangely unmerciful to those who disagree and to those who don't fit in."[9]

The United States is not the only Western country in which one can observe the return in strength of shame. The German philosopher Peter Sloterdijk complained that "here in our country also, conscience has become a hostile foreign country," suggesting that guilt feelings were diminishing.[10] In 2006 in the Netherlands a book was published, entitled *Taboo—100 feelings of which Dutch people are ashamed.* Feelings of shame were reported to be, on average, more prominent in the younger generation. Older respondents felt less shame about things "which were not your fault and thus shame is not necessary. You should be ashamed of things for which you are responsible."[11] In fact these older respondents were less motivated by feelings of shame than by feelings of guilt. The difference between the older and the younger generation could be due to a "cohort effect": the fact that an age cohort becomes less shame-prone as it grows older, but it could also indicate a real generation break in which it announces the rise of a more shame-prone society.

DIFFERENCES BETWEEN SHAME AND GUILT

Between guilt and shame there exist important differences. What are these? Let us enumerate some.

- In the case of guilt we experience "pangs of conscience": we know that we have transgressed a norm, we know that we have done something wrong or, on the contrary, failed to do something that could be morally expected of us. In the case of shame this is different. We don't feel criticized for having done (or refrained from doing) a particular act, but our whole personality—as such—is brought into question.
- In the case of guilt there is a reference to internalized norms of a Freudian *superego* (Über Ich). This superego is the person's conscience, which is the product of the individual's early socialization by the parents, who are the primary mediators of the norms of society. In the case of shame there is a reference to the person's *ego ideal* (Ichideal). The ego ideal consists of the ideal picture the person has formed of himself or herself. Although one seldom succeeds in completely realizing this ideal picture, for the individual it is a model of the person he or she wants to be or wants to become. One feels shame if one fails to live up to this ideal.
- In guilt there is an emphasis on the harm we have caused to others. In shame this is less the case. It is rather a mental pain caused by the low esteem in which we are held by others (or think to be held by others) and—consequently—by ourselves.
- The ways in which we deal with guilt and shame are also different. When we feel guilt we can offer compensation for what we have done and try to repair the wrongdoing. After this reparation the affair is closed. In shame this is not possible, because it is not a single act, but our whole self which is brought into question. Shame, therefore, is a deeper emotion: its ambition is not to return to the *status quo ante*, as is the case of guilt, but a desire rather to change our personality in order to bring it closer to our ego ideal.
- Another difference concerns the way in which both emotions are triggered. In guilt the emotion is evoked by a *voice* (of disapproval). This is normally the inner voice of conscience which represents the original parental voice and parental prohibitions. In the case of shame the emotion is rather evoked by a *look*: it is the other's eyes which trigger shame and lead to the concomitant feeling of one's secret inner self being exposed.

GUILT FEELINGS ARE NOT INNATE, BUT LEARNED

Each human society, small or large, needs some internal order to survive. This order can be maintained by repression and punitive measures. However, it is clear that no society can survive for a long time when its social order is exclusively based on these forms of external coercion. Although no society can function without fear of punishment by the authorities, other mechanisms are far more effective to regulate the behavior of the individual. Amongst these mechanisms are shame and guilt, which are both forms of anxiety which encourage the individual to adopt socially acceptable behavior. Although shame and guilt can lead to the same result, the psychological mechanisms that bring these results about are quite different. Shame and guilt are emotions—like disgust, fear, or sadness. But the difference with other emotions is that shame and guilt are *moral* emotions. They refer to accepted standards of behavior (and, in the case of shame, also to standards of outward appearance) in the surrounding society and penalize the person who transgresses societal norms. Of the two, shame seems more deeply ingrained in the human psyche and to precede guilt in human evolution. Guilt is not something innate in the human species, nor is it present in the form of "sin" in all human societies. "Whatever the origin of the concept of sin," writes the anthropologist Von Fürer-Haimendorf, "it certainly is not encountered in all human societies."[12] According to Jesse Prinz, "Guilt . . . may have analogues in dogs and non-human primates. The problem is that this is not evidence for innateness."[13] "Guilt is a product of nurture," he continues, "that builds on other emotions, a desire for affection, and a general capacity for learning."[14] In the same vein James Breasted writes that "man has been fashioning destructive weapons for possibly a million years, whereas conscience emerged as a social force less than five thousand years ago."[15] Margaret Mead equally observed that the capacity to experience guilt is a later development and may even not be present in many societies:

> We may say, on the basis of comparative cultural data, that the capacity to experience guilt, as a dominant psychological mechanism, is a human capacity which may be either developed or neglected by any given society, and cannot therefore be regarded as either universal or necessary, however desirable it may be found in terms of contemporary ethics.[16]

We should also be aware that guilt feelings have not always been the same. They changed in the course of history. In the beginning guilt was defined rather as *collective* guilt: it referred to the guilt of a people or a group—as was the case, for instance, in the Old Testament, where it refers to the guilt of the Jewish people vis-à-vis Yahweh. Guilt feelings as purely *individual* guilt feelings are rather a modern phenomenon and a concomitant of modern individualism. "In European high culture," writes Willi Oelmüller, "the concept of individual guilt experience and attribution of guilt is developing only slowly and [becomes] definitive only in modern times."[17]

ON THE ORIGINS OF GUILT AND SHAME CULTURES

Thus societies differ in the way in which their members are socialized. Socialization can take place by relying on guilt or on shame, or on a mixture of the two. There are societies which rely more on shame and others which rely more on guilt in the socialization process. The fact that our Western societies were labeled "guilt societies" was explained by the influence of Christianity which emphasized the importance of the individual conscience and of personal guilt. This became clear in the practice of confession—a one-to-one encounter between the sinner and god (the latter represented by the priest), in which the sinner confessed his guilt for having committed certain forbidden acts and god forgave the sinner after the completion of a penance, imposed by the priest. However, to explain Western "guilt society" exclusively by these Christian roots creates some problems: this explanation is challenged by several facts. In the first place there is the "chicken-and-egg" problem: is the emergence of the individual conscience a consequence of the rise of Christianity or are both developments caused by another, third, factor—for instance urbanization? This could explain why not only Christian theologians, but also non-Christian Stoic philosophers, such as Seneca (4 BCE–65 CE)[18] and Emperor Marcus Aurelius (121 CE–180 CE),[19] emphasized the role of the individual conscience in man's moral behavior. According to Michel Foucault,

> Spiritual guidance, examination of oneself, careful scrutinizing by the individual of his acts and thoughts, the way in which he speaks about it to someone else, asking advice from a guide and accepting the rules of conduct he proposes: all this is a quite ancient tradition. Christian authors neither hid this temporal priority, nor denied the kindred relationship between these practices and the exercises which they themselves prescribed.[20]

The rise of the new Christian religion in the Roman Empire, rather than being the cause of this guilt-based morality, was rather the continuation of an already existing spiritual trend, which was an expression of a newly emerging socio-economic and cultural order that promoted this new moral system. The rapid urbanization which took place in the Roman Empire could be a possible explanation. Dorothea Leighton and Clyde Kluckhohn emphasize, for instance, that "'Shame' naturally develops as a major sanction in societies . . . in which there is so little privacy and such constant face-to-face relationships among the people who really count in each other's lives that small peccadillos cannot be hidden."[21] In small, static, tribal, cattle-breeding and agricultural societies in which there are no big cities, moral norms are imposed on the basis of constant face-to-face relationships, which are prone to lead to a shame culture. Compare that with the city of Rome, which, in the second century of our common era, had about one million inhabitants, while other towns in the Roman Empire, such as Alexandria, Ephesus, Carthage, and Antioch, reached up to 200,000 inhabitants. Migrants who left their villages to live in big anonymous conglomerations could no longer be socialized by shame. They needed an inner compass: guilt. Urbanization could therefore be considered as one of the causes of the rise of a guilt culture, although other factors, such as education, culture, and religion, also played a role. *Mutatis mutandis* a process of de-urbanization could be an explanatory factor for the return of a shame culture in the Middle Ages.

> Rome began to shrink early in the fourth century just as Constantinople was expanding rapidly, and Rome continued to decline until its aqueducts were cut during the Gothic Wars of the sixth century. By then its population had dropped to perhaps 10,000 from an Augustan peak of around a million.[22]

This means that within a few centuries Rome would have lost 99 percent (!) of its population. Max Weber also explained the fall of the Roman Empire as a process of de-urbanization. "The later emperors fought the flight of the citizens to the countryside," he wrote.[23] "The city has gone," he continued, "the Carolingian age has no understanding of it at all as a specific concept of administrative law."[24] This process of de-urbanization implied a return to permanent face-to-face relations in small agricultural communities and an ensuing emphasis on socialization patterns which are characterized by shame rather than by guilt. This development could explain why, in the feudal Middle Ages, guilt culture increasingly gave way to a shame culture—notwithstanding the fact that during this period Europeans were organizing crusades to liberate the Holy Land and Catholicism was triumphant. Symbolic of this shame culture was the use of the pillory, a wooden frame with holes for the head and the hands, which was used to expose offenders to public ridicule and offense.

When, in the late Middle Ages and the Renaissance, Europe gradually re-urbanized, this shame culture was gradually replaced by a guilt culture, though without disappearing altogether. This process could also be observed in the American colonies. Peter Stearns, for instance, observes in colonial and early post-independence New England a shift from pervasive use of shame in dealing with children and miscreant adults to guilt, from the 18th to the early 19th century. As community cohesion declined, parents had to find new ways to internalize behavioral guidelines; they were able to use newly intensive love as the basis for instilling a greatly heightened level of guilt. A comparable shift, toward guilt rather than public shaming, describes innovations in the principles of social discipline and criminal justice in the same period.[25]

During the last two centuries this evolution from a shame culture to a guilt culture became a general pattern in most Western societies. According to a Dutch sociologist, "conscience is not a universal human, but as concerns Western Europe, an eighteenth century product."[26] It is interesting that the recent rise of shame has taken place despite a growing urbanization, under the influence of new cultural, educational, and technological factors which will be analyzed in this book.

STRUCTURE OF THE BOOK

Prologue: Guilt versus Shame (Chapters 1 and 2)

Chapter 1 poses the question of whether a guilt culture or a shame culture is preferable. A guilt morality has sometimes been accused of being too severe—an argument put forward not only by Nietzsche, but also by Freud. However, it is argued that this fear seems to be exaggerated, because in Western societies, rather than a supposed increase in guilt feelings, one can observe its gradual decrease and its progressive replacement by a shame morality. This shame morality is boosted by different factors, such as modern permissive child-rearing methods, the influence of the social media, and a rise in narcissism.

Chapter 2 analyzes the active side of shame: the practice of shaming. Recently shaming practices have made a comeback, particularly among young people who are using the social media to shame each other. Also governments are currently tempted to reintroduce shaming penalties in criminal law. The author analyzes the #MeToo movement, one of the most successful shaming actions in recent years, which is often presented as a tool of the powerless against the powerful. The author weighs the arguments for and against shaming.

Part I: The Rise of the Western Guilt Society (Chapters 3–7)

Modern individualism is the philosophical and ideological basis of the Western guilt culture. However, individualism is not an unequivocal concept.

In Part I the author tries to disentangle the different meanings of individualism and to explore how these different versions successively imposed themselves in Western society and contributed to the transformation of the Western guilt culture into a shame culture.

Chapter 3 explores the early stages of modern individualism. Religious, philosophical, and political individualism are discussed in turn—how they emphasize the moral value of the individual and give the individual conscience a central place. Special attention is paid to the emergence in the nineteenth century of an individualistic lifestyle, which considers the loner as its personality ideal. The loner took different forms: in the United States he was embodied in the pioneer and the cowboy, in Europe rather in the figure of the creative artist or 'bohemian.'

Chapter 4 analyzes economic individualism, which becomes dominant at the end of the nineteenth century with the emergence of modern industrial society. Economic individualism is often considered individualism's "ugly face." While political individualism emphasized the legal and political equality of citizens, economic individualism is at odds with the earlier forms of individualism by emphasizing the differences between citizens. It is argued that the economic individualism of capitalist society is a Janus-faced phenomenon: although it led to economic inequality, it also brought about an affluent society which permitted the masses to copy the 'conspicuous consumption' of the rich. Economic individualism created the new phenomenon of modern consumerism.

Chapter 5 analyzes the societal and psychological changes brought about by the new consumer society, which were first observed by David Riesman and his collaborators in *The Lonely Crowd.* Riesman described a new character type which emerged in the affluent society: the "other-directed person," whom he distinguished from the former "inner-directed person." Instead of following his individual conscience, the "other-directed person" is highly conformist, adapting his behavior to his peers rather than his parents. One can distinguish here the first signs of the emergence of a shame society.

Chapter 6 explores in more detail the influence of the consumer society and consumerism on the individual psyche, particularly the phenomenon that people soon become disaffected and bored in a "joyless economy" which does not satisfy their "deeper needs," as defined by Abraham Maslow. As a reaction they begin to turn their attention inward in search of their "authentic, true self."

Chapter 7 analyzes the consequences of this search for one's "authentic self," which supposes the existence of some "inner core" which one can discover through introspection. The author argues that this introduced a completely new form of individualism: expressive individualism. While the nineteenth-century *loner* sought spatial isolation, the modern individual, in search of his "authentic self," is in search of psychological isolation: he is not looking outward, but inward.

Part II: Narcissistic Individualism and the Rise of the Modern Shame Society (Chapters 8–11)

In this part the author describes the different phases of the modern shame revolution which is developing in parallel with increasing narcissism.

Chapter 8 analyzes the emergence of a new personality type which is characteristic of the emerging shame society: the narcissistic personality. Sociologists, like Amitai Etzioni and Robert Putnam, criticized the "rampant individualism" and the loosening of social ties which they observed in Western societies. The author argues that these are only side effects of a broader narcissism explosion.

Chapter 9 explores the narcissist's self-admiration, which is based on his or her looks. The narcissist is continually in search of the perfect body, a tendency which started after the Second World War as a trend to be healthy and to stay young. In recent years this tendency became an obsessive preoccupation with one's body, leading to a massive rise in plastic surgery. While women submitted to a weight-loss cult, men increasingly sought salvation in body sculpting and bodybuilding.

Chapter 10 analyzes how this body improvement trend has gone global. Even a man like Putin had his face botoxed. In China there has been a surge in eyelid operations to get more 'Western' eyes. Iran has become the paradise for 'nose jobs.' These global trends have been reinforced by the social media which offer the possibility of creating "improved selfies." These "improved selfies," particularly for the young generation, are a stimulus to seeking cosmetic surgery.

Chapter 11 analyzes a new phase in the narcissism explosion: the "happiness revolution." People, dissatisfied with the results of body improvement, developed a new ideal: happiness. In an individualist culture this pursuit of happiness is considered a purely individual enterprise. Happiness is presented as an act of pure will and not as something dependent on the surrounding society, fate, and/or circumstances. Happiness has become a question of choice and willpower. This individualistic search for happiness has completely neglected the political and societal causes of happiness. Companies soon followed this trend, appointing "Chief Happiness Officers" who had the task of promoting individual wellbeing without challenging the alienating structures of society.

Part III: The Development of a New Dialectic: "Old Shame" versus "New Shame" (Chapters 12–16)

In this part it is argued that although shame has become a major feature of contemporary Western society, it is not a static, but a dynamic phenomenon. In society one can observe trends which lead to shaming, as well as to de-shaming. We can therefore speak about "old shame" and "new shame." The development of "old shame" is explained using three examples: firstly, the growing sensitivity of society to the pain caused by anti-Black racism; secondly, the decrease in anti-gay prejudices, and, thirdly, efforts to end the stigmatization of people with disabilities. At the same time there are examples of "new shame," such as the stigmatization of obese people and of the so-called hikikomori—young, self-isolating hermits, who live with their parents and don't go to school or work. The author argues that "old shame" is diminishing because society is becoming more sensitive about the injustice of stigmata for ascribed statuses over which people have no control. On the other hand, new stigmata develop for statuses which one considers as a question of personal choice or a lack of willpower.

In chapter 12 the author explores anti-Black racism. Is this really on the way towards becoming "old shame"? This question is elaborated with reference to the works of Toni Morrison, Eldridge Cleaver, Frantz Fanon, and W. E. B. Du Bois. It shows how the victims of anti-Black racism used three strategies: first, conquering self-hate, second, a "re-evaluation struggle" in which one emphasizes one's pride—as, for instance, in the slogan "Black is beautiful"—and, third, civil and political action. However, for shame to become "old shame" a change in the attitude of the white population is also necessary. Such a change seems to be taking place as the broad worldwide support for the Black Lives Matter movement and the protests after the killing of George Floyd seem to show. This support came from the white, as well as the Black population. As regards the causes of this change the author mentions increased empathy in the white population, as well as what Samuel Huntington called "racial blurring"—the increase in mixed-race marriages. Despite these hopeful signs of progress, the author warns that it might still be too early to speak in this case of "old shame"—as long as the Black population is the victim of police brutality, discrimination in the housing and job markets, and humiliating "micro-aggressions."

Chapter 13 analyzes the de-shaming processes of two other stigmatized groups: LGBTQ people and people with disabilities. In both groups one can observe the same three strategies: turning the aggression outward, developing pride, and conducting social and political action. In the UK it was the imprisonment in 1954 of Peter Wildeblood, a gay journalist, which led to a movement to decriminalize gay sex. In the United States it was the Stonewall Riots in June 1969 which led to the Gay Pride movement, which gathered momentum to become a global movement. A similar development can be observed for people with disabilities. In 1968 disabled people in wheelchairs conducted "Rolling Squads" actions in Berkeley, which led to the Independent Living Movement and to the foundation of the Disabled People's International. While here too it may be too early to speak of "old shame," progress in the de-shaming of both groups is undeniable.

Chapter 14 analyzes an example of "new shame": the so-called fat shaming of obese people. This fat shaming takes aggressive forms and the obese person cannot reckon on any empathy, because his or her obesity is considered as a personal choice. If the person had more strength of character, so people tend to think, he or she wouldn't be obese. However, the author argues that this legitimation of the discrimination against obese people by making them personally responsible for their obesity is not justified, because obesity is not just a question of lifestyle or character, but has many still unknown causes, genetic and socio-economic, as well as physiological, and overcoming obesity is certainly not only a question of pure willpower.

Chapter 15 analyzes another example of "new shame": the case of the so-called hikikomori, a phenomenon which was first observed in Japan, but has also become more frequent in Western countries. These are young people who self-isolate and often stay for months and even years in their bedroom in their parents' home. As in the case of fat-shaming the hikikomori cannot count on any empathy, because their self-isolation is considered as a personal choice—what, in most cases, it isn't.

Chapter 16, the concluding chapter, explores the concepts of "self-esteem," "self-respect," and "respect," which are important if one wants to fight shame. While self-esteem is based on comparison with others, self-respect digs deeper in the self: one respects oneself not with reference to other people, but with reference to a standard. A third concept is "respect." This is different from "self-esteem" and self-respect," because here it is not oneself, but others, who are the judges. The author distinguishes "appraisal respect"—an assessment of the qualities of the other—and "recognition respect"—respect owed to all persons as human beings. The author concludes that the latter form of respect, which was defended by Immanuel Kant, is important in the fight against shame.

NOTES

1. English quotes from original French, German, Italian, Russian, and Dutch texts have been translated by the author.

2. Ruth Benedict, *The Chrysanthemum and the Sword—Patterns of Japanese Culture*, with a new Foreword by Ian Buruma (Boston and New York: Houghton Mifflin Company, 2005), p. 223.

3. Ibid., pp. 223–224.

4. Gershen Kaufman, *Shame—The Power of Caring*, (Rochester, VT: Schenkman Books, Inc; 1985), p. 29.

5. Peter Stearns, "Does American culture shame too much—or not enough?" *The Conversation*, November 7, 2017.

6. Ibid.

7. Bonnie Kristian, "Our political obsession with shame," *The Week*, February 6, 2019. https://theweek.com/articles/821655/political-obsession-shame.

8. Andy Crouch, "Andy Crouch: The Return of Shame," *Christianity Today*, March 10, 2015. https://www.christianitytoday.com/ct/2015/march/andy-crouch-gospel-in -age-of-public-shame.html. The complete text is available at https://andy-crouch.com /articles/the_return_of_shame.

9. David Brooks, "The Shame Culture," *The New York Times*, March 15, 2016. https://www.nytimes.com/2016/03/15/opinion/the-shame-culture.html.

10. Peter Sloterdijk, *Zeilen und Tage—Notizen 2008–2011*, (Berlin: Suhrkamp Verlag, 2014), p. 112.

11. Marcel Maassen and Frans Oosterwijk, *Taboe—100 gevoelens waar Nederlanders zich voor schamen*, (Amsterdam: TNS NIPO/Uitgeverij Balans, 2006), p. 181.

12. Christoph von Fürer-Haimendorf, "The sense of sin in cross-cultural perspective," *The Journal of the Royal Anthropological Institute*, 1974, Volume 9, p. 553.

13. Jesse J. Prinz, *Gut Reactions—A Perceptual Theory of Emotion*, (Oxford and New York: Oxford University Press, 2004), p. 128.

14. Ibid., p. 129.

15. James H. Breasted, *The Dawn of Conscience*, (New York and London: Charles Scribner's Sons, 1934), p. ix.

16. Margaret Mead, "Third Plenary Session on Collective Guilt," in J. C. Flugel (ed.), *Proceedings of the International Conference on Medical Psychotherapy, Volume III*, (London and New York: Columbia University Press, 1948), p. 64.

17. Willi Oelmüller, "Schwierigkeiten mit dem Schuldbegriff," in Hans Michael Baumgartner and Albin Eser (eds), *Schuld und Verantwortung—Philosophische und juristische Beiträge zur Zurechenbarkeit menschlichen Handelns*, (Tübingen: J. C. B. Mohr (Paul Siebeck), 1983), p. 19.

18. G. Molenaar writes that "In the writings of the younger Seneca the term *conscientia* occurs for the first time in the work of a formal representative of the Stoa." (G. Molenaar, "Seneca's use of the term *conscientia*," *Mnemosyne*, Vol. 22, Fasc. 2 (1969), p. 67).

19. In his *Meditations* Marcus Aurelius speaks about the individual conscience as "the very divinity seated within you, subordinating your private impulses to itself, examining your thoughts . . . " (Marcus Aurelius, *Meditations*, [New York: Knopf Doubleday, 2009], p. 14).

20. Michel Foucault, *Les aveux de la chair (Histoire de la sexualité 4)*, (Paris: Éditions Gallimard, 2018), p. 106.

21. Dorothea Leighton and Clyde Kluckhohn, *Children of the People: The Navaho Individual and His Development,* (Cambridge, MA: Harvard University Press, 1947), p. 106.

22. Greg Woolf, *The Life and Death of Ancient Cities: A Natural History,* (Oxford and New York: Oxford University Press, 2020), p. 405.

23. Max Weber, "Die sozialen Gründe des Untergangs der antiken Kultur," in Max Weber, *Schriften 1894–1922,* selected by Dirk Kaesler, (Stuttgart: Kröner Verlag, 2002), p. 65.

24. Ibid., p. 66.

25. Peter N. Stearns, "History of Emotions: Issues of Change and Impact," in Michael Lewis and Jeannette M. Haviland-Jones (eds), *Handbook of the Emotions,* (New York and London: The Guilford Press, 2000), pp. 21–22.

26. Paul Kapteyn, "Het geweten is een modern product," *De Gids,* 141, Nr. 9/10, 1978, p. 567.

Prologue: Guilt versus Shame

Chapter 1

What Is Shame and What Is Guilt and Which of the Two Is "Better"?

What exactly is "guilt" and what is "shame" and how do they relate to each other? To begin with: both are anxieties, intrapsychic tensions, and both play an important role in the socialization of individuals. When we speak here of "guilt" or "shame" we aren't referring to objective facts or events, but to the subjective *emotions* of the individual.[1] Guilt, according to Gerhart Piers, "is the painful internal tension generated whenever the emotionally highly charged barrier erected by the superego is being touched or transgressed."[2] Guilt has to do with the *transgression of norms* of the superego (the Freudian *Über Ich*). These norms are the product of the child's early socialization through the internalization of the parents' punishments, threatened punishments, or imagined punishments. These punishments or imagined punishments evoke aggression in the child, but this aggression is not turned outward, but inward, leading to the formation of the superego. Guilt is the feeling which one is likely to experience when one enters morally forbidden territory. Guilt is associated with "an inner voice of conscience" which represents the voices of the parents, the instances of the individual's primary socialization. An individual feels guilt when his behavior challenges the prohibitions of the punitive parents. Feelings of guilt cause psychic pain, a reason that we speak about "pangs of conscience." Guilt concerns a particular act or a negligent action which damages others. However, the individual can make amends for his transgression by repairing the damage he has caused.

Shame is different. "Shame arises out of a tension between the ego and the ego ideal," writes Gerhart Piers, "not between ego and superego as in guilt."[3] Shame is a feeling of inadequacy, of not being *à la hauteur* of one's ideal self-image. It is a feeling of failing to live up to the standards one has set oneself: it is not a transgression, as in guilt, but a feeling of a *shortcoming*. This feeling of inadequacy is often imposed by society, which means: by others. When one experiences shame one feels weak and exposed. This

1

feeling is stronger when the exposure happens suddenly and unexpectedly. Each of us has experienced feelings of shame and knows how deeply it can affect the psyche. Léon Wurmser, for instance, remembers the feelings of shame he experienced in his early childhood as a Jewish boy in Switzerland. These feelings of shame were induced by his classmates and boosted by the anti-Semitic Nazi propaganda coming from nearby Germany:

> When I was about seven I was dismayed to learn from other children that I was unacceptable because I belonged to another "race." Even though my family had lived in that little town for three generations, we still were treated as foreigners and intruders. For years my feeling of being an inferior, derided outcast was incessantly deepened by German propaganda from across the border a few miles away, heaping shame and contempt on all I was and knew. . . . I therefore know very well from my own inner life the significance of shame and disgrace.[4]

It is others who induce shame. This fact is also described by the French author André Gide (1869–1951) in one of his journals, where he writes:

> Too often someone else's prejudice obliges us and, if only our sensibility is greater than our force of character, we let ourselves be absorbed by the image that we are aware someone else has formed of us. Yes, the presence of others deforms us and, in spite of ourselves, we assume for a time the virtues or vices they attribute to us. . . . Thus we are carried by opinion.[5]

Sartre has formulated the same truth in the famous phrase: *L'enfer c'est les autres,* ("Hell is other people"), said by one of the main characters of his play *Huis clos* ("No Exit"). The phrase resumes his own thoughts on shame which he elaborated in his magnum opus *L'être et le néant* ("Being and Nothingness"), which was published in 1943.

> Let us think, for example, about shame. . . . It is the shameful apprehension *of* something and this something is *me*. I am ashamed of what I *am*. Shame realizes therefore an intimate relationship between me and myself: through shame I have discovered an aspect of *my* being. . . . Shame in its primary structure is shame *before someone*. . . . I am ashamed of myself for the way I appear to others. And by the very presence of others I am capable of judging myself as an object, because it is as an object that I appear to others. . . . This image ought, indeed, to be completely attributable to these others and should not "touch" me. I might feel irritation, anger about it, as before a bad portrait of myself which represents me as ugly or gives me an unattractive expression which I don't actually have. However, in that case I wouldn't be affected to my inner core: shame is, by its nature, *recognition*. I recognize that I *am* such as the other is seeing me.[6]

Sartre is formulating here some basic facts. First, that shame is induced by others who dehumanize me by making me into an object. Second, that although this should not "touch" me because I should know better, it affects me because I accept their negative view of myself. Third, that shame is a much deeper emotion than guilt, because it affects our "inner core," that is: our identity, our whole person, while guilt only concerns one aspect of our identity: our behavior.

GUILT: AN UNBEARABLE BURDEN?

Among philosophers and psychologists a debate is taking place about the respective emotional "costs and benefits" of shame and guilt as mechanisms of socialization and the question of which of the two might be preferable. This debate has been raging for a while and has become more heated since there are clear indications that in our Western societies the socializing role, traditionally fulfilled by guilt, is being been taken over, gradually and surreptitiously, by shame. This does not mean that guilt feelings have completely disappeared, but in recent years the balance between the two has clearly changed in favor of shame. The question is which of these two emotions is best fitted to socializing the individual, adapting them to the demands of society, without *over*-adapting them, while causing a minimum of psychological pain. Until recently, at least to the middle of the twentieth century, the conclusion was clear: Western societies were "guilt cultures" and the implicit message was that "this is how it should be." In 1959 the American psychologist Erik H. Erikson, for instance, still spoke without reservation about "our guilt-culture."[7] Most theorists valued the "guilt-prone" individual, who was considered an autonomous individual, freely choosing his path in life, led by his individual conscience. Ruth Benedict, for instance, was convinced of the superiority of the Western "guilt culture" vis-à-vis the Japanese and Asian "shame cultures."

However, this positive evaluation of Western "guilt culture" was far from unanimous. Friedrich Nietzsche (1844–1900) was one of the first to attack modern man's sense of guilt and bad conscience. In his essay "On the Genealogy of Morality," published in 1887, Nietzsche considered the individual conscience as "instincts of the wild, free, roaming man [which were] turned against man himself."[8] Describing the individual conscience as "instincts [which were] turned against man himself," Nietzsche could be seen as a precursor of Freud, who equally defined the conscience as the product of sexual and aggressive drives which were turned inward as a punishing instance against the individual's ego. Another writer who expressed his mistrust in guilt was William James (1842–1910), who thought that feelings of guilt, should they be too strong, would hinder the development of "healthy-mindedness."

> Within the Christian body, for which repentance of sins has from the beginning been the critical religious act, healthy-mindedness has always come forward with its milder interpretation. Repentance according to such healthy-minded Christians means *getting away from* the sin, not groaning and writhing over its commission. The Catholic practice of confession and absolution is in one of its aspects little more than a systematic method of keeping healthy-mindedness on top. . . . Any Catholic will tell us how clean and fresh and free he feels after the purging operation.[9]

It is telling that James, a non-Catholic, had such a positive view of the Catholic practice of confession as a means to alleviate a sense of guilt, which he considered contrary to "healthy-mindedness." Sigmund Freud (1856–1939) did not share Nietzsche's negative attitude toward guilt, but in his later work he seemed to share William James's fear that feelings of guilt could become too strong. In "Civilization and Its Discontents" (1930) he expressed his concern that feelings of guilt, which, as such, played a positive role in the socialization of the individual, could proliferate dangerously and become a source of psychological suffering. In this case, he wrote,

> The superego tortures the sinful ego with anxiety, itching for an opportunity to let it be punished by the outside world. At this second stage of development the conscience shows a characteristic, which did not exist in the first [stage] and which is not easy to explain. The more virtuous a person is, the stricter and more distrustful he will behave towards himself, so that in the end those who have made most progress in saintliness accuse themselves of the worst sinfulness.[10]

THE DECLINE OF GUILT

Even for Freud, "the inventor and father of the superego," guilt feelings were not innocent in case they should become too powerful. However, with hindsight Freud's fear of the development of an extremely punitive superego seems to be exaggerated. Although this tendency could be observed in certain rigorous protestant and Calvinist sects, it became increasingly rare with the progressive secularization of Western society. "Many of the objections to guilt . . . ," writes Hilary Bok, "are, I believe, objections only to one or another distorted form of guilt. Certainly only those distortions could be described as the vengeance of a tyrannical superego, a crippling manifestation of self-hatred, or a neurotic preoccupation with one's own iniquity at the expense of any concrete attempt at change."[11] In the same vein Vladimir Jankélévitch, a French philosopher, writes:

> The bad conscience is rare; so rare that it is, globally speaking, hardly a psychological experience. . . . With the exception of Boris Godunov and Macbeth everybody has in general a good conscience. It is well known that no one admits to being wrong, nor considers himself in any way guilty; everyone is convinced of his own right and of the wrongdoings done to him by others. Wicked or not, egoists are in general very happy, very satisfied with what they do and very often they enjoy excellent sleep; they never regret their meanness. . . .[12]

Here Jankélévitch has put his finger on an important fact: that guilt feelings in Western society—instead of increasing and therefore becoming unbearable, as Freud feared—have substantially *decreased* to the point that "no one admits to being wrong, nor considers himself in any way guilty." The French author Albert Camus (1913–1960), Nobel Prize in Literature winner, expressed the same idea in his novel *La Chute,* where he wrote: "The most natural idea of man, the one which comes to him naively, as from the very depths of his nature, is the idea of his innocence. . . . Everyone insists on being innocent, at all costs, even if he has to blame the whole of mankind and heaven itself."[13] His compatriot, the philosopher Paul Ricoeur (1913–2005), who, in his earlier work, still criticized Western society for its "overdose" of feelings of guilt, surprisingly praised guilt in one of his final interviews. When the interviewer asked him: "Why this change?" Ricoeur answered: "Undoubtedly because in many respects we are living now in a time in which there is a lack of guilt feelings, in the sense that certain persons tolerate the intolerable, and others don't feel guilt. We live in a culture in which there are people who don't have guilt feelings."[14] And he continued:

> To hurt means to hurt 'someone,' it is to cause someone to suffer. Thus, taking the measure of the harm done to someone else and relating this harm to myself as the author, makes guilt a healthy and positive feeling. In this respect I'm thinking of some very concrete problems. Judges, and particularly children's court judges, say that because feelings of guilt have disappeared, there are really very few possibilities of rehabilitation left. And this is true for each age category. We have today to deal with young adolescents who, for instance, feel no guilt for having killed.[15]

SHAME AS A TOOL OF EDUCATION

Apparently, the sense of guilt is becoming increasingly rare. The question is: why did feelings of guilt in the Western world decrease and what are the consequences? According to Helen Merrell Lynd one of the reasons for the decline of guilt is the emergence of new approaches in child rearing. She observed that

> Although the concept of guilt is prevalent in philosophical explanations of man's lot, contemporary methods of child rearing, of teaching, of social counseling—except perhaps in some religious groups—do not ostensibly attempt to develop and make use of a sense of guilt. Terms associated with guilt have tended to be dropped as inciters to desirable action. Sophisticated parents, teachers, or therapists no longer say that a child is good or bad. But the words good and bad have been replaced by mature and immature, productive and unproductive, socially adjusted and maladjusted. And when these words are used by the teacher, the counselor, or the therapist they carry the same weight as the earlier good and bad.[16]

Another author who blamed changed childrearing methods was the French psychoanalyst Cornelius Castoriadis, who observed that "the family is no longer a normative center: parents don't know what they should permit or forbid. And they have a bad conscience about forbidding, as well as about not forbidding."[17] And he continued: "But let us focus on this point: what does it mean to be a father? Is it simply to feed a family?"[18] Castoriadis deplored the fact that fathers no longer played their former normative roles. "At the same time . . . ," he observed, "there is a diminishing sense of reality for children . . . one should not deprive them, not frustrate them, not hurt them, one should always 'understand' them."[19] Children are overprotected, not to say "pampered," and unacceptable behavior is not corrected in time.

Helen Merrell Lynd observed that child rearing practices increasingly made use of a reference to the ego ideal, that is: to shame. However, an author who explicitly *recommended* these practices, is Herbert Morris. "A child hits a playmate," he writes, "he is told that that is a bad thing to do, that it is wrong to hit others; the next time he does it, he may be punished; he meets with 'you're a bad boy.'"[20] "But," he continues, "the parent may respond differently to the conduct. He may say to the child of whose conduct he disapproves, 'that is what an animal does, not a human being' and then turn away from the child . . . we have here the seeds of a morality, let us call it a 'shame morality.' . . . "[21] Morris formulates eight differences between a "shame morality" and a "guilt morality," which, according to him, would prove the superiority of a shame morality. They are interesting enough to quote them in full length.

> First, [in a shame morality] conduct is evaluated through comparison and contrast with a certain model identity."[22] "Second, the shame morality is a scale morality not, like guilt, a threshold morality. There is the conception of a good

toward which we may have travelled some distance but not the whole way. . . . Third . . . with shame we may focus on failure to achieve an ideal, perfection, some maximum whereas with guilt it is a minimum demand that has not been met. Fourth, shame unlike guilt, is not essentially tied to fault. . . . Shame . . . may arise through failure to do the extraordinary. We may feel either guilt or shame in behaving as a coward; we may feel shame and not guilt in failing to behave as a hero. Fifth . . . the shame response focuses on failing to be a worthy person as one conceives it, rather than on failing to meet one's obligations to others. . . .[23] Sixth . . . shame leads to creativity; guilt to restoration. Seventh, shame connects with sight and guilt with hearing . . . with shame we want to sink into the ground, we cannot stand the sight of us. With guilt the urge is to communicate, to be listened to, to confess. Eighth, shame links essentially to worth concepts and guilt does not. We may react to the shameful person with contempt; to the guilty we react with condemnation. . . . The shameful is not worthy of association; the guilty is still worthy but a price must be paid.[24]

Morris presents most of these eight differences between guilt and shame as that many arguments in favor of a shame morality. However, the question is: do they pass the test? The first three stress the importance of the *ego ideal* in the education process: it is a model one wants to emulate. One measures oneself against the model and as long as one feels that one is lagging behind the ideal one will increase one's efforts. This can indeed lead to creativity, as Morris writes, but also to depression when unrealistic and exaggerated expectations do not materialize. More importantly: Morris forgets that—as in the case of guilt feelings which can become unbearable when the super-ego is too severe—equally the ego ideal can become excessively demanding when the individual nurtures narcissistic delusions of glory and greatness. Shame, writes Morris, "may arise through failure to do the extraordinary." But should one aim "to do the extraordinary?" Extraordinary and even heroic acts are often spontaneously done by ordinary people who neither aim, nor plan to do the extraordinary. "We may react to the shameful person with contempt," writes Morris. At first sight this sounds okay: doesn't a shameful person *deserve* our contempt? However, in an environment in which shaming becomes an established practice shaming will not be restricted to those whose moral behavior deserves contempt. A shame society is a competitive society in which one can raise one's self-image by lowering the other's reputation. Contempt of others—deserved or not deserved—is a weapon in this war of reputations. "The shameful is not worthy of association," writes Morris: the shameful is stigmatized, isolated, and expelled from society, a treatment which can not only make people depressed, but even bring them to suicide. Compare this with the humane way a guilt society treats its offenders: after punishment even the most serious criminal gets the chance to be resocialized and reintegrated into society and to continue his life with a clean slate.

WHY MORAL GUILT IS
PREFERABLE TO MORAL SHAME

This last point is a reason for Martha Nussbaum preferring a socialization based on guilt over a socialization based on shame. "Moral guilt is so much better than shame," she writes, "because it can be atoned for, it does not sully the entirety of one's being. It is a dignified emotion compatible with optimism about one's own prospects."[25] "Thus in my account," she writes elsewhere, "guilt is potentially creative, connected with reparation, forgiveness, and the acceptance of limits to aggression."[26] She admits that "guilt can, of course, be excessive and oppressive, and there can be a corresponding excessive focus on reparation, one that is unhealthily self-tormenting. On the other side, shame of a specific and limited sort can be constructive, motivating a pursuit of valuable ideals, within a context where one already renounces the demands of narcissism. But in their role at a pivotal stage of a child's life, shame, with its connection to narcissism, would appear to be the emotion, of these two, that poses the bigger danger to development."[27] Nussbaum concludes: " . . . I am inclined to say that shame is always dangerous in the child-rearing process. Even if one is dealing with a persistent habit, a focus on guilt about bad acts, accompanied by an expression of love for the child, seems to be a wiser strategy than an appeal to shame, which can too easily seem debasing."[28]

Nussbaum rightly acknowledges that the ego ideal can have a positive influence, but only where it is free from the narcissism which leads to an inflated self-image and grandiose dreams of unlimited power. She shares the view of Heinz Kohut, who pleads not to suppress narcissistic needs, but rather to domesticate them and "to transform archaic grandiosity and exhibitionism into realistic self-respect and a moderate, but joyful self-esteem."[29] The problem, however, is that there are clear indications that in our society not the moderate, but the extreme forms of narcissism are on the rise.[30] While the guilt-prone individual is focused on his acts and the consequences of his acts for others, the narcissist is primarily focused on himself and not on his acts, nor on the consequences of his acts for others. His only concern is his own feelings. According to Richard Sennett, for the narcissist, "'What am I really feeling?' becomes a question which, in this personality profile, gradually detaches itself from and overrides the question 'What am I doing?'"[31] Apart from this navel gazing and the focus on his personal feelings, the narcissist's tendency to self-absorption leads him not so much to assess his actual behavior, but rather to indulge in grandiose dreams of his 'potential' and his 'innate qualities': "judgments are made about a person's 'promise,' about what he could do, rather than is doing now or has done."[32] While a guilt morality refers to the individual's actual behavior, the narcissist's shame morality refers rather to his limitless ambitions.

THE LINK BETWEEN GUILT AND RESPONSIBILITY

But there are more reasons to be skeptical about a shame morality. One of these is the fact that a shame morality—different from a guilt morality—refers not only to bad acts, but also to other deviations from the norm, which can be someone's social class, his physical appearance, sexual preference, disability, intelligence, etcetera. Most of these differences are not the result of a personal choice, which means that the individual cannot be held responsible for them. However, in a shame society that is exactly what happens. It tends to breed intolerance against people who deviate from the norm, imposing a suffocating conformity. "The final injunction," writes Gershen Kaufman, "is to be *popular* and *conform.* In a culture which esteems popularity and conformity, individuality is neither recognized nor valued. Being *different* from others becomes shameful. To avoid shame, one must avoid being different, or *seen* as different. The awareness of difference translates into feeling lesser, deficient."[33] A shame society is an eminently *competitive* society. Individuals not only compete to realize their often inflated self-images, but they also compete in convincing others and make them believe that they are "successful" and lead interesting and fulfilling lives. It is clear that in this competition many people, despite their sustained efforts, will be disappointed and that this disappointment will express itself in frustration, depression, or rage. For this reason it is not surprising that in our society both depression and aggression are on the rise. A guilt morality, on the contrary, is more "social" than a shame morality, because it is less self-oriented: it establishes a direct link between man's actions and the consequences these actions have for other people.

An additional concern is the fact that a shame morality has a tenuous relationship with the moral principle of responsibility. "Responsibility is a variant of guilt feeling," writes Helen Lewis.[34] Indeed. The root of the word "responsible" is "response" and this should be taken literally. It means that a person has to *answer* the question *why* he has done a certain act, because as a free person he had the choice to perform the act or to refrain from it. A guilt morality looks back to an individual's behavior and is therefore an eminently *ethical* morality. But responsibility does not only concern deeds and actions which are performed in the past. Equally, it concerns the eventual consequences of one's actions *in the future.* In recent decades this kind of responsibility has become increasingly important. It presupposes the existence of a societal bond and the willingness of individuals to take the interests of others into consideration—people they don't know: future generations or peoples living at the other side of the globe. In modern, technological society this kind of responsibility has massively increased. The climate crisis, caused by the warming of the atmosphere, is only one example. The COVID-19 pandemic is another. "Responsibility . . . ," writes Hans Jonas, "is a function of power and knowledge. . . . In the past both were so limited that as regards the future most had to be left to fate and the permanence of the natural order and all attention was focused on doing things here and now in the right way."[35] However, such a "benign neglect"—or, maybe, rather not so benign neglect— of the consequences of our actions for future generations or other peoples is no longer possible, because, as Jonas rightly observes,

> In this century one has reached the point, which has been long in the making, where the danger has become manifest and critical. With power and intellect comes responsibility. This has been clear from time immemorial for the field of human relations. The fact that recently this responsibility extends beyond that to the condition of the biosphere and the future survival of the human race, is just a result of the expansion of power over these things, which is primarily a power of destruction.[36]

One might ask oneself whether a society in which the sense of guilt—and with it: one's ability to feel responsible—are decreasing can foster this wider sense of responsibility, essential for sustained action to save humankind and our planet.[37] "It seems to me that the fact that in shame we are rejecting responsibility for what depends on us has less often been asserted—at least by philosophers," writes Ruwen Ogien.[38] Therefore, "shame cannot be considered as a commendable attitude in consequentialist theories which orient us toward the future. . . . "[39] He is right. The gradual transformation of our Western societies from guilt cultures into shame cultures could have many, still unknown, negative consequences—not only for the present generation, but also for future generations.

NOTES

1. "Guilt" can have both an objective and a subjective connotation. The judge can decide on the (objective) guilt of a criminal, while the criminal need not have any (subjective) sense of guilt. The same is true for (objective) shameful behavior which bystanders experience as "shameful" (e.g. someone urinating in public), while the person in question seems to be unashamed. In this chapter we refer to "guilt" and "shame" as subjective emotions.

2. Gerhart Piers and Milton B. Singer, *Shame and Guilt—A Psychoanalytic and Cultural Study,* (New York: W. W. Norton & Company, Inc., 1971), p. 16.

3. Ibid., p. 23. Piers and Singer distance themselves from the Freudian orthodoxy. For Freud the superego contained *both* the parental prohibitions and the ideal images. I go with Piers' and Singer's distinction between the superego on the one hand and the ego ideal on the other, which more successfully takes into account the differences between prohibitions on the one hand and ideals on the other, which play a major role in the development of guilt and shame respectively.

4. Léon Wurmser, *The Mask of Shame,* (Baltimore and London: The Johns Hopkins University Press, 1981), pp. 2–3.

5. André Gide, *Journals,* Volume 3: 1928–1939, (Urbana and Chicago: University of Illinois Press, 2000), p. 34, (Journal 1928).

6. Jean-Paul Sartre, *L'Être et le néant—Essai d'ontologie phénoménologique,* (Paris: Gallimard, 1973), pp. 275–276. (Emphasis in the original, MHVH).

7. Erik H. Erikson, *Identity and the Life Cycle,* (New York and London: W. W. Norton & Company, 1994), p. 27. (First published in 1959).

8. Friedrich Nietzsche, "Zur Genealogie der Moral," in Friedrich Nietzsche, *Werke in Drei Bänden,* Volume 2, (Munich: Carl Hanser Verlag, 1977), p. 825.

9. William James, *The Varieties of Religious Experience—A Study in Human Nature,* (New York and London: Penguin Books, 1982), p. 128.

10. Sigmund Freud, "Das Unbehagen in der Kultur," in Sigmund Freud, *Studien-ausgabe* Volume IX, *Fragen der Gesellschaft, Ursprünge der Religion,* (Frankfurt am Main: S. Fischer Verlag, 1974), p. 252.

11. Hilary Bok, *Freedom and Responsibility,* (Princeton, NJ: Princeton University Press, 1998), p. 178.

12. Vladimir Jankélévitsch, *La mauvaise conscience,* (Paris: Aubier-Montaigne, 1966), p. 7.

13. Albert Camus, *La chute,* (Paris: Gallimard, 1956), p. 86.

14. Paul Ricoeur, "Le sentiment de culpabilité: sagesse ou névrose?" Dialogue avec Marie de Solemne, in Marie de Solemne, *Innocente culpabilité,* (Paris: Éditions Dervy, 1998), p. 27. Ricoeur's change of position is not an "about-face," but rather an expression of the fact that he lived through a period in which guilt was increasingly being replaced by shame. In 1985 another French author, Jacques Goldberg, could, for instance, still write: "As concerns the question of whether shame and inferiority feelings have become more powerful than guilt feelings, certain authors are in a hurry to answer this question in a too assured [i. e. positive, MHVH] way . . . " (Jacques Goldberg, *La culpabilité axiome de la psychanalyse,* [Paris: Presses Universitaires de France, 1985], p. 16).

15. Paul Ricoeur, "Le sentiment de culpabilité: sagesse ou névrose?," op. cit., p. 13.

16. Helen Merrell Lynd, *On Shame and the Search for Identity,* (New York: Harcourt, Brace and Company, 1958), p. 18.

17. Cornelius Castoriadis, "Psychanalyse et société," in Cornelius Castoriadis, *Domaines de l'homme—Les carrefours du labyrinthe 2,* (Paris: Éditions du Seuil, 1986), p. 114.

18. Ibid., p. 117.

19. Ibid.

20. Herbert Morris, "Guilt and Shame," in Herbert Morris, *On Guilt and Innocence—Essays in Legal Philosophy and Moral Psychology,* (Berkeley, Los Angeles, London: University of California Press, 1979), p. 60.

21. Ibid.

22. Ibid.

23. Ibid., p. 61.

24. Ibid., p. 62.

25. Martha C. Nussbaum, *Upheavals of Thought—The Intelligence of Emotions,* (Cambridge and New York: Cambridge University Press, 2005), p. 216.

26. Martha C. Nussbaum, *Hiding from Humanity—Disgust, Shame, and the Law,* (Princeton and Oxford: Princeton University Press, 2004), p. 208.

27. Ibid.

28. Ibid., p. 214.

29. Heinz Kohut, "Überlegungen zum Narzißmus und zur narzißtischen Wut," in Heinz Kohut, *Die Zukunft der Psychoanalyse,* (Frankfurt am Main: Suhrkamp Verlag, 1975), p. 210.

30. William Wan, "America is a nation of narcissists, according to two new studies," *The Washington Post,* July 3, 2018, and Sadie F. Dingfelder, "Reflecting on narcissism—Are young people more self-obsessed than ever before?" *Monitor on Psychology,* Vol. 42, No. 2, February 2011. https://www.apa.org/monitor/2011/02/narcissism.

31. Richard Sennett, *The Fall of Public Man—On the Social Psychology of Capitalism,* (New York: Vintage Books, 1978), p. 325.

32. Ibid., p. 327.

33. Gershen Kaufman, *Shame—The Power of Caring,* op. cit., p. 29. (Emphasis in original, MHVH).

34. Helen B. Lewis, *Shame and Guilt in Neurosis,* (New York: International Universities Press, 1971), p. 29. See also D. Stanley-Jones, who writes that "at a higher level, guilt may be sublimated as a sense of responsibility, it forms the basis of our ethical sense of moral values." (D. Stanley-Jones, "The Biological Origin of Love and Hate," in Magda B. Arnold (ed.), *Feelings and Emotions—The Loyola Symposium,* [New York and London: Elsevier, 1970], p. 30).

35. Hans Jonas, *Das Prinzip Verantwortung—Versuch einer Ethik für die technologische Zivilisation,* (Frankfurt am Main: Suhrkamp Verlag, 1984), p. 222.

36. Ibid., p. 248.

37. Hannah Arendt clearly refers to this link between responsibility and a guilt morality when she writes: "That deeds possess such an enormous capacity for endurance, superior to every other man-made product, could be a matter of pride if men were able to bear its burden, the burden of irreversibility and unpredictability, from which the action process draws its very strength. That this is impossible, men have always known. They have known that he who acts never quite knows what he is doing, that he always becomes 'guilty' of consequences he never intended or even foresaw, that no matter how disastrous and unexpected the consequences of his deed he can never undo it, that the process he starts is never consummated unequivocally in one single deed or event, and that its very meaning never discloses itself to the actor

but only to the backward glance of the historian who himself does not act." (Hannah Arendt, *The Human Condition,* [Chicago and London: The University of Chicago Press, 1958], p. 233).

38. Ruwen Ogien, *La honte est-elle immorale?* (Paris: Bayard, 2002), p. 160.

39. Ibid., p. 161.

Chapter 2

New Shaming Practices

Back to the Past?

Shame is a painful feeling. This feeling can emerge spontaneously in an embarrassing situation, but it can also be deliberately evoked by others with the intention to hurt. This process is called *shaming.* Shaming is a common practice in shame societies, where it can be used by individuals, by groups, or by the state. An example of shaming by a group is the *volksgericht,* a popular tribunal which took place in November 1961 in Staphorst, a Dutch village. Staphorst is a special village. In the Netherlands its inhabitants have a reputation which is somewhat similar to the Amish in the United States. The inhabitants adhere to a strict and fundamentalist splinter of the Dutch Reformed Church. They reject watching TV, visiting bars, and oppose vaccination against polio. The victims of the shaming action were two married persons in the village who had a relationship with each other, which was considered a violation of the norms of the small community. One evening the woman was taken out of her bed in her nightgown and put on a manure cart. The man, who had had fled to a neighboring town, was brought back in a cattle wagon. At midnight the two made a tour of two and a half hours through the village on the manure cart. They were insulted and vituperated by about one thousand villagers who had stayed up for the occasion.[1] People threw dirt and dung on the couple, who had to promise to end their relationship, which they did after being threatened to be thrown in the cold water of the canal if they refused.[2] There were angry reactions in the Dutch media. Commentators spoke about "excesses from a dark past."[3] And, indeed, in the Netherlands, at that time an example of a modern guilt society, the popular tribunal of Staphorst seemed rather a remnant of an eighteenth-century shame society, a residue of a definitively bygone age.[4] However, such atavistic practices were not confined to the Netherlands. In August 2007 in Belfast (Northern Ireland) an alleged drug dealer was tarred and feathered. "The victim was tied to a lamppost, and masked men poured tar over him and covered him in feathers

15

as women and children looked on. A placard around his neck declared: 'I'm a drug dealing scumbag.'"[5]

THE COMEBACK OF SHAMING PRACTICES

Events, which in 1961 or in 2007 still seemed to be remnants of a bygone age, destined to fade away and to disappear forever under the steamroller of an advancing modernity, made in recent years a comeback with a vengeance. Ironically, this comeback was made possible by new, advanced technological devices and related services, particularly the Internet, the smartphone, and the social media. Exposure on a manure cart has been replaced by exposure on the Internet where the victim is not exposed to one thousand spectators, but to tens of thousands of unknown people, who can watch the most private pictures and read the accompanying shaming messages. This is especially a concern for the young generation who are, as it were, "at the frontline" of this phenomenon—both as actors and as victims. Shame "is an emotion used by people also to hurt each other," writes the Dutch sociologist Johan Goudsblom. "Children are very good at it," he continued, "they can shame each other terribly, and they can also suffer terribly from shame. They have both a great receptivity for shame, as well as a huge potential for shaming."[6]

However, modern forms of shaming are not only practiced by adolescents. It can also be tempting for governments to use this tool. The United States is a case in point. Marc Hauser speaks, for instance, about "punishment through shame, a form of retribution that has been revived in the last decade, bringing back visions to many legal scholars of public floggings, burnings, and decapitations."[7] One commentator went so far as to compare today's America with "pre-2001 Afghanistan (where the Taliban, like American judges, reintroduced public shame sanctions)."[8] These punishments through shame are often called "scarlet-letter punishments"—a reference to the novel *The Scarlet Letter* by the American author Nathaniel Hawthorne (1804–1864), in which a woman, Hester Prynne, accused of adultery, has to wear the letter A for adulteress on her dress. "In recent times," wrote Hauser, "these punishments have taken on a variety of forms, including bumper stickers for individuals convicted of drunk driving, full-body placards for individuals caught shoplifting, and registration of sex offenders with the department of public safety."[9] According to Hauser, "there are at least three reasons why this form of punishment has been on the rise, primarily in the United States: skepticism that prison time and fines function as deterrents, concern that overcrowding in the prisons requires a cheaper solution, and intuitive beliefs that shaming is just desert for the public's sense of moral outrage—shaming is a form of revenge."[10]

There are legal reservations concerning the reintroduction of shaming penalties into criminal law. Apart from this there exist also psychological reservations. Martha Nussbaum wrote that there are "some reasons for skepticism about the current revival of interest in 'shaming penalties' for offenses such as drunk driving, soliciting prostitutes, and so on. Societies that use shaming penalties to mock criminal offenders reinforce primitive shame at the frailties of the human being. In the case of the particular offender, this may prove psychologically damaging. . . . "[11] She added: "In general . . . most people have too much shame already; what they need is to develop confidence in their capacity to make reparation."[12] Making reparation, however, is characteristic of criminal law which is based on guilt, not on shame. Nussbaum mentioned still other reasons to be skeptical about shaming. "In particular, it is difficult to calibrate the quantity of punishment to the quantity of the offense."[13] While a non-shaming penalty for a crime or an offense can be measured relatively precisely in prison time or the amount of a fine, it is difficult to attribute a circumscribed "amount of shame" which is proportional to the crime or offense, because it has the tendency to be disproportional to the action of the individual. There exist, therefore, different reasons for viewing the "return of shame" as a tool of criminal law in our modern societies with skepticism. There is, finally, an additional argument against shaming: this is the fact that those who deserve most to be shamed are often impervious to shame. Powerful people, such as politicians, celebrities, the super-rich, seem often to be immune. Shame is a sanction for the small fish, not the big fish.

SHAMING: THE TWO-EDGED SWORD
OF THE #METOO MOVEMENT

Does this mean that there is no place at all for shaming practices? One has to acknowledge that there are powerful actors who are literally "unashamed," who deserve to be shamed. Shaming could then become a tool in the hands of the weak and oppressed against the powerful. With the advent of social media each individual has access to a weapon that enables any small David to take on any powerful Goliath. In order to shame someone a person doesn't need to be rich, famous, or powerful: creating a hashtag on Twitter which goes viral is often sufficient. This availability of new, technologically advanced shaming tools has provoked great excitement.

Something of real consequence was happening. We were at the start of a great renaissance of public shaming. After a lull of almost 180 years (public punishments were phased out in 1837 in the United Kingdom and in 1839 in the United States), it was back in a big way. When we deployed shame, we were utilizing an immensely powerful tool. It was coercive, borderless, and increasing in speed and influence. Hierarchies were being leveled out. The silenced were getting a voice. It was like the democratization of justice.[14]

An example of this "democratization of justice," in which the silenced "were getting a voice," was the #MeToo movement. This movement went viral on social media in October 2017 after allegations of rape and sexual assault were made against Hollywood producer Harvey Weinstein. The hashtag #MeToo became a worldwide rallying cry of women who spoke out against their sexual aggressors.[15] In the last three months of 2017 the hashtag #MeToo was tweeted more than five million times.[16] Soon heads were rolling. One year later the *New York Times* reported that in the United States the #MeToo movement had brought down 201 powerful men, many of whom had lost their jobs following the accusations. These included Hollywood celebrities, CEOs, politicians, and TV anchors. Nearly half of their replacements were women.[17] The movement seemed unstoppable. In January 2019 *Vox* published a list which was even longer, with the names of 262 celebrities who since April 2017 had been accused of sexual misconduct. The list contained names of well-known actors and film directors, such as Sylvester Stallone, Lars von Trier, Dustin Hoffman, Oliver Stone, Gérard Depardieu, and Roman Polanski.[18] From the very beginning the impact of the movement was worldwide. In Italy the corresponding hashtag was #QuellaVoltaChe (The Time That), in France #BalanceTonPorc (Denounce Your Pig), in Spain #YoTambién. The movement became viral also in countries not known for a feminist fervor, such as India, Egypt, and Iran. The *Los Angeles Times* spoke, tellingly, about "a global primal scream."[19]

However, the movement didn't receive only support. In January 2018 a group of 100 women published an open letter in the French paper *Le Monde*. Signatories of this statement included Catherine Millet, a writer, and the French actress Catherine Deneuve. They wrote that "After the Weinstein affair an awareness of sexual violence against women was necessary."[20] That said, they regretted that "this freedom of speech is turning today into the opposite: we are told to speak appropriately, to silence whatever makes us angry, and women who refuse to follow such orders are regarded as traitors, accomplices."[21] They continue,

In fact, #MeToo has conducted in the press and on social media a denunciation and public accusation campaign against individuals who, without being given the opportunity to respond or defend themselves, are set on the same level as sexual predators. This summary justice already has its victims, men are sanctioned in the exercise of their profession, forced to resign, etc., when all they have done is to have touched a knee, tried to steal a kiss, spoken about "intimate" things during a professional dinner or sent messages with a sexual connotation to a woman for whom the attraction was not mutual.[22]

The signatories emphasized that "an insistent or clumsy flirtation is not a crime."[23]

Was this open letter the expression of what in Anglo-Saxon eyes was a "Latin" or "typically French"—that means: exaggerated—tolerance for the game of seduction? Wasn't France, after all, the country where Juliette Gréco could sing "Déshabillez-moi" ("Take off my clothes")? However, these 100 women were not the only ones to air their doubts. Other women followed, such as, for instance, Katie Roiphe, who published an article in *Harper's Magazine,* titled "The Other Whisper Network—How Twitter feminism is bad for women." Roiphe wrote that Twitter "has energized the angry extremes of feminism." She added that "the world Twitter feminists are envisioning—scrubbed clean of anyone hitting on anyone, asking for phone numbers, leaning over to kiss someone without seeking permission—seems not that substantively far away from the world of Mike Pence saying he will never eat alone with a woman who is not his wife."[24]

However, despite their criticism these critics did not minimize the importance of the movement. The #MeToo movement was, indeed, some kind of a "Great Awakening," or, for that matter, a small cultural revolution: "giving the voiceless a voice." Women, who had been raped or sexually assaulted and who had never dared to speak out, all of a sudden found not only the courage to speak out, but also a medium through which they could express themselves. The moment was significant: it was, on the one hand, an unprecedented global wave of *shaming* of alleged sexual predators. It was, on the other hand, an unprecedented global wave of *de-shaming*: women, who often for many years had been too timid and too ashamed to speak about their experience—even with relatives—spoke out openly, mentioning the names of their aggressors, even of those at the top of the power pyramid. In this sense the movement was a huge catharsis, an unprecedented cleansing of the emotions. However, one should not close one's eyes to the negative aspects of the movement: for the victims of sexual harassment or sexual assault shaming the alleged aggressors was not only a way of speaking out, but also a form of revenge. And one question was: were their testimonies always based on facts? Should one accept an allegation of sexual harassment at face value, because it was made by a woman? The hashtag #BelieveWomen, which went viral on Twitter, urged the visitor to believe the women unconditionally.

However, might an allegation not be revenge for another event, such as being passed over for a promotion, or for not being hired, being fired, or a love affair turned sour? And should the attacked person not have the right to be heard, to tell his side of the story—if there was any story—according to the principle a*udi et alteram partem* (hear the other side) of fair justice? Another problem was confusion about the offenses. Could touching a knee or stealing a kiss be called sexual harassment and justify someone being exposed on Twitter as a sexual predator? "Many of the incidents of harassment were too minor to warrant opprobrium," wrote *The Guardian,* adding that one "lost a sense of nuance."[25] An example were complaints aired by women about Joe Biden's allegedly sexist behavior. One of these, Caitlyn Caruso, said Joe hugged her "just a little bit too long." "Men reading this account," wrote the (female) journalist, "will surely wish to know *exactly* how long it takes for a consoling hug to become a shocking perpetuation of the harm of sexual assault. Two seconds? Four? How long is too long?"[26] She wrote that the rules had become "a moving target, one becoming more exacting by the day. But they seem to be these: Physical contact of any kind between an unmarried man and woman . . . is *streng verboten.* The exception is the straight-armed handshake. . . . At least on that point our new sexual mores are more liberal than the Taliban's."[27] Soon became clear that the #MeToo movement could have dramatic consequences. A few weeks after the hashtag became viral, Kathleen Parker wrote:

> As the #MeToo movement gained momentum the past weeks—and more than a dozen powerful men accused of sexual misconduct were suspended, fired or banished into the outer darkness, it was reasonable to wonder where it would all end. On Wednesday afternoon, it ended for Kentucky State Rep. Dan Johnson on a remote bridge, where he shot himself with a .40-caliber handgun. In an apparent suicide note posted (briefly) on Facebook, he wrote: 'GOD knows the truth, nothing is the way they make it out to be. . . . I cannot handle it longer . . . BUT HEAVEN IS MY HOME.'[28]

He was referring to accusations published two days earlier that he had fondled a seventeen-year-old friend of his daughter, as she was sleeping on a couch during a New Year's Eve sleepover. This was not the only case. On September 28, 2020, Taku Sekine, a thirty-nine-year-old chef of Japanese origin, who headed two trendy restaurants in Paris, committed suicide. He had killed himself after being accused of attempted rape on the social media.[29] People were shocked. Marie Burguburu, a lawyer, wrote in *Le Monde* that "in a state where there is a rule of law one doesn't take right in one's own hands and one doesn't repair an injustice by committing another injustice. In a democracy only a tribunal can establish guilt, which cannot be declared, but must be proven."[30]

The movement had other, unexpected consequences. In a survey, conducted in early 2019 in the United States, "19% of men said they were reluctant to hire attractive women for jobs involving close interpersonal interactions with men (jobs involving travel, say), and 27% said they avoided one-on-one meetings with female colleagues. . . . "[31] The male sex was clearly on the defensive and was trying to reduce the risk of being caught in a compromising situation. Was this new puritan apartheid becoming the new normal? There were more fundamental questions, such as: is shaming the right approach? Do the flaws of this approach not outweigh the benefits? Should one not distinguish between minor offenses and criminal acts? Do social media provide the appropriate forum to come forward with these allegations? Should one not rather bring the alleged perpetrators of sexual crimes and sexual assaults to justice (as was the case with Harvey Weinstein), where they can defend themselves and where an independent judge and not the victim pronounces the judgment? That said, it is clear that justice systems should be made better adapted, making it easier for victims of rape and sexual assault to file a complaint. Victims should be provided legal and psychological support and it would be recommendable to install specialized tribunals.

SHAMING: DEMOCRATIZATION OF JUSTICE OR KANGAROO COURT?

The idea that new shaming methods are a "democratization of justice" is defended by Jennifer Jacquet, the author of the book *Is Shame Necessary?* Her book, which has the telling subtitle: *New Uses for an Old Tool,* is a long plea to re-introduce shame punishments. Her argument runs as follows:

> Some people see shaming as an outmoded tool, useful at some point but no longer needed. Others see shaming as similar to nuclear technology: effective but also potentially dangerous and likely to fall into the wrong hands. For shaming's role in the twenty-first century, we should think less about the traditional forms of shaming—the stocks or the scarlet letter—and more about what shaming might become. Mimes who shamed bad driving in Bogotá led to a decrease in traffic accidents. Shaming tax delinquents led to an increase in tax revenue. Labels that singled out salty foods in Finland significantly decreased salt consumption.[32]

The examples this author gives of modern forms of effective shaming are rather disparate. Her first example, for instance, refers to the policy of Antanias Mockus, the mayor of the Colombian capital Bogotá, who hired 420 mime artists to make fun of traffic violators, which is thought to have led to a reduction of more than 50 percent of traffic fatalities.[33] However, the actions of the mime artists were humorous and should rather be considered as "pedagogical humor" than as acts of shaming. Her second example: shaming tax delinquents, is different. Research showed that of two groups of tax delinquents those who were informed that their neighbors received information on their delinquent status were more likely to pay off their debt. However, only the "small fish"—those owing up to $2,500 were likely to pay. The "big fish," owing more, didn't.[34] This seems to confirm the fear mentioned by the authors of the research, namely that "many people worry that the publication of the lists [with the names of tax delinquents, MHVH] could backfire by insulting individuals who are in temporary financial hardship, making them less likely to pay once they are back on their feet."[35] "Shaming practices come at a cost," they wrote: "the violation of privacy. Governments face a trade-off between privacy and increasing the effectiveness of tax collection."[36] They further mentioned the "real risk" that "in some cases social media may amplify penalties to the point of greatly outweighing the crime."[37] One may, therefore, doubt whether shaming is an effective tool against tax delinquents, as Jacquet argues, because the big offenders, those who are the most shameless, apparently tend to escape, while the small offenders, those who could face temporary financial problems, run the risk of being exposed on social media. Jacquet's third example of "effective shaming" is even more dubious. It refers to an action in Finland to reduce the salt intake of the population. In this action a major role was played by the biggest Finnish newspaper *Helsingin Sanomat,* which since the late 1970s had been publishing a series of articles denouncing salt as harmful for health. It led to salt-labelling legislation which came into effect on June 1, 1993.[38] It is not clear what the role of "shaming" might have been here. The paper's action may be better described as a successful information campaign.

WHY SHAMING COMPANIES IS DIFFERENT
FROM SHAMING INDIVIDUALS

Jacquet formulates a number of conditions for a modern way of shaming, giving it a "role in the twenty-first century." She emphasizes situations in which "our values change more quickly than the institutions designed to enforce them, shaming companies or governments can be the first step toward institutionalizing formal rules and punishment, as it was in the case of banning child labor."[39] Here Jacquet has a point. Often criminal law can't keep up with changing norms in society. Environmental law, for instance, has developed only slowly, most of the time lagging behind the requirements of the situation, which offered polluters the opportunity to act with impunity. In the absence of pre-existing laws and regulations, shaming might be a tool to put pressure on governments to change the law. Jacquet enumerates "seven habits of effective shaming," which are:

> The transgression should (1) concern the audience, (2) deviate widely from desired behavior, and (3) not be expected to be formally punished. The transgressor should (4) be sensitive to the group doing the shaming. And the shaming should (5) come from a respected source, (6) be directed where possible benefits are highest, and (7) be implemented conscientiously.[40]

Jacquet's condition that the shaming practice should come "from a respected source" seems to refer to the actions of international NGOs, such as *Greenpeace* or *Amnesty International.* But what about a group of fundamentalist Christians who organize a picket line at the entrance of an abortion clinic, shaming, harassing, and intimidating the visitors to the clinic, mostly women who are in a fragile situation? For these Christians abortion is a transgression which "concerns the audience," "deviates widely from desired behavior," is "not formally punished," and their shaming action "is directed where possible benefits are highest," being "implemented conscientiously." The religious group will also certainly consider itself to be a "respected source." Moreover, who would be the arbiter in a society that is deeply divided by culture wars for determining whether a shaming group is a "respected source"? These are pertinent questions. Jacquet makes some additional remarks that could take some of the heat off. She emphasizes that shaming should not only be effective, but also permissible and refers to the "Goldilocks principle." Goldilocks is a character in the children's story *The Three Bears,* who tastes different bowls of porridge and prefers the bowl which is neither too hot, nor too cold. It indicates the human tendency to choose moderate, "middle of the road" options, which means that "shaming should not be too weak or too strong, too brief or too permanent, used too infrequently or too often."[41] "Shaming," she continues, "should also work to stigmatize bad practice, rather than focusing overtly on specific people or institutions. Shaming the bad practices of institutions, companies, or countries is probably not just more effective in terms of bringing about large-scale changes in behavior . . . but shaming groups is probably more acceptable. Groups are less prone to emotional suffering in the face of shaming, because groups do not have 'human dignity' the way that individuals do."[42] Again: it depends on *the kind* of group which is the target of these shaming practices. Economic groups, such as multinationals, indeed, don't have human dignity, as Jacquet writes. But what about ethnic or religious groups? Norbert Elias wrote: "It is a universal fact that individuals, who have done nothing to deserve it, are shamed (or for that matter praised), simply because they belong to a group which is said to deserve shame (or praise)."[43] Elias, a German Jew, knew this from his own experience. In 1933 he fled Nazi Germany. His mother was killed in Treblinka. Shaming groups is, therefore, not an innocent activity: these groups consist of individuals and shaming individuals is always a kind of aggression which causes psychological suffering. It is exactly for this reason that shaming practices were abolished, as Jon Ronson rightly reminds us:

> The common assumption is that public punishments died out in the new great metropolises because they'd been judged useless. Everyone was too busy being industrious to bother to trail some transgressor through the city crowds like some volunteer scarlet letter. But at the archives I found no evidence that public shaming fell out of fashion as a result of newfound anonymity. I did, however, find plenty of people from centuries past bemoaning its outsized cruelty, warning that well-meaning people, in a crowd, often take it too far. . . . They didn't fizzle out because they were ineffective. They were stopped because they were far too brutal.[44]

It is because of their brutality that shaming practices were stopped. And in our century this brutality has not diminished. On the contrary: due to social media it has grown exponentially. Shaming persons should, therefore, be avoided. One should focus explicitly on their behavior and sanction transgressive behavior. If there is a role to play for shaming practices, it should be in targeting companies, governments, or institutions which are lacking a personal character. At the same time it remains questionable whether in these cases the term "shaming" would still be appropriate. Shaming is a psychological device and its targets are individual human beings. "Shaming" a company is, therefore, not an adequate term. It should rather be labeled "causing reputational damage." There is no multinational which has committed suicide after having been shamed. Multinationals seem to have understood this better than Jacquet. They, themselves, don't speak about shame, but rather about "reputational damage," which is quite different.[45]

NOTES

1. Bert Monster, "Staphorst herdenkt laatste volksgericht," *Reformatorisch Dagblad,* November 9, 2011.

2. Cf. John Griffiths, "Review Essay: Village Justice in the Netherlands," *Journal of Legal Pluralism,* 22, 1984.

3. Bert Monster, "Staphorst herdenkt laatste volksgericht," op. cit.

4. The event brings to mind the words of David Riesman, who wrote that "one of the interesting semantic expressions of our own disenchantment is that of bewailing our society as 'impersonal.' What would the member of the village group or small town not give at times for an impersonal setting where he was not constantly part of a web of gossip and surveillance?" (David Riesman, "Individualism Reconsidered," in David Riesman, *Individualism Reconsidered*, [New York: Doubleday Anchor Books, 1955]), p. 23.

5. "Man tarred and feathered in Belfast," *The Irish Times,* August 28, 2007. https://www.irishtimes.com/news/man-tarred-and-feathered-in-belfast-1.811373 This was still a common "punishment" used in the 1970s, and even later—including in 2018. See Jane Scott, "Vigilante justice is a brutal reminder of dark days," *Belfast Telegraph,* April 30, 2018. https://www.belfasttelegraph.co.uk/news/northern-ireland/vigilante-justice-is-a-brutal-reminder-of-dark-days-36856716.html.

6. J. Goudsblom, "De functies van schaamte," *De Gids,* 158, No. 5, May 1995, p. 335.

7. Marc D. Hauser, *Moral Minds—How Nature Designed Our Universal Sense of Right and Wrong,* (New York: HarperCollins, 2006), p. 105.

8. James Q. Whitman, *Harsh Justice: Criminal Punishment and the Widening Divide Between America and Europe,* (Oxford and New York: Oxford University Press, 2003), p. 4.

9. Marc D. Hauser, *Moral Minds—How Nature Designed Our Universal Sense of Right and Wrong,* op. cit., p. 105.

10. Ibid.

11. Martha C. Nussbaum, *Upheavals of Thought—The Intelligence of Emotions,* op. cit., pp. 228–229.

12. Ibid., p. 229.

13. Ibid., p. 229, note 114.

14. Jon Ronson, *So You've Been Publicly Shamed,* (New York: Riverhead Books, 2015), p. 10.

15. Nadia Khomani, "#MeToo: how a hashtag became a rallying cry against sexual harassment," *The Guardian,* October 20, 2017. https://www.theguardian.com/world/2017/oct/20/women-worldwide-use-hashtag-metoo-against-sexual-harassment.

16. Anisa Subedar, "Has #MeToo divided women?" *BBC,* August 17, 2018. https://www.bbc.com/news/blogs-trending-44958160.

17. Audrey Carlsen, Maya Salam, Claire Cain Miller, Denise Lu, Ash Ngu, Jugal K. Patel, Zack Wichter, "#MeToo Brought Down 201 Powerful Men. Nearly Half of their Replacements Are Women," *New York Times,* October 23, 2018, updated October 29, 2018. https://www.nytimes.com/interactive/2018/10/23/us/metoo-replacements.html.

18. "Sexual Harassment Assault Allegations List," *Vox,* updated January 9, 2019. https://www.vox.com/a/sexual-harassment-assault-allegations-list.

19. Noga Tarnopolsky and Melissa Etehad, "A global primal scream: #MeToo," *Los Angeles Times,* October 18, 2017. https://www.latimes.com/world/middleeast/la-fg-global-me-too-20171018-story.html.

20. Collectif de 100 femmes, "Nous défendons une liberté d'importuner, indispensable à la liberté sexuelle," *Le Monde,* January 9, 2018, (updated January 13, 2018), https://www.lemonde.fr/idees/article/2018/01/09/nous-defendons-une-liberte-d-importuner-indispensable-a-la-liberte-sexuelle_5239134_3232.html.

21. Ibid.

22. Ibid.

23. Ibid.

24. Katie Roiphe, "The Other Whisper Network—How Twitter feminism is bad for women," *Harper's Magazine,* March 2018. https://harpers.org/archive/2018/03/the-other-whisper-network-2/.

25. Moira Donegan, "How #MeToo revealed the central rift within feminism today," *The Guardian,* May 11, 2018. https://www.theguardian.com/news/2018/may/11/how-metoo-revealed-the-central-rift-within-feminism-social-individualist.

26. Claire Berlinski, "#MeToo Dead Ends," *The American Interest,* Vol. XIV, No. 6, July/August 2019, p. 35.

27. Ibid., p. 36.

28. Kathleen Parker, "Kathleen Parker: Shame making a comeback with a vengeance," *Times Union,* December 16, 2017. https://www.timesunion.com/opinion/article/Kathleen-Parker-Shame-making-a-comeback-with-a-12436036.php.

29. Kim Hullot-Guiot, "Suicide du chef Taku Sekine, accusé d'agression sexuelle," *Libération,* September 30, 2020. https://next.liberation.fr/food/2020/09/30/suicide-du-chef-taku-sekine-accuse-d-agression-sexuelle_1801025.

30. Marie Burguburu, "Face aux violences faites aux femmes, ne plus se taire mais arrêter ce phénomène de délation," *Le Monde,* October 9, 2020.

31. "The #MeToo Backlash," *Harvard Business Review,* September-October 2019. https://hbr.org/2019/09/the-metoo-backlash.

32. Jennifer Jacquet, *Is Shame Necessary? New Uses for an Old Tool,* op. cit., pp. 172–173.

33. Sarah Marsh, "Antanias Mockus: Columbians fear ridicule more than being fined," *The Guardian,* October 28, 2013. https://www.theguardian.com/public-leaders-network/2013/oct/28/antanas-mockus-bogota-mayor The actions of the artists can be watched on YouTube https://www.youtube.com/watch?v=6YcK05z--n8.

34. Ricardo Perez-Truglia and Ugo Troiano, "Shaming Those Who Skip Out on Taxes," *New York Times,* April 15, 2015. https://www.nytimes.com/2015/04/15/opinion/shaming-those-who-skip-out-on-taxes.html.

35. Ibid.

36. Ibid.

37. Ibid.

38. "Finland—Salt Action Summary," *World Action on Salt & Health,* March 2009. http://www.worldactiononsalt.com/worldaction/europe/finland/.

39. Jennifer Jacquet, *Is Shame Necessary? New Uses for an Old Tool,* op. cit., p. 173.

40. Ibid.

41. Ibid.

42. Ibid., p. 174.

43. Norbert Elias, *Etablierte und Außenseiter,* (Frankfurt am Main: Suhrkamp Verlag, 1993), p. 182.

44. Jon Ronson, *So You've Been Publicly Shamed,* op. cit., p. 54.

45. Royal Dutch Shell, which in 2015 abandoned an Antarctic drilling project after actions of Greenpeace, mentioned as one of the reasons for abandoning the project not shame, but "damage to reputation." (Louise Rouse, "Comment: Shell's retreat from the Arctic—what tipped the scales," *Unearthed,* September 29, 2015). https://unearthed.greenpeace.org/2015/09/29/comment-shells-retreat-from-the-arctic -what-tipped-the-scales/?_ga=2.140930034.1980850405.1601020889-678670445 .1601020889.

PART I

The Rise of the Western Guilt Society

Chapter 3

The Changing Character
of Individualism

Until recently Western society was predominantly a guilt society. The formation of a guilt society began in the seventeenth century and continued through the eighteenth and nineteenth centuries. It was a complex phenomenon shaped by multiple causes, some of which could be labeled "materialist," such as a change in housing conditions. The middle class built bigger houses. These houses had not only more rooms, but some of these were used as *cabinets*—private rooms for study, rest, and contemplation. Women also got their own private rooms, called *boudoirs*. "Why has guilt ascended on the moral stage? Perhaps it became more important as we began to have more opportunities to be physically isolated from the group, since some argue that guilt is experienced in solitude, without reference to an audience."[1] Spatial isolation went in tandem with a rise in individualism. Individualism is a social outlook which doesn't take God or society as its point of departure, but the human individual. We can distinguish different forms of individualism, such as religious, philosophical, political, and economic individualism, and individualism as a lifestyle. Not only do these have their own characteristics, but also they emerged in different periods. In this chapter we will analyze religious, philosophical, and political individualism and individualism as a lifestyle. In the next chapter we will turn to economic individualism. In the remaining chapters of Part I we will analyze how in recent years these different forms of individualism morphed into two new kinds of individualism: "expressive individualism" and "narcissistic individualism," which, instead of triggering guilt feelings, rather trigger shame. While Asian shame cultures develop in collectivist societies, this new Western shame culture is different, because it develops in a highly individualistic societies.

31

RELIGIOUS INDIVIDUALISM: LUTHER'S INFLUENCE

Norbert Elias has pointed to the fact that "in ancient languages there [was] no equivalent for the word 'individual.' At the stage of the Athenian and the Roman republics, affiliation to the family, the tribe, or the state, played an indispensable role in the idea of man."[2] This was still the case in the Middle Ages. "The medieval concept *individual,*" he writes, "did not yet . . . specifically refer to human beings."[3] However, this changed in the Renaissance and the advent of religious individualism, which is commonly associated with the Reformation. Ernst Troeltsch, a German sociologist, emphasized the important influence of Protestantism and pointed to the fact that "it has been described, in terms, sometimes of censure, sometimes of admiration, as the parent of the Individualism which is characteristic of the modern world."[4] The Reformation began on October 31, 1517, the day that Luther nailed his 95 Theses to the door of the Wittenberg Castel church. In these Theses Luther attacked the practice of the so-called indulgences—the papal granting of remission from temporal punishment in purgatory after death for sins which remained after absolution by the priest in the confessional. This "indulgence" practice had become a real business in the late Middle Ages. Luther attacked this business in his Theses. "They preach only human doctrines," he wrote, "who say that as soon as the money clinks into the money chest, the soul flies out of purgatory."[5] However, Luther's Theses were not only an attack on the practice of indulgences, but—at a deeper level—they announced a restoration of human guilt. In his 6th Thesis he wrote, for instance, that "the pope cannot remit any guilt, except by declaring and showing that it has been remitted by God. . . . "[6] And in the 76th Thesis he again insisted "that papal indulgences cannot remove the very least of venial sins as far as guilt is concerned."[7] Christians could not get rid of their guilt by paying money to the church, such was Luther's message: they had personally to atone for their sins and repair the damage they had done. By eliminating the chance to buy a good conscience and avoid punishment in purgatory, Luther restored guilt, and with the same stroke he restored the individual as a morally responsible person.[8]

> If Luther did not really say the words which became most famous: "Here I stand," legend again rose to the occasion; for this new credo was for men whose identity was derived from their determination to stand on their own feet, not only spiritually, but politically, economically, and intellectually. . . . Luther's emphasis on individual conscience prepared the way for the series of concepts of equality, representation, and self-determination which became in successive secular revolutions and wars the foundations not of the dignity of some, but of the liberty of all.[9]

However, although Luther's individualism was showing the way for these later developments, he would confine it mainly to the religious domain. He neither preached that individuals could shape society at their discretion, nor formulated a right of rebellion for citizens, considering that the existing authorities had been installed by God. It was rather the more radical protestant sects—the Anabaptists, the Calvinists, and the Quakers—who gave this early protestant individualism a political translation by making the individual conscience the yardstick with which to judge a government.[10] An additional reason for this could be that these sects were often persecuted by the authorities. Max Weber wrote of these radical protestant sects that they were characterized by "the absolute rejection of all demands made by the state which 'go against one's conscience,' and the demand of freedom of conscience as an absolute right of the individual *against* the state. . . . "[11] For these protestant sects neither loyalty, nor tradition were the foundations of the state, but the individual and the individual conscience. The importance of religion to the emergence of modern individualism and modern democracy is also emphasized by Tocqueville, who wrote: "Almost all the efforts modern people have made toward freedom, they have made because of the need to manifest or defend their religious beliefs. It is religious passion which pushed the Puritans to America and brought them to wanting to govern there themselves."[12] However, it was not only (protestant) religion which gave a boost to this early individualism. Technical progress also played a major role, particularly the invention of the printing press. "In the early 16th century, religious reformer Martin Luther and his protégés exploited the unique features of printing for the first mass-mediated publicity campaign for the Protestant Reformation."[13] The major role played by the printing press in advancing individualism is widely acknowledged, for instance by media expert Marshall McLuhan: "McLuhan argued that the spread of literacy and printing enhanced individuality. . . . "[14]

PHILOSOPHICAL AND POLITICAL INDIVIDUALISM: DESCARTES, LOCKE, AND BENTHAM

Radical protestant individualism set the way for philosophical individualism, which was already evident in the philosophy of René Descartes (1596–1650). In a time in which old certainties and dogmas were no longer valid Descartes sought a new foundation for his philosophy. But what could this foundation be, he asked, in a period characterized by skepticism, growing uncertainty, and doubt? If everything is uncertain and I doubt everything, argued Descartes, there remains only one certainty and that is the fact that I doubt. To doubt means to think. *Je pense donc je suis:* when I think, I am sure that I exist.[15] Descartes founded his philosophy not on God or a metaphysical real-ity, but on the individual thinking person. However, like Luther's individual-ism, which was restricted to the realm of religion, Descartes' individualism was confined to the realm of philosophy. It was John Locke (1632–1704), who was himself a Calvinist, who made the individual the basis of his politi-cal system in his famous *Second Treatise of Government.* Locke constructed a state of nature in which all individuals are equal and subjected to no one. Endowed with reason these individuals agreed on a contract which estab-lished a political community. This didn't mean that they gave up their origi-nal freedoms: the newly erected political community had the obligation to preserve and defend their natural rights. For Locke the state is there to serve the individual and the individual is not there to serve the state. This means that Locke recognized a right to revolution, writing that "the people gener-ally ill-treated, and contrary to right, will be ready upon any occasion to ease themselves of a burden that sits heavy upon them."[16] This new political indi-vidualism is the ideological foundation of both the American and the French Revolution, and in the nineteenth century this individualism will become the dominant political philosophy in the United States and Europe. It will also become more radical. Locke was in favor of representative government, but he thought that a census would be necessary in order to prevent the have-nots from using their political power to confiscate the property of the rich. According to him this would go against the reason why the state had been installed. He was quite explicit on this in his *Second Treatise,* where he wrote: "The great and chief end, therefore, of men's uniting into common-wealths, and putting themselves under government, is the preservation of their prop-erty."[17] He added that "the supreme power cannot take from any man any part of his property without his own consent. . . . "[18] Locke was an opponent of universal suffrage. His political individualism excluded the have-nots from a say in the day-to-day running of government. Although in the nineteenth century a gradual enlargement of the franchise took place,[19] one had to wait until the twentieth century before universal male and female suffrage was introduced in most Western countries.

Jeremy Bentham (1748–1832) took an even more radical stance than John Locke, arguing that a "common interest" independent from the interests of the individual did not exist.

> The interest of the community is one of the most general expressions that can occur in the phraseology of morals: no wonder that the meaning of it is often lost. When it has a meaning, it is this. The community is a fictitious *body,* com-posed of the individual persons who are considered as constituting as it were its *members.* The interest of the community then is, what?—the sum of the interests

of the several members who compose it. It is in vain to talk of the interest of the community, without understanding what is the interest of the individual.[20]

Alan Bloom seemed to be describing this extremely individualistic Benthamite world, when he wrote: "America is experienced not as a common project but as a framework within which people are only individuals, where they are left alone."[21] But are there only individual interests and is a common interest a mere illusion? Daniel Bell criticized Bentham's extreme individualism:

> Jeremy Bentham had denied there was such an entity as a community. It was, he said, a fictitious body. But there is a real distinction between a social decision and the sum total of individual decisions. . . . It is . . . clear that what an individual often wants for himself . . . in the aggregate becomes a nightmare. So the balance of private appetite and public responsibility is a real one.[22]

THE INDIVIDUALISTIC LIFESTYLE: THE *LONER* AS THE INDIVIDUALISTIC PERSONALITY IDEAL

The United States is often considered to be a country in which, from the beginning, individualism was an essential part of its psychological makeup. However, Barry Shain points to the fact that late-eighteenth-century Americans still "awarded the public's needs preeminence over the immediate ones of discrete individuals. Local communities catered little to the particular wants of individuals, and the autonomous self was thought to be at the core of human sinfulness. For Revolutionary-era Americans, that self was neither an ultimate ethical category nor a center of moral worth."[23] This began to change in the early nineteenth century, when individualism, apart from being the foundation of political liberalism, was increasingly touted as a personality ideal. The popular hero was the loner who left civilized society behind him in a restless search for new challenges and adventures. An example of this nineteenth-century hero was the American cowboy, roaming the endless prairies, defending himself with great courage against the attacks by enemies and bandits.

> America is . . . the inventor of that most mythic individual hero, the cowboy, who again and again saves a society he can never completely fit into. The cowboy has a special talent—he can shoot straighter and faster than other men—and a special sense of justice. But these characteristics make him so unique that he can never fully belong to society. His destiny is to defend society without ever really joining it. . . . It is as if the myth says you can be a truly good person, worthy of admiration and love, only if you resist fully joining the group.[24]

The cowboy fascinated not only Americans, but also Europeans. It was not an American, but a German author, Karl May (1842–1912), who created the iconic characters of Winnetou and Old Shatterhand. However, the cowboy was not the only heroic model. Other examples of these individualistic *loners* were famous explorers, such as Henry Stanley or David Livingstone, who ventured into the dark, dangerous, and unknown jungle of Africa. This kind of lifestyle individualism was widely touted in nineteenth-century American literature. Ralph Waldo Emerson (1803–1883), for instance, wrote:

> Society everywhere is in conspiracy against the manhood of every one of its members. Society is a joint-stock company, in which the members agree, for the better securing of his bread to each shareholder, to surrender the liberty and culture of the eater. The virtue in most request is conformity. Self-reliance is its aversion. . . . Whoso would be a man must be a nonconformist.[25]

And Emerson concluded:

> We must go alone. . . . At times the whole world seems to be in conspiracy, to importune you with emphatic trifles. Friend, client, child, sickness, fear, want, charity, all knock at once at thy closet door, and say, "Come out unto us." But keep thy state, come not into their confusion.[26]

Society breeds conformity, such was Emerson's message; a true man should not be dependent on society, he should be self-reliant and nonconformist and not let himself be tied to social obligations. Robert Putnam relativizes this absolute individualism. "We Americans," he wrote, "like to think of ourselves as 'rugged individualists'—in the image of the lone cowboy riding toward the setting sun, opening the frontier. But at least as accurate a symbol of our national story is the wagon train, with its mutual aid among a community of pioneers."[27] However, what these nineteenth-century thinkers touted was not so much moral egoism, as free thinking and nonconformity.

This praise of individualism and critique of conformity can also be found in the work of the American novelist James Fenimore Cooper (1789–1851), who wrote that "individuality is the aim of political liberty,"[28] adding that "all greatness of character is dependant [sic] on individuality. The man who has no other existence than that which he partakes in common with all around him, will never have any other than an existence of mediocrity."[29] These American authors tout the self-reliance of the autonomous individual, who should not only distance himself from the crowd, but also not let himself be influenced by an unstable and changeable public opinion, because—in Emerson's words, "it is easy in the world to live after the world's opinion; it is easy in solitude to live after our own; but the great man is he who in the midst of the crowd keeps with perfect sweetness the independence of solitude."[30]

The same celebration of the individual can be found in the poems of Walt Whitman (1819–1892). In 1855 Whitman published a poem collection, entitled *Leaves of Grass* of which the first poem, "Song of Myself," begins with the words: "I celebrate myself."[31] In this poem Whitman expresses his aversion to conformity and tradition, urging the individual to form his own opinion:

> You shall no longer take things at second or third hand . . . nor look through the eyes of the dead . . . nor feed on the spectres in books,
> You shall not look through my eyes either, nor take things from me,
> You shall listen to all sides and filter them for yourself.[32]

In Europe one could find a similar celebration of the lonely hero in Charlotte Brontë's novel *Jane Eyre,* where Jane exclaims: "I care for myself. The more solitary, the more friendless, the more unsustained I am, the more I will respect myself."[33]

AMERICAN INDIVIDUALISM AND THE "FRONTIER THESIS"

In the United States the glorification of the independent individual was influenced by the "frontier thesis," this is the theory that the formation of the individualistic American character was a product of America's specific geographical situation, namely the availability of the "frontier"—the existence of a vast, empty space in the West which was open to almost continuous expansion. According to Frederick Jackson Turner (1861–1932), who was the historian who formulated this theory, the frontier was "the meeting point between savagery and civilization."[34] "This expansion westward," he wrote, "with its new opportunities, its continuous touch with the simplicity of primitive society, furnish the forces dominating American character."[35] But how exactly, in what way, did the frontier mold the American character?

> The most important effect of the frontier has been in the promotion of democracy here and in Europe. As has been indicated, the frontier is productive of individualism. Complex society is precipitated by the wilderness into a kind of primitive organization based on the family. The tendency is anti-social. It produces antipathy to control, and particularly to any direct control. The tax-gatherer is viewed as a representative of oppression.[36]

The individualistic American *pioneer* who ventured into the unknown, savage territories of the frontier was here presented as the standard bearer of democracy. But was that true? Was the "don't mess with us" anti-government spirit of the pioneers and their exclusive reliance on the small circle of family and friends really conducive to democracy? Tocqueville had some doubts. He rather feared the advent of a new despotism:

> I seek to trace the novel features under which despotism may appear in the world. The first thing that strikes the observation is an innumerable multitude of men equal and alike, incessantly endeavoring to procure the petty and paltry pleasures with which they glut their lives. Each of them, living apart, is a stranger to the fate of all the rest—his children and his private friends constitute to him the whole of mankind; as for the rest of his fellow-citizens, he is close to them, but he sees them not—he touches them, but he feels them not; he exists but in himself and for himself alone; and if his kindred still remain to him, he may be said at any rate to have lost his country. Above this race of men stands an immense and tutelary power, which takes upon itself alone to secure their gratifications, and to watch over their fate. That power is absolute, minute, provident, and mild.[37]

Tocqueville criticized the individualistic loner on the grounds that he had lost the social bonds with other citizens which are indispensable for political individualism. His impoverished social life, restricted to family and friends, instead of boosting democracy, would, according to Tocqueville, more likely undermine a healthy democracy and pave the way for a "soft" authoritarian regime. A similar critique can be found in Hannah Arendt, who wrote:

> To live an entirely private life means above all to be deprived of things essential to a truly human life: to be deprived of the reality that comes from being seen and heard by others . . . to be deprived of the possibility of achieving something more permanent than life itself. The privation of privacy lies in the absence of others; as far as they are concerned, private man does not appear, and therefore it is as though he did not exist. Whatever he does remains without significance and consequence to others, and what matters to him is without interest to other people.[38]

EUROPE'S INDIVIDUALISTIC MODEL: THE BOHEMIAN AND CREATIVE ARTIST

The individualistic loner was a model not only in America, but also in Europe. But here the geographical situation was different. In these old and established nation states there was no empty space available and an experience, such as that of the American "frontier," was unknown,[39] although the overseas colonies offered an opportunity for adventurous men and women to leave the civilized world behind. However, in Europe there were other options available. The nineteenth-century Romantic Movement had its own individualistic hero: the bohemian artist, who—like the American pioneer—didn't care about traditions, good manners, and conventions, and stood out from the crowd. The creative artist—the painter, the poet, the musician, the novelist—was the Romantic ideal "new man." To be creative one had to be individualistic. In this context Charles Taylor talked about "expressivism."

> Artistic creation becomes the paradigm mode in which people can come to self-definition. The artist becomes in some way the paradigm case of the human being, as agent of original self-definition. Since about 1800, there has been a tendency to heroize the artist, to see in his or her life the essence of the human condition, and to venerate him or her as a seer, the creator of cultural values.[40]

Romanticism supposed that each person had a unique, intrinsic source that wanted to be expressed. This emphasis on man's creativity had an anti-Enlightenment focus: "The greatest men are not the knowers," wrote Allan Bloom, "but the artists, the Homers, Dantes, Raphaels and Beethovens. Art is not imitation of nature, but liberation from nature."[41] Unlike the scientist who wants to discover the laws of nature, the creative person is himself a legislator who makes his own laws by expressing his deepest personal feelings and emotions. "Expressivism was the basis for a new and fuller individuation. This is the idea which grows in the late eighteenth century that each individual is different and original, and that this originality determines how he or she ought to live. . . . Each person is to be measured by a different yardstick, one which is properly his or her own."[42] But even if "we are called to live up to our originality,"[43] this doesn't mean that everyone is equally "original." Only those who are gifted with special talents can really claim to express this originality. The artist, often a bohemian living outside what is commonly called "civilized society," who feels neither at home with the bourgeoisie, nor with the common people, is the model to emulate. "The artist has defined himself as someone who expresses his identity by distancing himself from the accepted rules. [This means] a break with the bourgeois world defined by its conformism [and] . . . distancing himself equally from the crowd, considered to be gregarious. . . . "[44]

The idea that the artist could embody the ideal of the individualist, is also defended by Oscar Wilde in his essay "The Soul of Man under Socialism," which was published in 1899.

Art is the most intense mode of Individualism that the world has known. I am inclined to say that it is the only real mode of Individualism that the world has known . . . alone, without any reference to his neighbours, without any interference, the artist can fashion a beautiful thing; and if he does not do it solely for his own pleasure, he is not an artist at all.[45]

Wilde warned that the artist should not try to be popular or to adapt himself to popular tastes. " . . . Art should never try to be popular. The public should try to make itself artistic."[46] Hannah Arendt writes in the same vein that "the last individual left in a mass society seems to be the artist . . . he is, after all, the authentic producer of those objects which every civilization leaves behind as the quintessence and the lasting testimony of the spirit which animated it."[47] W. Somerset Maugham shares this opinion. "The artist is a lone wolf," he writes. "His way is solitary. It is to his own good that the pack should drive him out into the wilderness."[48] However, these creative loners are not only artists, but also nonconformist intellectuals who dared to challenge the accepted truths of their contemporaries. It is, for instance, telling that Karl Marx, who is considered the father of modern collectivism, concluded the preface of his major work *Capital* with the following quote: "*Segui il tuo corso, e lascia dir le genti*" (Follow your own way and let the people talk).[49] It would be hard to imagine a better motto to express individualistic nonconformity.

Modern psychological research has confirmed the basic tenets of this kind of creative individualism. In the first place it confirms the fact that the creative individual is a loner. "Why do people want to create?" asks Gregory Feist. His answer: "Some people are willing to forego social relationships and economic well-being to create lasting works."[50] "Highly creative people are generally not sociable and outgoing, but they are independent, confident, and assertive."[51] The creative person knows what he wants and has a belief in his ability to succeed: "Highly creative people . . . possess a definite and strong sense of self-efficacy, if not in general than at least in the domain of their expertise."[52] And—last, but not least: the creative person is also a nonconformist. "Conservatism and conformity continue to conflict with creativity," writes Feist.[53] An interesting case of such a creative loner is John Locke, the father of modern individualism and modern liberal democracy. Locke, who was not married and had no children, lived in exile in Holland between 1683 and 1688. In a letter, sent from Amsterdam, he praised his solitude in the following words:

My satisfaction in those many solitary howers I spent alone, industriously avoiding company, to that degree, that it was reproached to me here, that I was a man by my self. . . . Coffeehouses it is well known I loved and frequented little in England, lesse here. I speake much within compasse when I say I have not been in a Coffee house as many times as I have been months here, having noe great delight either in the conversation or the liquor. . . . My time was most spent alone, at home by my fires side, where I confesse I writ a good deale, I thinke I may say, more than ever I did in soe much time in my life. . . .[54]

It was this individualistic lifestyle which became a model to emulate in the nineteenth century.

NOTES

1. Jennifer Jacquet, *Is Shame Necessary? New Uses for an Old Tool,* op. cit., pp. 29–30.

2. Norbert Elias, "Wandlungen der Wir-Ich Balance," in Norbert Elias, *Die Gesellschaft der Individuen,* (Frankfurt am Main: Suhrkamp Verlag, 1991), p. 212.

3. Ibid., p. 214.

4. Ernst Troeltsch, *Protestantism and Progress—A Historical Study of the Relation of Protestantism to the Modern World,* (Boston: Beacon Press, 1958), p. 149.

5. Martin Luther, "Ninety-Five Theses or Disputation on the Power and Efficacy of Indulgences," in *Selected Writings of Martin Luther, Volume I, 1517–1520,* edited by Theodore G. Tappert, (Minneapolis: Fortress Press, 2007), Thesis 27, pp. 53–54.

6. Ibid., p. 52.

7. Ibid., p. 58.

8. In the words of Max Stirner (1806–1856), a German individualist anarchist, "The Catholic is satisfied when he follows an order; the Protestant acts 'to the best of his knowledge, according to his conscience.'" (Max Stirner, *Der Einzige und sein Eigentum,* [Stuttgart: Philipp Reclam Jun., 1972], p. 97).

9. Erik H. Erikson, *Young Man Luther—A Study in Psychoanalysis and History,* (New York: W. W. Norton & Company, 1962), p. 231. See also Adam B. Seligman, *Modernity's Wager—Authority, the Self, and Transcendence,* (Princeton and Oxford: Princeton University Press, 2000), p. 105: "The great struggles of Martin Luther were precisely over the foundations of justification, ultimately to be sought in the realm of an internal conscience imbued with Divine grace. Again and again in Luther's writings the workings of conscience are contrasted with law and made the bedrock of a good Christian life. . . . "

10. Ernst Troeltsch writes that Calvinist peoples "until the present day are characterized by a strongly developed, independent individuality, initiative, and a sense of responsibility for their actions . . . " (Ernst Troeltsch, *Gesammelte Schriften. Erster Band: Die Soziallehren der christlichen Kirchen und Gruppen,* [Tübingen: Scientia Verlag Aalen, 1965], p. 671).

11. Max Weber, "'Kirchen' und 'Sekten,'" in Max Weber, *Schriften 1894–1922,* op. cit., p. 236.

12. Letter of Tocqueville to Louis de Kergorlay of October 18, 1847. In Tocqueville, *Lettres choisies, Souvenirs 1814–1859,* (Paris: Gallimard, 2003), p. 589.

13. Joshua Meyrowitz, "Medium Theory: An Alternative to the Dominant Para-digm of Media Effects," in Robin L. Nabi and Mary Beth Oliver (eds), *The SAGE Handbook of Media Processes and Effects,* (Los Angeles and London: SAGE Publications, Inc., 2009), p. 521.

14. Ibid.

15. René Descartes, *Discours de la méthode,* (Paris: Livre de poche, 1970), p. 61. Descartes' formula is usually summarized as follows: "*Dubito ergo cogito, cogito ergo sum.*" (I doubt, therefore I think, I think, therefore I am).

16. John Locke, *Second Treatise of Government,* edited by C. B. Macpherson, (Indianapolis and Cambridge: Hacket Publishing Company, Inc., 1980), § 224, p. 113.

17. Ibid., § 124, p. 66.

18. Ibid., § 138, p. 73.

19. Cf. Marcel H. Van Herpen, "Early Liberals and Universal Suffrage—Their Fear of Populists and 'Dangerous' People," *Cicero Foundation Great Debate Paper,* No. 19/01, June 2019. http://www.cicerofoundation.org/lectures/Marcel_H_Van_Herpen _Early_Liberals_Fear_of_Populists.pdf.

20. Jeremy Bentham, *The Principles of Morals and Legislation,* with an introduction by Laurence J. Lafleur, (New York and London: Haffner Press, 1973), p. 3.

21. Allan Bloom, *The Closing of the American Mind,* (New York and London: Simon & Schuster, Inc., 1987), p. 85.

22. Daniel Bell, *The Cultural Contradictions of Capitalism,* (London: Heinemann, 1979), p. 21.

23. Barry Alan Shain, *The Myth of American Individualism—The Protestant Origins of American Political Thought,* (Princeton: Princeton University Press, 1994), pp. 3–4.

24. Robert N. Bellah, Richard Madsen, William M. Sullivan, Ann Swidler, and Steven M. Tipton, *Habits of the Heart—Individualism and Commitment in American Life,* (Berkeley, Los Angeles, London: University of California Press, 1996), p. 145. Note that there exists a *prima facie* resemblance to the lonely lifestyle, praised by the Stoics—including its supposed moral superiority. Seneca (c. 4 BCE–65 CE) wrote, for instance: "You are asking what you should avoid most of all? The masses . . . I never return home in the same moral state in which I left . . . " (Seneca, "Aus den Briefen an Lucilius," in Seneca, *Vom glückseligen Leben,* [Stuttgart: Albert Kröner Verlag, 1978], p. 194). And he continued: "Retreat into yourself as much as you can . . . " (p. 195). However, the difference is that the Stoic sought solitude for study and reflection, the American loner for incessant action.

25. Ralph Waldo Emerson, "Self-Reliance," in Ralph Waldo Emerson, *Self-Reliance and Other Essays,* (Mineola, NY: Dover Publications, Inc., 2017), p. 21.

26. Ibid., p. 30. Emerson did not only preach an individualistic lifestyle, he was also a living example of it. In a lecture, William James reminded his audience of Emerson's aversion to conformity: "After you have seen men a few times, he could say, you find most of them as alike as their barns and pantries, and soon as musty and dreary." (William James, "Address at the Centenary of Emerson," in William James, *Pragmatism and Other Writings,* [New York and London: Penguin, 2000], p. 312). Virginia Woolf pointed to the fact that Emerson's praise of a lonely lifestyle was,

maybe, less a question of choice than of character, writing that "he was conscious of a 'signal defect.' . . . Either he was without 'address' or there was a 'levity of the understanding' or there was an 'absence of common sympathies.' At any rate, he felt a 'sore uneasiness in the company of most men and women . . . " (Virginia Woolf, "Emerson's Journals," in Virginia Woolf, *Books and Portraits,* [Frogmore, St Albans: Triad Panther Books, 1979], p. 86).

27. Robert D. Putnam, *Our Kids—The American Dream in Crisis,* (New York and London: Simon & Schuster, 2016), p. 206.

28. James Fenimore Cooper, *The American Democrat,* with an introduction by H. L. Mencken, (Indianapolis: Liberty Fund Inc., 1981), p. 231.

29. Ibid., p. 232.

30. Ralph Waldo Emerson, "Self-Reliance," op. cit., p. 23. See also Christopher Lasch, "Nostalgia: The Abdication of Memory," in Christopher Lasch, *The True and Only Heaven: Progress and Its Critics,* (New York and London: W. W. Norton & Company, 1991), p. 94: "The novels of James Fenimore Cooper showed how the solitary hunter, unencumbered by social responsibilities, utterly self-sufficient, uncultivated but endowed with a spontaneous appreciation of natural beauty, could become the central figure in the great American romance of the West." Richard Sennett observed that the ability of Americans to maintain the independence of solitude "in the midst of the crowd" was promoted by the design of nineteenth-century railway carriages. "The nineteenth-century European railway carriage," he writes, "placed its six to eight passengers in a compartment where they faced each other, a seating plan derived from the large horse-drawn coaches of an earlier era." (Richard Sennett, *Flesh and Stone—The Body and the City in Western Civilization,* [New York and London: W. W. Norton & Company, 1996], p. 343). "The American railroad carriage," he continued, "as developed in the 1840s, puts its passengers in a position which virtually assured the desire to be left alone in silence. Without compartments, the American railroad carriages turned all passengers looking forward, staring at one another's backs rather than faces . . . it struck Old World visitors that one could cross the North American continent without having to address a word to anyone else, even though there were no physical barriers between people in the carriage" (p. 344).

31. Walt Whitman, *Song of Myself,* (New York: Dover Publications, Inc., 2001), p. 1.

32. Ibid., p. 2.

33. Charlotte Brontë, *Jane Eyre,* (Mineola, NY: Dover Publications, 2002), p. 296.

34. Frederick Jackson Turner, *The Frontier in American History,* (New York: Henry Holt and Company, 1921), p. 3.

35. Ibid.

36. Ibid., p. 30.

37. Alexis de Tocqueville, *Democracy in America,* Translation Henry Reeve, Penn State Electronic Classics Series, 2002.

38. Hannah Arendt, *The Human Condition,* (Chicago and London: The University of Chicago Press, 1958), p. 58.

39. With the exception of Russia. But in the nineteenth century in that country about one half of the peasants were serfs, bound to the land. There were not many free

people available. In order to colonize the vast territories of Siberia and the Far East an oppressive government built penal colonies where the prisoners had to perform forced labor.

40. Charles Taylor, *The Ethics of Authenticity,* (Cambridge, MA, and London: Harvard University Press, 1991), p. 62.

41. Allan Bloom, *The Closing of the American Mind,* op. cit., p. 181.

42. Charles Taylor, *Sources of the Self—The Making of the Modern Identity,* (Cambridge: Cambridge University Press, 1992), p. 375.

43. Ibid., p. 375.

44. Pierre Rosanvallon, *La société des égaux,* (Paris: Éditions du Seuil, 2011), p. 307.

45. Oscar Wilde, "The Soul of Man under Socialism," in Oscar Wilde, *The Soul of Man under Socialism and Selected Critical Prose,* (London and New York: Penguin, 2001), p. 142.

46. Ibid.

47. Hannah Arendt, "The Crisis of Culture," in Hannah Arendt, *Between Past and Future—Eight Exercises in Political Thought,* with an Introduction by Jerome Kohn, (New York and London: Penguin Books, 2006), p. 197.

48. W. Somerset Maugham, *A Writer's Notebook,* (London: William Heinemann Ltd., 1991), p. 304.

49. Karl Marx, *Das Kapital,* Volume One, (Berlin: Dietz Verlag, 1969), p. 17.

50. Gregory J. Feist, "The Function of Personality in Creativity—The Nature and Nurture of the Creative Personality," in James C. Kaufman and Robert J. Sternberg, *The Cambridge Handbook of Creativity,* (Cambridge: Cambridge University Press, 2010), p. 122.

51. Ibid., p.121.

52. Ibid.

53. Ibid., p. 122.

54. John Locke, Letter to Thomas Herbert, Eighth Earl of Pembroke, Amsterdam, 28 November / 8 December 1684, in John Locke, *Selected Correspondence,* edited by Mark Goldie, (Oxford and New York: Oxford University Press, 2007), p. 99.

Chapter 4

Economic Individualism

Individualism's "Ugly Face"?

The emergence of the Western guilt culture is closely associated with increasing individualism. However, individualism is not an unambiguous concept. In the preceding chapter we have seen that political individualism is based on the equal worth and equal rights of the individual, and was, therefore, defined as the common project of equal citizens. As such it was quite different from the lifestyle ideal of the individualist loner—regardless of how this loner was conceived: cowboy, explorer, artist, or intellectual. The model of the individualistic loner seemed to be completely at odds with political individualism's premises. Instead of emphasizing man's equality, in effect, it did the opposite: it emphasized the difference and the uniqueness of a special group of people, namely the creative, nonconformist loners. Individualism is, therefore, a multifaceted and often contradictory phenomenon. The contradiction between political individualism and the idealized model of the individualistic loner is duplicated in another contradiction which emerged in the nineteenth century, namely between political individualism on the one hand and economic individualism on the other. Economic individualism was not new. It emerged during the Renaissance with the rise of an economically independent urban bourgeoisie. However, it became dominant during the industrial revolution, when a new class of capitalist entrepreneurs emerged. These new capitalists agreed wholeheartedly with Locke's thesis that private property is a natural right of the individual, a right which Locke based on the labor with which the individual transforms nature. The labor of this new class of capitalists was their entrepreneurial activity, which, in order to be effective, needed maximum freedom. This meant that it should be free from government interference. This was clearly at odds with the tenets of political individualism which explicitly tasked the state to actively defend citizens' rights. However, rather than an active state, which defended the natural rights and freedoms of citizens, the new entrepreneurial class preferred a passive state or a "minimal

45

state" which gave them maximum leeway and maximum freedom of action.[1] In their view the state should restrict its economic interference to some basic tasks, such as monetary policy, levying protective import tariffs, and the enforcement of contracts. The new economic individualism—Macpherson speaks, tellingly, about "possessive individualism"[2]—glorified *homo oeconomicus*, the rational individual who calculates his maximum profit. This *homo oeconomicus* is competitive and narrowly self-interested, not hesitating to exploit those who are dependent on him. Christopher Lash describes how this new, competitive, economic individualism became triumphant at the end of the nineteenth century:

> The nineteenth-century cult of success placed surprisingly little emphasis on competition. It measured achievement not against the achievements of others but against an abstract ideal of discipline and self-denial. At the turn of the century, however, preachments on success began to stress the will to win. The bureaucratization of the corporate career changed the conditions of self-advancement; ambitious young men now had to compete with their peers for the attention and approval of their superiors.[3]

Ruth Benedict was even more critical of this new form of individualism, comparing it with the behavior of prison inmates. "In our own generation," she wrote, "extreme forms of ego-gratification are culturally supported. . . . Arrogant and unbridled egoists as family men, as officers of the law and in business, have been again and again portrayed by novelists and dramatists . . . their courses of action are often more asocial than those of the inmates of penitentiaries. In terms of the suffering and frustration that they spread about them there is probably no comparison."[4] Economic individualism is the ideological expression of an emerging bureaucratic industrial society in which two classes—capitalists and wage-laborers—increasingly oppose each other and in which the ruling class doesn't feel inhibited by regulations.

ECONOMIC INDIVIDUALISM VERSUS POLITICAL INDIVIDUALISM?

It is interesting that the Founding Fathers of the young American republic had already warned against this phenomenon, denouncing the formation of a class society, or—what they called—*factions*. "By a faction," wrote James Madison, "I understand a number of citizens whether amounting to a majority or minority of the whole, who are united and actuated by some common impulse of passion, or of interest, adverse to the rights of other citizens, or to the permanent and aggregate interests of the community."[5] And he added:

" . . . The most common and durable source of factions has been the . . . unequal distribution of property."[6] If political individualism was individualism's moral, modern, and enlightened "pretty face," and the individualistic loner its "ethically neutral face," economic individualism, which promoted man's egoism, was rather individualism's "ugly face." "Whereas a belief in political individualism did not require one to turn against the best interests of others," writes Stephanie Walls, "economic individualism was understood as a zero-sum game in which one must lose for another to win."[7] Economic individualism had a negative effect on societal bonds. While political individualism makes the individual citizen responsible for society as a whole, realizing a political project together with his fellow-countrymen, economic individualism is self-centered and preoccupied with the gratification of one's own desires and wishes.

This economic individualism was boosted by the emergence of a modern industrial society at the end of the nineteenth century and particularly by the rapid urbanization with which it was accompanied. New York City, for instance, which in 1880 had 1,206,299 inhabitants, grew in the period 1880–1920 to a metropolis of 5,620,048.[8] European capitals, such as Berlin and Paris, equally showed unprecedented growth. Paris grew from 1,696,000 inhabitants in 1861 to 2,650,000 in 1900.[9] Berlin almost doubled its population between 1880 and 1920, growing from 1,123,749 to 1,902,509 inhabitants.[10] The sociologist Georg Simmel emphasized the role of the modern metropolis as an incubator of individualism. In his study on the psychological influence of the metropolis he wrote that "the consequences for the independence of the individual of the mutual reserve and indifference [and of] the psychological conditions of life in great conglomerations are nowhere more intensively experienced than in the dense crowd of the metropolis, because the physical closeness and intimacy makes the psychological distance all the more vivid. . . . "[11]

However, the emergence of economic individualism did not mean that it replaced political individualism. Both existed side by side. The point is that economic individualism had a negative influence on political individualism. Instead of offering a level playing field the increasing economic inequality gave rich people, who had the financial means and the leisure time to conduct expensive and time-consuming election campaigns, an advantage. This contradiction between political individualism and economic individualism, the professed equality of political rights on the one hand and the existing economic inequality in civil society on the other, had already been heavily criticized in the nineteenth century. It became, for instance, a central issue in the work of Karl Marx (1818–1883).[12] Economic individualism led also to a weakening of the guilt culture. In the economic rat race in which there were only winners and losers it was important to be on the winners' side. Even if this implied using dubious methods the winners were not excessively tormented by a guilty conscience.[13]

HERBERT HOOVER ON EQUALITY OF OPPORTUNITY

How could political individualism, which emphasized the equality of citizens and was in favor of an active role for the state, be reconciled with economic individualism, which advocated a minimal role for the state? And—more importantly—how could one prevent political equality being undermined by the growing economic inequality? In his book *American Individualism*, published in 1922, Herbert Hoover suggested that he had found a solution to this problem. Hoover, who would become America's thirty-first president in 1929, confessed that he was "an individualist—an unashamed individualist."[14] "But let me say also," he continued, "that I am an American individualist. For America has been steadily developing the ideals that constitute progressive individualism."[15] Hoover acknowledged that economic individualism posed a problem. "No doubt," he wrote, "individualism run riot, with no tempering principle, would provide a long category of inequalities, of tyrannies, dominations, and injustices."[16] But he reassured his readers that American individualism actually had such a "tempering principle."

> Our individualism differs from all the others because it embraces these great ideals: that while we build our society upon the attainment of the individual, we shall safeguard to every individual an equality of opportunity to take that position in the community to which his intelligence, character, ability, and ambition entitle him; that we keep the social solution free from frozen strata classes. . . .[17]

According to Hoover the principle of "equality of opportunity" would prevent America from becoming a class society, because talented working class people had the opportunity to study or to start a business and improve their situation. Social mobility was the magic phrase which would prevent America from becoming a class society.[18] But was the fact that a capitalist society permitted some of its most active and intelligent members to leave their class and join the ruling political and economic elite sufficient proof that there were no "frozen strata classes"? What about the great mass of workers who were left behind? These questions would become even more pressing when in 1929—seven years after the publication of his book—Hoover became president. In September of the same year he would be confronted with the New York stock exchange crash which would lead to the Great Depression. Neither "equality of opportunity," nor "social mobility" offered a solution for the mass unemployment and deep impoverishment of the American population. The much-touted "minimal state" of economic individualists was unable to solve the huge problems caused by the Depression. However, even the crash was insufficient reason for Hoover to change his ideas. As evidence that substantial equality of opportunity still existed in the United States Hoover observed: "Of the twelve men comprising the President, Vice-President, and Cabinet, nine have earned their own way in life without economic inheritance, and eight of them started with manual labor."[19] Richard Hofstadter, a political analyst, commented ironically: "Hoover's idea of an adequate statistical sample was pretty meager. . . . "[20] According to Christopher Lasch, "Americans clung to an utterly unrealistic conception of society as a ladder, which anyone with energy and ambition could hope to climb, whereas it should have been apparent that those at the top had pulled the ladder after them."[21]

Hoover's successor, Franklin Delano Roosevelt, would start the New Deal, an ambitious and successful program of government intervention, based on the "Three R's"—a program of Relief, Recovery, and Reform, which included public works and provided financial security to retirees, farmers, the unemployed, and people with disabilities. The New Deal would usher in a new era in which the principle of the state having a distributive function became widely accepted—even, although reluctantly, by the most ardent defenders of economic individualism. One of these, Friedrich Hayek, wrote that "no political term has suffered worse . . . than individualism."[22] "It not only has been distorted by its opponents into an unrecognizable caricature . . . but has been used to describe several attitudes toward society which have as little in common among themselves as they have with those traditionally regarded as their opposites."[23] Hayek admitted that "the belief that individualism approves and encourages human selfishness is one of the main reasons why so many people dislike it."[24] However, he concluded, "we must face the fact that the preservation of individual freedom is incompatible with a full satisfaction of our views of distributive justice."[25] One can agree with him that even in the best of all worlds a *full* satisfaction of our views of distributive justice will be unlikely. But this doesn't mean that in a society based on economic individualism one does not need an active policy of redistributive justice to reduce economic inequality. With the advent of the modern welfare state after the Second World War the hardest sides of economic individualism seemed to have been—finally, and as was hoped: definitively—overcome. However, in the 1970s economic individualism made its comeback with a vengeance, when, after the oil crisis of 1973, neoliberal market fundamentalism became the leading ideology. This ideology "acquiesced in, or even embraced, greed as a dominant human motivation, which believed that most policy issues had market-based solutions, and which favoured only the most minimal regulation. . . . The practical workhorse of market fundamentalism was Economic Man, an unappealing mammal who responded only to financial incentives. Greedy, selfish and potentially lazy, he exemplified *possessive individualism.*[26] This new wave of economic individualism would lead twenty years later to an upsurge of populism which threatened to undermine the very foundations of political individualism.[27]

CONSPICUOUS CONSUMPTION: THE EMERGENCE OF THE NEW CONSUMERISM

In the United States the high tide of economic individualism, the period between 1870 and 1900, is usually referred to as the Gilded Age. It was a period of rapid economic development, boosted by massive industrialization, nationwide urbanization, and revolutionary technological inventions, such as the telegraph, the automobile, and electricity. From a nation of small, independent farmers America became a modern, industrial society. The Gilded Age was known for its rich tycoons, such as the Morgans, Vanderbilts, Rockefellers, Carnegies, Goulds, and Harrimans, who were known as the "robber barons." They "were held to be uneducated and uncultivated, irresponsible, rootless and corrupt, devoid of refinement or of any sense of noblesse."[28] At the same time they were envied, because " . . . the new plutocracy had set standards of such extravagance and such notoriety that everyone else felt humbled by comparison."[29] The robber barons had money, a lot of money, and they wanted the world to know it by showing off their wealth in an ostentatious way. Scrooge McDuck—also known as Dagobert Duck in Germany and the Netherlands and Picsou in France—was the cartoon character that the Walt Disney Company modeled on this figure, and children around the world could see how Scrooge McDuck literally swam in a pool filled to the brim with golden coins and banknotes. The robber barons might not have done that, but they had other means of showing off their newly acquired wealth, such as building splendid castle-like mansions in Newport, Rhode Island, organizing sumptuous feasts, investing in expensive art collections, and founding philanthropic organizations. The new rich spent their leisure time traveling abroad, with a preference for the French Riviera and the casino at Monte Carlo. For the new millionaire gambling was a means "to prove that he had money to burn. If he was rich, he could not lose. If he dropped ten or fifty thousand, he showed to his audience that he was a man who could lose such sums."[30]

This process of "conspicuous consumption" of the new rich was analyzed by the sociologist Thorstein Veblen in his book *A Theory of the Leisure Class,* published in 1899. According to Veblen the conspicuous consumption of this rich leisure class set a model for the rest of society. This was not to imply that this leisure class would per se be a moral model or an example of good taste. On the contrary. Often the uncultivated new rich had a preference for extravagant and gaudy objects, if not for outright kitsch. Veblen wrote for instance, referring to their pets, that "the commercial value of canine monstrosities, such as the prevailing styles of pet dogs both for men's and women's use, rest on their high cost of production and their value to their owners lies chiefly in their utility as items of conspicuous consumption."[31] What ultimately counted was their wealth. "The leisure class stands at the head of the social structure in point of reputability, and its manner of life and its standards of worth therefore afford the norm of reputability for the community. The observance of these standards . . . becomes incumbent upon all classes lower in the scale."[32] Through its conspicuous consumption the leisure class became the standard bearer of a new phenomenon: *consumerism*, which included not only the consumption of goods, but also of services and the use of leisure time.

> There are . . . measurable degrees of conformity to the latest accredited code of the punctilios as regards decorous means and methods of consumption. Differences between one person and another in the degree of conformity to the ideal in these respects can be compared, and persons may be graded and scheduled with some accuracy and effect according to a progressive scale of manners and breeding. The award of reputability in this regard is commonly made in good faith, on the ground of conformity to accepted canons of taste in the matters concerned. . . .[33]

HOW CONSUMERISM BREEDS CONFORMITY

The superrich became the trendsetters not only for *what* should be consumed, but also for *how* it should be consumed. This was, of course, not a completely new phenomenon. In feudal societies similarly members of the nobility enjoyed a much more luxurious lifestyle than the common people. But in a feudal society this conspicuous consumption remained the privilege of the "happy few" and the great mass of the population, mostly serfs, farmers, and artisans, knew that this would never be available to them. The mass production of goods, which began to develop around the turn of the twentieth century, changed this overnight. The invention of the assembly line and Fordist work organization created a new kind of society: a consumer economy, and, with it, *consumerism*. During the 1920s the US economy grew 42 percent. The United States became the world's economic powerhouse, producing almost half of the world's output. Average income rose from $6,460 to $8,016 per person.[34] The consumerist appetite was whetted by generous credit facilities. "Previously one had to save in order to buy. But with credit cards one could indulge in instant gratification. The system was transformed by mass production and mass consumption, by the creation of new wants and new means of gratifying those wants."[35]

In the beginning this consumerism was an offshoot of economic individualism: the more successful one's economic career the greater one's ability to show off this success in conspicuous consumption and to distinguish oneself from those lower down the ladder, who were less well off. This early consumerism had a *prima facie* similarity with the nineteenth-century individualist personality ideal because in the same way it did not emphasize the similarities between individuals, but rather their differences. However, the quality of these differences was not the same. The nineteenth-century personality ideal celebrated the individualistic loner who expressed himself through his adventurous lifestyle or his creative activity. He was considered completely unique. Twentieth-century consumerist individualism, on the contrary, was neither active nor creative, but a question of *passive consumption* of goods and services produced and made available by modern industrial society. It was a reason for Hannah Arendt to criticize Marx, who assumed that when people are liberated from exhausting, "necessary" labor, they will use their energy to nourish "higher" activities. "A hundred years after Marx we know the fallacy of this reasoning," she wrote, "the spare time of the *animal laborans* is never spent in anything but consumption, and the more time left to him, the greedier and more craving his appetites."[36]

While the creative romantic individualist was a loner who distanced himself from society, the modern consumer wholeheartedly embraced modern society, which could satisfy almost all his wishes. This consumer expressed his individualism not by his activities or his work, but by the choices he made with regards to his consumption. In these choices he did not express some creative "inner self," but, rather, he followed the dominant tastes of his society, in particular the tastes of the superrich. And when he became aware that these consumption models could not be emulated, he tried to copy models closer at hand in a never ending effort "to keep up with the Joneses." "Keeping up with the Joneses" implied a differentiation of sex roles at a time in which men were still the primary breadwinners. "The familiar theme of conspicuous consumption," observed Erving Goffman, "describes how husbands in modern society have the job of acquiring socio-economic status, and wives the job of displaying this acquisition."[37]

Despite the urge to distinguish oneself, conformity was the defining characteristic of this consumerism. This was the case for even the superrich, who sought the company of likeminded and preferably equally rich people with whom they could share their extravagant patterns of consumption and leisure which were far beyond the reach of the common man. Robert Bellah and his co-authors speak in this context about "lifestyle enclaves."

The term "lifestyle" . . . they write, "is linked most closely to leisure and consumption and is usually unrelated to the world of work. It brings together those who are socially, economically, or culturally similar, and one of its chief aims is the enjoyment of being with those who "share one's lifestyle." . . . Lifestyle is fundamentally segmental and celebrates the narcissism of similarity. It usually explicitly involves a contrast with others who "do not share one's lifestyle." For this reason, we speak not of lifestyle communities . . . but of lifestyle enclaves. Such enclaves are segmental in two senses. They involve only a segment of each individual, for they concern only private life, especially leisure and consumption. And they are segmental socially in that they include only those with a common lifestyle.[38]

However, despite this conformism within the social in-group there remained an urge to distinguish oneself vis-à-vis the out-group—particularly, but not only, at the top of the hierarchy. When the superrich noticed that other groups began to adopt their modes of consumption and leisure, they felt obliged to invent ever more extravagant ways of consumption. This was not only the case for the consumption of goods, but equally for the way they spent their leisure time. This trend can be observed in their preference for certain branches of sport. When tennis became more popular and was no longer an elite sport, they switched to golf. When golf became more popular they began to switch to polo. Their holiday destinations, too, changed. When mass tourism began to invade the idyllic paradises they had reserved for themselves, they searched ceaselessly for even more exotic and faraway places to spend their leisure time.

That said, there were also countervailing trends. David Riesman has pointed to the fact that abundance led to a certain consumption fatigue. "It has, I believe, been the bounteousness of modern industry," he wrote, "especially in America, which has done more than almost anything else to make conspicuous consumption obsolete here. It would go much too far to say that consumption bores us, but it no longer has the old, self-evident quality. . . . "[39] "Boring" as it may have become, consumption occupied nevertheless such an important place in American family life that "Steve Jobs revealed that the question of which washing machine to purchase could dominate his family's dinner table for weeks. (Nor did the brilliant inventor find this fact problematic; he offered it as an example of democratic deliberation)."[40] However, it was a fact that the conspicuous consumption by the fast expanding group of new millionaires was looked down upon by 'old money.' "In this situation, the more established wealth and its auxiliary leaders of high taste sought to fight back, not by a futile outspending, but by a conspicuous underspending."[41] We have seen, in this chapter, how economic individualism weakened the importance of guilt feelings and gave rise to a consumerist society. In the next chapter we will analyze how this new consumerism, in its turn, affected individualism and was one of the causes of a change of character.

NOTES

1. A modern protagonist of this economic individualism is the American author Ayn Rand. In an essay, titled "Let Us Alone!" she writes "that the only way a government can be of service to national prosperity is by keeping its hands off." Cf. Ayn Rand (ed.), *Capitalism: The Unknown Ideal,* (New York: New American Library, 1967), p. 141.

2. Macpherson criticizes liberal individualism, because it defines "the individual as essentially the proprietor of his own person or capacities, owing nothing to society for them. The individual was seen neither as a moral whole, nor as part of a larger social whole, but as owner of himself. . . . Society consists of relations of exchange between proprietors. Political society becomes a calculated device for the protection of this property and for the maintenance of an orderly relation of exchange." (C. B. Macpherson, *The Political Theory of Possessive Individualism—Hobbes to Locke,* [London, Oxford, New York: Oxford University Press, 1972], p. 3).

3. Christopher Lasch, *The Culture of Narcissism—American Life in An Age of Diminishing Expectations,* (New York: Warner Books, 1979), pp. 113–14.

4. Ruth Benedict, *Patterns of Culture,* (Boston and New York: Houghton Mifflin Company, 1934), p. 277.

5. Alexander Hamilton, James Madison, John Jay, *The Federalist Papers,* (New York, Ontario, London: New American Library, 1961), Paper #10, p. 78.

6. Ibid. p. 79.

7. Stephanie M. Walls, *Individualism in the United States—A Transformation in American Political Thought,* (New York and London: Bloomsbury Academic, 2015), p. 87.

8. Cf. Campbell Gibson and Kay Jung, "Table 23. Nativity of the Population for the 50 Largest Urban Places: 1870 to 2000," (Historical Census Statistics on the Foreign-Born Population of the United States: 1850–2000), Washington DC 20233–8800: US Census Bureau Population Division, February 2006. https://www.census.gov/population/www/documentation/twps0081/tables/tab23.xls Even if one considers that Brooklyn City, which in 1880 had 566,663 inhabitants, merged with New York City in 1898, this meant that in the period 1880–1920 the population of New York more than tripled.

9. Cf. Paris Atlas Historique. http://paris-atlas-historique.fr/resources/tableau+population.jpg.

10. "Bevölkerungsentwicklung Berlin," Berlingeschichte Stadtentwicklung. https://berlingeschichte.de/stadtentwicklung/texte/4_13_bvoelent.htm.

11. Georg Simmel, "Die Großstädte und das Geistesleben," in Georg Simmel, *Aufsätze und Abhandlungen 1901–1908,* Volume I, (Frankfurt am Main: Suhrkamp Verlag, 1995), p. 126.

12. Marcel H. Van Herpen, *Becoming Marx - How the Young Karl Marx Became a Marxist,* (Maastricht: Cicero Foundation Press, 2016), p. 164: "For Marx it is the tragedy for modern man that he can realize his social essence in an abstract, formal way—in the state. On the other hand, in civil society—the sphere in which he daily lives and works—he acts on the basis of pure egoistic self-interest."

13. An exponent of this economic individualism is Donald Trump, who thinks in terms of losers versus winners. "I know that sounds harsh," he writes, "but let's face it—some people *are* losers." (Donald Trump, *How to Get Rich,* [New York: Ballantine Books, 2005], p. 88).

14. Herbert Hoover, *American Individualism,* (New York: Doubleday, Page & Company, 1922), p. 7.

15. Ibid., pp. 7–8.

16. Ibid., p. 8.

17. Ibid., p. 9.

18. Robert Nisbet wrote that Americans, instead of a class consciousness, had a "level consciousness." "Unlike class consciousness, level consciousness makes for a high degree of individualism with respect to aspirations and life chances; it does not promote feelings of identification or collective involvement. The principal motive of the level conscious individual is to pass up and out of the level in which he finds himself. He is, so to speak, on the make. He lives in an atmosphere of competition . . . Level consciousness creates awareness of one's differences from others, rather than similarities, and in this respect the individual is constantly moved by distinctions he invents between himself and the others, by preoccupation, even anxiety with these distinctions." (Robert A. Nisbet, "The Decline and Fall of Social Class," in Robert A. Nisbet, *Tradition and Revolt—Historical and Sociological Essays,* [New York: Vintage Books, 1970], p. 125).

19. Quoted in Richard Hofstadter, *The American Political Tradition,* (New York: Vintage Books, 1948), pp. 297–98.

20. Ibid., p. 298.

21. Christopher Lasch, *The Revolt of the Elites and the Betrayal of Democracy,* (New York and London: W. W. Norton & Company, 1995), p. 56. The belief of Americans in the principle of equality of opportunity seems to be indestructible. Michael Sandel wrote, for instance, that "the rhetoric of rising now rings hollow. In today's economy, it is not easy to rise. Americans born to poor parents tend to stay poor as adults. Of those born in the bottom fifth of the income scale, only about one in twenty will make it to the top fifth; most will not even rise to the middle class." However, he continued, "seventy percent of Americans believe the poor can make it out of poverty on their own, while only 35 percent of Europeans think so." (Michael J. Sandel, *The Tyranny of Merit—What's Become of the Common Good?* [New York and London: Allen Lane, 2020], p. 23).

22. F. A. Hayek, *Individualism and Economic Order,* (Chicago: University of Chicago Press, 1958), p. 3.

23. Ibid.

24. Ibid., p. 13.

25. Ibid., p. 22.

26. Paul Collier and John Kay, *Greed Is Dead—Politics After Individualism,* (London and New York: Allen Lane, 2020), p. 14.

27. On this populist backlash see my book *The End of Populism—Twenty Proposals to Defend Liberal Democracy,* (Manchester: Manchester University Press, 2021).

28. Richard Hofstadter, *The Age of Reform—From Bryan to F.D.R.,* (New York: Vintage Books, 1955) p. 141.

29. Ibid., p. 147.

30. John Kenneth Galbraith, *The Age of Uncertainty,* (London: British Broadcasting Corporation, 1977), p. 70.

31. Thorstein Veblen, *The Theory of the Leisure Class—An Economic Study of Institutions,* New York: B. W. Huebsch, 1922), p. 142.

32. Ibid., p. 84.

33. Ibid., p. 51.

34. Cf. Kimberly Amadeo, "1920s Economy—What Made the Twenties Roar," *The Balance,* January 3, 2020. https://www.thebalance.com/roaring-twenties-4060511.

35. Daniel Bell, *The Cultural Contradictions of Capitalism,* (London: Heinemann, 1979), p. 21.

36. Hannah Arendt, *The Human Condition,* op. cit., p. 133. (Emphasis in text, MHVH).

37. Erving Goffman, *The Presentation of Self in Everyday Life,* (London and New York: Penguin Books, 1990), p. 107.

38. Robert N. Bellah, Richard Madsen, William M. Sullivan, Ann Swidler, and Steven M. Tipton, *Habits of the Heart—Individualism and Commitment in American Life,* op. cit., p. 72.

39. David Riesman, "New Standards for Old," in David Riesman, *Individualism Reconsidered,* (New York: Doubleday & Company, Inc., 1955), p. 156.

40. Susan Neiman, *Why Grow Up? Subversive Thoughts for an Infantile Age,* (London and New York: Penguin Books, 2016), p. 41.

41. David Riesman, "New Standards for Old," op. cit., p. 157.

Chapter 5

The "Other-Directed Person"

Conformity Instead of Individualism?

The new consumer society reached its apotheosis in the decades following the Second World War. The new affluence had a deep influence on lifestyle and personality ideals. The model to emulate was no longer the creative person or the self-reliant loner who distanced himself from society, but an individual who wanted to distinguish himself by his consumption choices. Rather than by originality this consumption pattern was characterized by conformity with the prevalent tastes and fashions: the "new man" of the consumer society was clearly a conformist.

RIESMAN'S "LONELY CROWD"

The psychological make-up and personality of this "new man" is described by David Riesman and two collaborators in their famous study *The Lonely Crowd*. In this book the authors distinguish the modern "other-directed person" from the nineteenth-century and early-twentieth-century "inner-directed person."

> The other-directed person's tremendous outpouring of energy is channeled into the ever expanding frontiers of consumption, as the inner-directed person's energy was channeled relentlessly into production. Inner-directed patterns often discouraged consumption for adults as well as children.[1]

While the inner-directed person was the prevalent character type in a society which emphasized production, the other-directed person represents a society which emphasizes consumption. But that was not all. There were more differences between these two character types. According to Riesman, after his primary socialization the inner-directed person developed a psychological mechanism which he called a "psychological gyroscope." "This instrument," he writes, "once it is set by the parents and other authorities, keeps the inner-directed person, as we shall see, 'on course' even when tradition, as responded to by his character, no longer dictates his moves."[2] The inner-directed person can make use not only of this "psychological gyroscope," he also has self-discipline and is production-driven, because "the task of production is no longer left to an external group sanction or situational pressure but is installed as a drive in the individual. . . . "[3] The inner-directed person is characterized by a protestant work ethic and a guilt morality, because when he does not live up to the standards he has set himself, he "may respond to these demands by guilt. . . . "[4] His attitude to work is one of "long-term commitment" which requires "long-term investment," because, explains Riesman, "to build a railroad or an Indian civil service or the intellectual system of a Comte, a Clerk Maxwell, or a Marx was not an affair of a few months."[5]

In the modern consumer society this inner-directed person gave way to a new personality type: that of the other-directed person. According to Riesman this type of character "seems to be emerging in very recent years in the upper middle class of our larger cities. . . . "[6] The formation of this new character type was not only the consequence of the consumer society, but also of new child-rearing practices, characterized by the spread of permissive child care, leading to a relaxation of parental discipline. "Under these newer patterns the peer-group (the group of one's associates of the same age and class) becomes much more important to the child, while the parents make him feel guilty not so much about violation of inner standards as about failure to be popular or otherwise to manage his relations with these other children."[7] Riesman considers this influence of the peer-group a determining factor for the emergence of the new character type of the "other-directed" person.

> *What is common to all the other-directed people is that their contemporaries are the source of direction for the individual.* . . . This mode of keeping in touch with others permits a close behavioral conformity, not through drill in behavior itself, as in the tradition-directed character, but rather through an exceptional sensitivity to the actions and wishes of others.[8]

The other-directed person lacks the "gyroscope" of the inner-directed person. Instead he has a "radar" which enables him to pick up signals which come from his direct environment—particularly from his peer-group. This character type breeds conformity, because "approval itself, irrespective of content, becomes almost the only unequivocal good in this situation: one makes good when one is approved of."[9] Riesman did not mention it explicitly, but he puts his finger on another important issue: the gradual transformation of a "guilt culture" into a "shame culture." In effect, the "gyroscope" of the inner-directed person corresponds with the individual conscience in a guilt culture, while the "radar" of the other-directed person is instead an instrument to adapt oneself to the tastes and preferences of one's peers in order to avoid shame.

This replacement of a guilt culture by a shame culture has also been observed by other authors, who equally point to changes in childrearing policies, particularly to the diminished role of the father in the education of the child. This was behind the German psychiatrist Alexander Mitscherlich speaking about a "fatherless society." According to him the traditional father would have transmitted two things to the child: "A schedule for adapted behavior would have been developed, which we call *conscience* ('Superego'), and, secondly, a capacity to confront life would have been transmitted by the father to the son."[10] According to Mitscherlich this would no longer be the case, because "in the North American system of cultural models of behavior one can observe a clear contempt for the father."[11] This "clear contempt" for the father which Mitscherlich observes in the United States seems a bit exaggerated. Edward Shorter has a different view. He points to "a fundamental shift in the willingness of adolescents to learn from their parents . . . parents are losing their role as educators. The task passes instead to the peers. . . . The parents become friends (an affective relationship), not representatives of a lineage (a functional relationship). If this is so, we are dealing with an unprecedented pattern."[12] For Shorter the parents themselves become some kind of friendly "peers."

Also Christopher Lasch sees this diminished role of the father, but for him this is not the result of a spontaneous retreat, but rather of societal changes characterized by the increasing dependence of the nuclear family on external experts:

> Thus the family struggles to conform to an ideal of the family imposed from without. The experts agree that the parents should neither tyrannize over their children nor burden them with "oversolicitous" attentions. They agree, moreover, that every action is the product of a long causal chain and that moral judgments have no place in child rearing. This proposition, central to the mental health ethic, absolves the child from moral responsibility, while leaving that of his parents undiminished. Under these conditions, it is not surprising that many parents seek to escape the exercise of this responsibility by avoiding confrontations with the child and by retreating from the work of discipline and character formation. Permissive ideologies rationalize this retreat.[13]

THE OTHER-DIRECTED PERSON: A NEW CHARACTER
TYPE ADAPTED TO THE SERVICE ECONOMY

Riesman's book had an immediate and profound impact. Many readers of the book tended to interpret inner-directness and other-directness as two moral models, of which the first was considered superior. However, in a preface, written in 1969—nineteen years after the first edition—Riesman distanced himself from these moralistic interpretations and warned against an idealization of the inner-directed person. Riesman was right: it was not the sociologist's role to prescribe or idealize a social character, because social characters as such cannot be "chosen"—they are often the products of social factors which are beyond the influence of the individual. The sociologist is rather someone who "takes the temperature of the patient" and when he prescribes some cure, he does so hesitatingly, conscious of his own limitations and fallibility. One should also not forget that Riesman's two character types were "ideal types" as conceived by Max Weber: crystallizations of bundles of character traits which one would seldom find in this pure form in reality.[14]

Riesman insists that in the modern post-industrial society a different kind of education is developing which is adapted to prepare the young generation for new occupational roles. The members of this generation have less need to develop an inner "gyroscope," because their work involves less and less working with materials and increasingly the management of one's relations with clients on the one hand and colleagues and superiors on the work floor on the other hand. This new emphasis on the management of personal relations led to all kinds of self-help books, of which Dale Carnegie's *How to Win Friends and Influence People*, published in 1936, is one of the best known. In this book, which became a world bestseller, Carnegie wrote that "dealing with people is probably the biggest problem you face, especially if you are in business."[15] "Dealing with people" didn't mean for Carnegie that one should blindly follow others and adapt oneself. It was also a question of influencing, if not outright manipulating other people. In the words of Carnegie: "Say to yourself over and over: 'My popularity, my happiness and sense of worth depend to no small extent upon my skill in dealing with people.'"[16]

TOCQUEVILLE ON THE AMERICAN CHARACTER

In his time Alexis de Tocqueville had already observed a prominent feature of the American character: its materialism. It was described by him in Volume II of *Democracy in America* under the heading "Why the Americans are so restless in the midst of their prosperity." "In America," he wrote, "I saw the freest and most enlightened men placed in the happiest circumstances that the world affords; it seemed to me as if a cloud habitually hung upon their brow, and I thought them serious and almost sad, even in their pleasures."[17] Why? The chief reason was that they "are forever brooding over advantages they do not possess. It is strange to see with what feverish ardor the Americans pursue their own welfare, and to watch the vague dread that constantly torments them lest they should not have chosen the shortest path which may lead to it."[18] "At first sight," he continued, "there is something surprising in this strange unrest of so many happy men, restless in the midst of abundance."[19] Tocqueville concluded: "He who has set his heart exclusively upon the pursuit of worldly welfare is always in a hurry, for he has but a limited time at his disposal to reach, to grasp, and to enjoy it."[20] The materialist streak in the American character, observed by Tocqueville a century earlier, was able to be fully satisfied after the Second World War when consumer goods, previously reserved for the "happy few," became available to the broader public. Even people with modest incomes could buy on credit and they did not hesitate to use their new purchasing power—buying new cars and the latest electrical equipment, such as TVs, gramophones, vacuum cleaners, refrigerators, and washing machines. The postwar boom period lasted about thirty years, not only in America, but also in Europe. The Germans spoke of a *Wirtschaftswunder*—an "Economic Miracle"—and the French of the *Trente Glorieuses*—the "Glorious Thirty Years." However, did this spending spree bring the expected happiness?

MASLOW'S MESSAGE: MAN DOESN'T LIVE BY BREAD ALONE

One of the first to cast doubt on the benefits of extravagant consumption was the psychologist Abraham Maslow. In an article, published in 1943, he developed a hierarchy of human needs. At the lower end of this pyramid were the "basic needs," such as food, drink, and shelter. If these physiological needs are relatively well gratified, he argued, there emerges a second set of needs: the "safety needs." When these are more or less satisfied, "love needs" follow—the need for love, affection, and belongingness. Next come the "esteem needs": in the first place the need for self-esteem, and in the second place the need for esteem from others in the form of reputation, recognition, and respect. On top of this come the "need for self-actualization" and "the desires to know and understand." The essential message of Maslow's theory was that "man does not live by bread alone." The availability of food was necessary on a basic level, but, once this basic need was gratified, other, "higher" needs emerged. The highest needs of this pyramid were the need for self-actualization and the need to know and understand. The gratification of the lower needs wouldn't lead to real satisfaction, because, according to Maslow, "even if all these needs are satisfied, we may still often (if not always) expect that a new discontent and restlessness will soon develop, unless the individual is doing what he is fitted for. A musician must make music, an artist must paint, a poet must write, if he is to be ultimately happy. What a man *can* be, he *must* be. This need we may call self-actualization."[21] The need for self-actualization was "the desire to become more and more what one is, to become everything that one is capable of becoming."[22] However, unlike the authors of the Romantic era, Maslow did not attribute this need only to creative people.

> The specific form that these needs will take will of course vary greatly from person to person. In one individual it may take the form of the desire to be an ideal mother, in another it may be expressed athletically, and in still another it may be expressed in painting pictures or in inventions. It is not necessarily a creative urge although in people who have any capacities for creation it will take this form.[23]

In his book *Motivation and Personality,* published in 1954, Maslow elaborated this theory further. He once more emphasized that the gratification of basic needs gave no lasting satisfaction, writing that " . . . one of the possible consequences of basic need gratifications may be boredom, aimlessness, anomie and the like. Apparently we function best when we are striving for something that we lack, when we wish for something that we do not have, and when we organize our powers in the service of striving toward the gratification of that wish. The state of gratification turns out to be not necessarily a state of guaranteed happiness or contentment."[24] These lines could be read as an early criticism of the emerging consumer society and its dominant character: the other-directed person. What might be made of, for instance, the following remark? "Young people are unsure of themselves, not yet formed, uneasy because of their minority position with their peers (their private opinions and tastes are more square, straight, metamotivated, i.e., virtuous, than average). They are secretly uneasy about cruelty, meanness, and mob spirit so often found in young people, etc."[25] Without mentioning him, Maslow seems here to be criticizing Riesman, arguing that other-directed young people are better and more virtuous than supposed and in their hearts less influenced by the "mob spirit" of their peers, and therefore capable of aiming higher in order to satisfy their higher needs.[26]

Maslow showed the way out of the consumer society, not rejecting it, but relativizing its importance. What he *did* criticize implicitly was the gratification, almost exclusively, of basic physiological needs and security needs at the expense of spiritually and psychologically "higher" needs. Wasn't this precisely what was happening in the consumer society? And were Riesman's other-directed persons and their conformist lifestyle not the result of this society? Maslow's theory means, in fact, a return to the Romantic ideal of the creative individual, although he "democratizes" the Romantic ideal by giving a broader definition of creativity. The person who seeks his self-actualization doesn't need to be a genius, is his message. It is enough that he should seek his self-actualization in his own way. Was Maslow's critique listened to? That is another question, as we shall see in the next chapter.

NOTES

1. David Riesman, *The Lonely Crowd—A Study of the Changing American Character*, with Nathan Glazer and Reuel Denney, (New Haven and London: Yale University Press, 1978), p. 78.

2. Ibid., p. 16.

3. Ibid., p. 43.

4. Ibid., p. 67.

5. Ibid., p. 115.

6. Ibid., p. 19.

7. Ibid., p. 21.

8. Ibid., pp. 21–22. (Emphasis in original, MHVH).

9. Ibid., p. 48.

10. Alexander Mitscherlich, *Auf dem Weg zur vaterlosen Gesellschaft—Ideen zur Sozialpsychologie,* (Munich: Piper & Co. Verlag, 1980), p. 179. (Emphasis in original, MHVH).

11. Ibid., p. 184.

12. Edward Shorter, *The Making of the Modern Family,* (New York: Basic Books, Inc., 1975), pp. 276–77.

13. Christopher Lasch, *Haven in a Heartless World—The Family Besieged,* (New York: Basic Books, Inc., 1979), pp. 172–173. The "absence of the fathers" in the educational process is a recurrent theme in the sociological literature of the 1970s. Peter Berger, for instance, writes: "Rebellious youth is not fighting against any fathers; on the contrary, it is outraged by the *absence* of parental figures and familial warmth in the bureaucratic institutions that envelop it." (Peter L. Berger, "The Blueing of America," in Peter L. Berger, *Facing Up to Modernity—Excursions in Society, Politics, and Religion,* [Harmondsworth and New York: Penguin Books, 1979], p. 64).

14. This is confirmed by Riesman. "At any rate," he writes, "the typological concepts of *The Lonely Crowd* - [are] 'ideal-type' concepts, in Max Weber's sense. . . . " (David Riesman, "The Study of National Character: Some Observations on the American Case," in David Riesman, *Abundance for What? & Other Essays,* [Garden City, NY: Doubleday, 1964], p. 564).

15. Dale Carnegie, *How to Win Friends and Influence People,* (London: Vermilion, 2006), p. xiv.

16. Ibid., p. xx.

17. Alexis de Tocqueville, *Democracy in America,* Volume II, (New York: Alfred Knopf, 1945), p. 136.

18. Ibid.

19. Ibid., p. 137.

20. Ibid.

21. A. H. Maslow, "A Theory of Human Motivation," *Psychological Review,* 50, 370–396, 1943. https://psychclassics.yorku.ca/Maslow/motivation.htm.

22. Ibid.

23. Ibid.

24. A. H. Maslow, *Motivation and Personality,* (New York: Harper & Row, 1970), pp. xiv–xv.

25. Ibid., p. xx.

26. Susan Neiman comes closer to Riesman's position, writing: "When consuming goods rather than satisfying work becomes the focus of our culture, we have created (or acquiesced in) a society of permanent adolescents." The adolescent is for her the example of the non-productive consumer. (Cf. Susan Neiman, *Why Grow Up? Subversive Thoughts for an Infantile Age,* op. cit., p. 19).

Chapter 6

Joyless Consumption

Maslow argued that "one of the possible consequences of basic need gratifications may be boredom, aimlessness, anomie and the like." A consumer society might have a *prima facie* attractiveness, but, as Maslow rightly remarked, man does not live by bread alone, and once each family has got a car, a color TV, a washing machine, a refrigerator, and all the rest, one realizes that something is still missing. But what?

WILLIAM JAMES AND THE BOREDOM
OF MATERIAL ABUNDANCE

This situation brought to mind an imaginary experience, described by William James in a lecture, titled "What Makes a Life Significant," delivered in 1900 at Harvard.

> A few summers ago I spent a happy week at the famous Assembly Grounds on the borders of Chautauqua Lake. The moment one treads that sacred enclosure, one feels one's self in an atmosphere of success. Sobriety and industry, intelligence and goodness, orderliness and ideality, prosperity and cheerfulness, pervade the air.[1]
>
> You have no zymotic diseases, no poverty, no drunkenness, no crime, no police. You have culture, you have kindness, you have cheapness, you have equality. . . . You have, in short, a foretaste of what human society might be, were it all in the light, with no suffering and no dark corners.[2]
>
> I went in curiosity for a day. I stayed for a week, held spell-bound by the charm and ease of everything, by the middle-class paradise, without a sin, without a victim, without a blot, without a tear.[3]

But what happened? Let us see what James had to say.

And yet what was my own astonishment, on emerging into the dark and wicked world again, to catch myself quite unexpectedly and involuntarily saying: "Ouf! What a relief! . . . This order is too tame, this culture too second-rate, this goodness too uninspiring. . . . Let me take my chances again in the big outside worldly wilderness with all its sins and sufferings. There are the heights and the depths and the steep ideals, the gleams of the awful and the infinite; and there is more hope and help a thousand times than in this dead level and quintessence of every mediocrity.[4]

The well-ordered and prosperous society which William James found on the edges of Chautauqua Lake was for him an example of mediocrity and a source of boredom. Maslow concluded that what man needed deep inside was "self-actualization." James, though in different words, said essentially the same: man, to be truly alive, needs challenge, needs "heights and depths" and "steep ideals."[5]

A JOYLESS ECONOMY?

In her book *The Human Condition,* published in 1958, Hannah Arendt was one of the first to criticize the emerging postwar consumer society. We already quoted her statement that "the hope that inspired Marx . . . that free time eventually will emancipate men from necessity and make the *animal laborans* productive—rests on the illusion of a mechanistic philosophy which assumes that labor power, like any other energy, can never be lost, so that if it is not spent and exhausted in the drudgery of life it will automatically nourish other, 'higher,' activities."[6] "A hundred years after Marx," she continued, "we know the fallacy of this reasoning; the spare time of the *animal laborans* is never spent in anything but consumption, and the more time left to him, the greedier and more craving his appetites."[7] Arendt expressed her fear "that eventually no object of the world will be safe from consumption and annihilation through consumption."[8] A similar critique was to be formulated by Herbert Marcuse, a philosopher of the Frankfurt School, in his book *One-Dimensional Man,* which became an iconic book of the 1960s protest generation. At the time of publication of Marcuse's book the rich and prosperous society, which in 1900 for William James was still an object of pure imagination, had become a reality. But this was not a reason to celebrate. According to Marcuse the new consumer society had led to a flat, "one-dimensional" culture in which higher needs and values had disappeared. "The achievements and the failures of this society invalidate its higher culture," wrote Marcuse.[9] And he continued:

If the individuals are satisfied to the point of happiness with the goods and services handed down to them by the administration, why should they insist on different institutions for a different production of different goods and services? And if the individuals are pre-conditioned so that the satisfying goods also include thoughts, feelings, aspirations, why should they wish to think, feel, and imagine for themselves? True, the material and mental commodities offered may be bad, wasteful, rubbish—but *Geist* and knowledge are no telling arguments against satisfaction of needs.[10]

Marcuse's verdict was without appeal: in the consumer society "high culture becomes part of the material culture," and what we witness is the "assimilation of the ideal with reality," with the result that "the great words of freedom and fulfillment . . . turn into meaningless sounds."[11] Hannah Arendt and Herbert Marcuse were not the only critics of the emerging consumer society. There were others, such as Tibor Scitovsky, who, in his book *The Joyless Economy,* analyzed the reasons behind Americans' growing disaffection with the new prosperity. He observed, that "the middle of the twentieth century may well turn out to have been the high point of our national existence. We saw ourselves in the forefront not only as a nation, but also as individuals. The American consumer was on top of the world, freely spending the world's highest income on the world's most copied and coveted life-style."[12] However, did this mean that the prosperous American consumer was satisfied? Not at all. Scitovsky observed an "increasing frustration with our freely chosen lives," and he asked: "Could it not be that we seek our satisfaction in the wrong things, or in the wrong way, and are then dissatisfied with the outcome?"[13] A question to which he gave an affirmative answer. American consumers were bored, he concluded, because "our American life-style provides much comfort, but little stimulation."[14] One chapter of Scitovsky's book had—tellingly—the title "Is It Too Dull?"[15]

However, according to Albert Hirschman this disaffection with consumerism was a normal process. "My basic point is easily stated," he wrote, "acts of consumption, as well as acts of participation in public affairs, which are undertaken because they are expected to yield satisfaction, also yield disappointment and dissatisfaction . . . any pattern of consumption or of time use carries within itself, to use the hallowed metaphor, 'the seeds of its own destruction.'"[16] "Don't we all know," he continued, " . . . that disappointment and discontent are eternally the human lot, regardless of achievements . . . humans, in contrast to animals, are never satisfied . . . it is their very nature to be intrinsically unsatisfiable, insatiable."[17] For Hirschman this disaffection with consumerism was, as such, not a typical American phenomenon, but rather part of a more general "human condition." "The world I am trying to understand . . . ," wrote Hirschman, "is one in which men think they want one thing and then upon getting it, find out to their dismay that they don't want it nearly as much as they thought or don't want it at all and that something else, of which they were hardly aware, is what they really want."[18] The Dutch poet Mischa de Vreede (1936–2020), who in the period 1983–1984 stayed as a writer-in-residence at the University of Michigan in Ann Arbor, wrote the following commentary about her experience in the United States:

> Soon I learned that compassion there is a character trait that one cannot allow oneself to possess. Virtually none of the people I met knew what empathy was or could project himself in another's situation. That is not only true on a personal level: if you ask me lack of compassion is public enemy number one here. Maybe for the sake of self-preservation; or maybe only those who have a little empathy are able to leave their country, people, native language and culture to start a new and hopefully better life elsewhere. But one knows only what one wants to know, looks no further than one's own house, backyard, career, and consumption pattern. 'Where did you buy it?' they ask when they like something and this is meant as a compliment. The art of living is the art of shopping, of having the good things and a healthy body.[19]

THE CONSUMPTION ADDICTION

The Dutch poet wrote about the consumerism, the lack of empathy, and the loss of social bonds of the Americans she met. Similar observations were made by William James, Hannah Arendt, Herbert Marcuse, Tibor Scitovsky, and Albert Hirschman. Living in a consumer's paradise with its almost exclusive focus on the gratification of their basic needs, Americans were confronted with feelings of malaise, alienation, and dissatisfaction. However, did the citizens of the consumer society come to the same conclusion? Apparently not. Their first reaction to these feelings of malaise was not to diminish their consumption, but, on the contrary, to forge ahead with *more* consumption. Christopher Lasch pointed to this vicious circle, built into the capitalist consumer society, "which continually tries to create new demands and new discontents that can be assuaged only by the consumption of commodities."[20] In the perpetuation of this addiction, advertising played a major role, because it "makes the consumer an addict, unable to live without increasingly sizeable doses of externally provided stimulation."[21] This addiction led, for instance, to the profile of the "compulsive shopper" for whom "shopping serves as a means of "alleviating loneliness," "dispelling boredom," and "relieving depression."[22]

When these consumption addicts manage to face their situation they feel a desperate urge to fill the psychological void which they feel inside. But how? Unlike the inner-directed persons who used to solve their problems autonomously, the other-directed persons felt that they were not capable of dealing with the situation. Therefore they increasingly turned for help to psychologists, therapists, and coaches, who replaced the peer-group. Refusing to be considered patients they claimed the label "client" for themselves, professing an autonomy which, in reality, they didn't possess. These clients told their therapists that they had lost "their sense of self" or their "true self" and asked for help in order to be able to discover their "real self." Maybe it was no coincidence that this search for the "true self" began in the 1970s when the postwar boom period came abruptly to an end with the two oil crises of 1973 and 1979 and the consumer society, together with the welfare state, began to be called increasingly into question.

THE SEARCH FOR THE "TRUE SELF"

The malaise of the consumer society was caused by feelings of emptiness and a lack of purpose. These feelings were accompanied and strengthened by feelings of loneliness. It is, for instance, no coincidence that the two bestselling books on the changing American character were David Riesman's *The Lonely Crowd* and Robert D. Putnam's *Bowling Alone.* Although the time interval between the two publications is exactly fifty years, the titles of these books point to the same problem: the growing *loneliness* of the average American. While in American nineteenth-century literature the individualist loner was still hailed as the typical American hero, in the twentieth century his loneliness was increasingly considered a social pathology. Tibor Scitovsky, whose book was published in 1976, had already addressed this problem.

A striking confirmation of our great tendency to keep to ourselves is the migration of the aged. Most people in most countries stay put on retirement because they want to be near their friends, relatives, acquaintances and former colleagues, whose company they want and cherish all the more when the routine of human contacts of their profession and workplace are disrupted. We do the very opposite. Many retired Americans move to a milder climate in California, Florida, or Mexico, others buy a camper or trailer and spend months, even years, moving from one trailer camp to another, and still others buy themselves into retirement homes, apparently willing to relinquish the company of all those they spent their active life with, whether as daily gossips or nodding acquaintances. The implication of that choice is that their human contacts were either not too numerous, or not very strong, or not very precious. We are much more mobile, of course, socially and geographically, than most societies . . . and our great mobility during our active life keeps us from forming strong friendships which bind others to their home towns. Whatever the reason, the footlooseness of the American aged confirms the statistics on our lack of company.[23]

The malaise, caused by the consumer society, coupled with the alienation, caused by endemic loneliness, led to anxious soul searching in which the Romantic idea reemerged that each person had a unique "essence." American sociologist Edward Shils wrote:

> There is a belief, corresponding to a feeling that within each human being there is an individuality, lying in potentiality, which seeks an occasion for realization but is held in the toils of the rules, beliefs, and roles which society imposes. In a more popular, or vulgar recent form, the concern "to establish one's identity," "to discover oneself," or "to find out who one really is" has come to be regarded as a first obligation of the individual." . . . "To be "true to oneself" means . . . discovering what is contained in the uncontaminated self, the self which has been freed from the encumbrance of accumulated knowledge, norms, and ideals handed down by previous generations.[24]

Everyone was supposed to possess such a unique "true self" or "real self"—a hidden treasury in everyone's soul, which would be present from the very moment of one's birth—pure and noble and not yet spoiled by the purported negative influence of society. This search for the "true self" meant a democratization of the nineteenth century ideal of the creative person or "lonely hero," because *everyone* was supposed to have the potential to become such a unique person.

PHILIP RIEFF'S "PSYCHOLOGICAL MAN"

One of the first authors to write about the emergence of this search for the "true self" was Philip Rieff. In his book *The Triumph of the Therapeutic*, published in 1966,[25] he described the emergence of what he called "Psychological Man." This "Psychological Man" was the individual who was searching for his "true self." Conscious of the fact that he couldn't do this alone, he turned for help to professionals. According to Rieff the therapy offered by these professionals was value-free: its sole function was to liberate the hidden energy and potential of the individual. "A man can be made healthier without being made better," he wrote, "rather, morally worse. Not the good life but better living is the therapeutic standard. It is a popular standard, not difficult to follow, as Americans . . . were the first to recognize in any significant number."[26] Rieff's "psychological man" was a far cry from the nineteenth century ideal of the "creative individual" or "lonely hero." These were work oriented individuals who tried to live up to high standards and elevated ideals. Rieff's "psychological man," on the contrary, is not reaching for the stars, but is satisfied with who he is and it was the task of the therapist to reveal his "real" personality to him, not to prescribe or suggest lofty ideals which might prove unattainable. The therapist reveals the "is" and not the "ought." "In the age of psychologizing," wrote Rieff, "clarity about oneself supersedes devotion to an ideal as the model of right conduct."[27]

However, not everyone was convinced of the merits of this inward spiritual movement. The American author Tom Wolfe wrote a highly critical article in the *New York Magazine,* titled "The 'Me' Decade and the Third Great Awakening," in which he criticized this solipsistic focus on one's own personality. "The saga of the Me Decade," he wrote, "begins with . . . the 30-year boom. Wartime spending in the United States in the 1940s touched off a boom that has continued for more than 30 years."[28] This unknown, new prosperity led to a situation that "by the 1960s the common man was also getting quite interested in this business of 'realizing his potential as a human being.'" Wolfe did not hide his skepticism: "The new alchemical dream is: changing one's personality—remaking, remodeling, elevating, and polishing one's very *self* . . . and observing, studying, and doting on it."

In one respect Wolfe's criticism was biased: the goal of the therapy was not "changing one's personality," nor "remaking" or "remodeling" it, but rather *discovering* it. The client's self didn't need to be changed, but rather to be *found*. It was already there, but had to be explored as a hidden treasure. This idea that everyone had a "real self" or an "authentic self," which would reveal his "potential," was clearly inspired by eighteenth century philosophers, such as Rousseau, whose "natural man" equally had many qualities that were lost in civilization.[29] David Riesman didn't think that the search for one's authentic self would bring hidden treasures to the surface. On the contrary. He wrote "that a life devoted to the gratification of impulse and to the expression of a supposedly *authentic self* is often empty."[30] Rieff called those who were searching for their true self, "psychological men." Maybe it would be better to call them "therapy men," because they were not only clients of professional psychologists, but also of self-appointed coaches, spiritual healers, self-help gurus, and outright charlatans, as we will see in the next chapter.

These different developments were just as many stepping stones towards the development of a shame society. The other-directed person who became the dominant psychological profile of the younger generation, was less guided by his own conscience than by the influence of his peer group. Conformity with the values and practices of the peer group became imperative. The sanction for nonconformity was shame, rather than guilt. This trend was reinforced by the advent of modern consumerism: it was less a question of guilt if one couldn't "keep up with the Joneses" than a question of shame. And when a growing disaffection with consumerism led to the wish to discover one's "inner self," this didn't lead to a restoration of the "psychological gyroscope" (Riesman), but rather to a new dependence—this time on coaches and self-help gurus.

NOTES

1. William James, "What Makes a Life Significant," in William James, *Pragmatism and Other Writings,* (New York and London: Penguin Books, 2000), p. 287.
2. Ibid., p. 288.
3. Ibid.
4. Ibid.
5. Leszek Kołakowski wrote that "one might say that boredom is the price we pay for curiosity: if we were never bored, we would never be curious. In other words, our capacity to be bored is an essential part of our humanity, we are human because we can be bored." (Leszek Kołakowski, "On Boredom," in Leszek Kołakowski, *Freedom, Fame, Lying and Betrayal—Essays on Everyday Life,* [London and New York: Penguin Books, 1999], p. 91).
6. Hannah Arendt, *The Human Condition,* (Chicago and London: The University of Chicago Press, 1958), p. 133.
7. Ibid.
8. Ibid.
9. Herbert Marcuse, *One-Dimensional Man—Studies in the Ideology of Advanced Industrial Society,* (London and New York: Routledge, 1991), p. 59.
10. Ibid., p. 53.
11. Ibid., p. 61.
12. Tibor Scitovsky, *The Joyless Economy—A Inquiry into Human Satisfaction and Consumer Dissatisfaction,* (New York and London: Oxford University Press, 1976), p. 3.
13. Ibid., p. 4.
14. Ibid., p. 150.
15. In happiness research, boredom is generally associated with unhappiness and activity with happiness. Ruut Veenhoven, for instance, writes: "The happy more often feel 'energetic' and the unhappy more often 'apathetic.' . . . Though the happy are typically more active than the unhappy, they do not tend to feel more overburdened." (Ruut Veenhoven, *Conditions of Happiness,* (Dordrecht, Boston, Lancaster: D. Reidel Publishing Company, 1984), p. 284.
16. Albert O. Hirschman, *Shifting Involvements—Private Interest and Public Action,* (Princeton, New Jersey: Princeton University Press, 1982), p. 10.
17. Ibid., p. 11.
18. Ibid., p. 21.
19. Mischa de Vreede, column in *NRC Handelsblad,* June 28, 1984.

20. Christopher Lasch, "New-Class 'Permissiveness' or Capitalist Consumerism?" in Christopher Lasch, *The True and Only Heaven—Progress and Its Critics,* (New York and London: W. W. Norton & Company, 1991), p. 518.

21. Ibid., p. 519.

22. Ibid., p. 522.

23. Tibor Scitovsky, *The Joyless Economy—A Inquiry into Human Satisfaction and Consumer Dissatisfaction,* op. cit., pp. 196–197.

24. Edward Shils, *Tradition,* (Chicago: The University of Chicago Press, 1981), p. 11.

25. Philip Rieff, *The Triumph of the Therapeutic—Uses of Faith after Freud,* (Chicago and London: Chicago University Press, 1987).

26. Ibid., p. 58.

27. Ibid., p. 56.

28. Tom Wolfe, "The 'Me' Decade and the Third Great Awakening," *New York Magazine,* August 23, 1976. https://nymag.com/news/features/45938/.

29. Rousseau's "natural man" or *homme sauvage* had an inborn drive, called by him *perfectibilité*—a drive to make himself more perfect—which resembled Maslow's "self-actualization" and Rieff's "potential." However, unlike Maslow and Rieff, who considered self-actualization and "realizing one's potential" among man's highest needs, for Rousseau the human drive to become more perfect was "the source of all man's misery . . . It is that . . . which makes him in the long run the tyrant over himself and nature." (Jean-Jacques Rousseau, "Sur l'origine de l'inégalité," in Jean Jacques Rousseau, *Œuvres Complètes,* Volume II, [Paris: Gallimard, 1964], p. 142).

30. David Riesman, "Egocentrism—Is the American Character Changing?" *Encounter,* August-September 1980, p. 27.

Chapter 7

Expressive Individualism and Its Holy Grail

"Authenticity"

According to Philip Rieff, the new "Psychological Man" was searching for his "true self." In order to find this "true self" he needed therapies. The catchword of these therapies was "authenticity." "Authenticity" was the new Holy Grail, the hidden treasure the therapist promised his client would find at the end of the therapy. Charles Taylor even spoke about "The Age of Authenticity" and didn't hide his enthusiasm.

> Let's call this the Age of Authenticity. . . . I believe, along with many others, that our North Atlantic civilization has been undergoing a cultural revolution in recent decades. The 60s provide perhaps the hinge moment, at least symbolically. It is on one hand an individuating revolution, which may sound strange, because our modern age was already based on a certain individualism. But this has shifted on to a new axis, without deserting the others. As well as moral/spiritual and instrumental individualisms, we now have a widespread "expressive" individualism. This is, of course, not totally new. . . . What is new is that this kind of self-orientation seems to have become a mass phenomenon.[1]

However, Taylor regretted that "the shift is often understood, particularly by those most disturbed by it, as an outbreak of mere egoism, or a turn to hedonism." "But I think," he continued, "this misses an important point."[2] And this is, according to him, the fact that in the culture of authenticity "each one of us has his/her own way of realizing our humanity, and that it is important to find and live out one's own, as against surrendering to conformity with a model imposed on us from outside, by society, or the previous generation, or religious or political authority."[3] Taylor is right: if the new "authenticity fashion" were to liberate the younger generation from imposed models of conformity, it would, indeed, be a positive development. However, what if this new trend imposed itself as a new fashionable model and itself became only an expression of a new conformity?

THE SEARCH FOR THE AUTHENTIC "INNER CORE"

A problem in this authenticity movement was that "authenticity" had connotations of the natural, the unspoilt: a kind of hidden treasure to be found in an "inner core." But did such an authentic "inner core" exist? Hartmut Rosa, a German sociologist, expressed his doubts. Moreover, he spoke even about an "authenticity terror" and pointed to "the practical problem that individuals are not capable of discerning precisely this supposed 'inner core': not only does it turn out to be elusive, but apparently [it is] also changeable. Time and time again, people find that they are 'different beings' in different contexts and can become different people; and under the conditions of the highly dynamic late modern society the requirement, based on the idea of authenticity, to find out *who, in reality we are,* collides with the . . . demand to 'reinvent' and creatively define ourselves each time anew."[4]

Rosa's statement that people are finding themselves to be "different beings in different contexts" may be an exaggeration. Although he is right that the vagueness of the concept "authenticity," indeed, poses a problem, as well as the supposition that this authentic "inner core" would be completely immune to change. However, the main question is: does such an "inner core"—something purely individual, which is independent from society—exist? Could it be what people used to call "character"? Character is something personal and characters are different. But a "character" doesn't need to be "discovered," nor is it something hidden. It expresses itself spontaneously. So, if this "inner core" is not a person's character, what is it? Jürgen Habermas gave a tentative answer. "Individualization is just the opposite of socialization," he wrote. "Only in a situation of mutual recognition can a person build and reproduce his own identity. Even the person's most *inner core* is internally connected to the wide periphery of a ramified network of communicative relations."[5]

THE MORAL AMBIGUITY OF "AUTHENTICITY"

Habermas rightly emphasized that man's "inner core"—if it exists—is not a pure "essence," independent from societal influences, but something that is formed in a dialogue with its social environment—in the first place with the parents, but also with other persons. The philosopher Alan Gewirth came to a similar conclusion.

An especially influential kind of internal aspiration, deriving from the Romantic movement, has taken "authenticity" to be the prime object of aspiration. . . . The central ideas are that there is a core self which defines or demarcates what one is as a unique person, as having a certain identity; one is conscious of this core self and the demands it makes on one to live up to it; and these demands are the proper objects of one's aspirations, so that self-fulfillment consists in this way in being "authentic" or true to oneself. . . . This conception of aspiration-fulfillment can be interpreted in several different ways. In one way it embodies an emphasis on a kind of individualist spontaneity wherein what is supremely important is to "do one's own thing"; it may reflect an extreme egoism in its disregard of the needs of other persons, and it may also be imprudent in its neglect of the calculation of consequences. . . . The drive for such ideal authenticity also incurs the danger of vacuity. Unless one can tie the self to a content or a conception of value that gives it significance, the ideal may result either in contemplating one's navel or in striking out toward whatever object arouses one's fancy.[6]

Gewirth is referring here to the important question of the ultimately negative moral implications of the drive for authenticity. He warns of the dangers of "extreme egoism," "imprudence," and "vacuity." He goes further than Rieff, who mentioned only the moral neutrality of the concept. Rieff considered that each individual was free to choose the way of life that fitted him best, regardless of the moral consequences. It was in this vein that Rieff wrote: "A man can be made healthier without being made better, rather morally worse." However, one should not forget that this amoral stance was based on *implicit* moral considerations. These implicit moral considerations were, in the first place, a fundamental respect for the individual's freedom and autonomy and, secondly, a recognition of the choices another person made, regardless of the quality of these choices—even in those cases that we didn't accept them. The question is whether this implicit moral base is strong enough to justify morally wrong choices. Charles Taylor, who recognized this implicit moral base, wrote:

What we need to understand here is the moral force behind notions like self-fulfillment. . . . Once we try to explain this simply as a kind of egoism . . . we are already off the track. . . . What we need to explain is what is peculiar to our time. It's not just that people sacrifice their love relationships, and the care of their children, to pursue their careers. . . . The point is that today many people feel *called* to do this, feel they ought to do this, feel their lives would be somehow wasted or unfulfilled if they didn't do it.[7]

Taylor is defending these choices as follows:

People in the culture of authenticity . . . give support to a certain kind of liberalism. . . . This is the liberalism of neutrality. One of its basic tenets is that a liberal society must be neutral on questions of what constitutes a good life. The good life is what each individual seeks, in his or her own way, and government would be lacking in impartiality, and thus in equal respect for all citizens, if it took sides on this question.[8]

One can agree with Taylor that respect for the individual's autonomy and personal choices is in itself a good thing. But does this mean that this liberal neutrality must always prevail? Allan Bloom wrote that

> The great majority of students, although they as much as anyone want to think well of themselves, are aware that they are busy with their own careers and their relationships. There is a certain rhetoric of self-fulfillment that gives a patina of glamor to this life, but they can see that there is nothing particularly noble about it. This turning in on themselves . . . is a new degree of isolation that leaves young people with no alternative to looking inward. The things that almost naturally elicit attention to broader concerns are simply not present.[9]

Taylor recognizes this problem, writing that "we struggle to realize higher and fuller modes of authenticity against the resistance of the flatter and shallower forms."[10] These "flatter and shallower forms" consist of the self-centered forms, while the "higher and fuller modes of authenticity" include those which take into account the interests of others, because Taylor insists that "authenticity is not the enemy of demands, coming from beyond the own self, but it presupposes such demands."[11] In the same vein Hartmut Rosa wrote " . . . If *autonomy* means that we determine ourselves, so the norm of *authenticity* should guarantee that we can determine ourselves 'in the right way,' namely in such a way that we can *realize ourselves.*"[12] There is clearly a limit to Taylor's "liberal neutrality" as concerns the choices the authentic person makes. Should society, for instance, passively stand by when a significant segment of the youth population chooses to use hard drugs or risks killing themselves through anorexia?[13]

THE NEW AUTHENTICITY MARKET

The search for authenticity gave rise to a new market, particularly in the United States, where the psychological "turn inward" was a byproduct of increasing feelings of loneliness. "One quarter of Americans (26 per cent)," wrote Theodore Zeldin, "classify themselves as chronically lonely,"[14] adding: "No country has taken loneliness more seriously than America, none has created so many specialist organizations to combat it, but at the same time nowhere has examination of one's inner self become such a widespread passion."[15] Because the demand for professional help to find one's real "inner self" grew massively, the supply side mushroomed equally. Writing about these new professionals, Christopher Lasch said: "Recent studies of professionalization show that professionalism did not emerge . . . in response to clearly defined social needs. Instead the new professions themselves invented many of the needs they claimed to satisfy."[16] The "authenticity market," therefore, was not only demand driven, but also—and maybe even more so—supply driven. Real and self-appointed experts entered this market and flooded it with seminars, courses, therapies, and wellness sessions, promising their clients that they would "find themselves." However, instead of a greater autonomy, it led to an increased dependence. In the first instance, this was evident in child-rearing practices and education. According to Lasch, "The cult of authenticity reflects the collapse of parental guidance and provides it with amoral justification. It confirms . . . the parent's helplessness to instruct the child in the ways of the world or to transmit ethical precepts. . . . It legitimizes . . . the appropriation of child-rearing techniques by the "helping professions."[17] The professionals became a new elite, a new caste of priests who pretended to have a secret knowledge which enabled them to discover and interpret their clients' authentic "real self."

> The elite would get under the skin of the masses by making them feel that they did not understand themselves, that they were inadequate interpreters of their own experience of life. . . . Judgments about potential ability are much more personal in character than judgments of achievement. An achievement compounds social and economic circumstances, fortune and chance, with self. Potential ability focuses only on the self. The statement "you lack potential" is much more devastating than "you messed up." It makes a more fundamental claim about who you are.[18]

The new professionals had a psychological grip on their clients comparable to the power of a catholic priest in the confessional: they "got under the skin" of their clients. This aspect was overlooked by Carl Cederström, who—rightly—wrote: "The happiness fantasy . . . that has dominated the rich West for almost a century . . . is a fantasy of self-actualization, according to which there is only one way to become happy, and that is by reaching your full potential as a human being. It is to live in a spirit of authenticity, where you are called upon to live *your* life, as opposed to someone else's life."[19] He continued: "These are some of the moral values that seem to undergird happiness today: be real, enjoy yourself, be productive—and most important, don't rely on other people to achieve these goals, because your fate is, of course, in your own hands."[20]

Cederström clearly underestimates the new dependence created by the wellness therapists, a dependence emphasized by Julia de Funès, a French philosopher. "Everywhere where the 'me' is present," she writes, "coaching is expanding. As the expansion of the 'me' turns out to be unlimited, coaching encounters no limits: a coach for leadership, seduction, makeovers, health, food, sport, marital love, sex, stress management, conflict management, emotional management, tidying up, gardening, decoration. . . . These coaches take us in the hand as a mother her child, or a master his dog: infantilization or dressage, or 'no matter'!"[21] Therapists, instead of helping their clients, may instead worsen and aggravate their problems: "Many people who consult psychotherapists are suffering from an excess of individuality. They feel isolated and disconnected, they lack a clear sense of belonging to social groups, and they are missing the sense of purpose a group would give. Often they attempt to compensate by developing their individuality to absurd degrees: rejecting the goals, standards, and policies of society. Unfortunately, too many psychologists encourage them in this direction by idealizing a self-sufficient, self-contained, autonomous, independent personhood."[22] However, "to concentrate all one's efforts on making oneself into a grand creation—whether through therapy or not—points the individual away from the world into himself. His self may then open itself to him in splendor, but that vision will eventually reveal itself to be a mirage blinding him to the approaching abyss."[23] The dangers of the authenticity fad could not be better expressed: the danger that an insane navel gazing leads to an extreme form of individualism which isolates the individual from his fellow men. In the end the authenticity movement didn't bring freedom, nor authenticity, it rather created a new, shame-inducing dependence, for influenceable, other-directed persons.

NOTES

1. Charles Taylor, *A Secular Age,* (Cambridge, MA, and London: The Belknap Press of Harvard University Press, 2007), p. 473.

2. Ibid., p. 474.

3. Ibid., p. 475.

4. Hartmut Rosa, *Resonanz—Eine Soziologie der Weltbeziehung,* (Berlin: Suhrkamp, 2016), p. 43. (Emphasis in the original, MHVH).

5. Jürgen Habermas, "Lawrence Kohlberg und der Neoaristotelismus," in Jürgen Habermas, *Erläuterungen zur Diskursethik,* (Frankfurt am Main: Suhrkamp Verlag, 1991), p. 97. (My emphasis, MHVH).

6. Alan Gewirth, *Self-Fulfillment,* (Princeton, New Jersey: Princeton University Press, 1998), pp. 48–49.

7. Charles Taylor, *The Ethics of Authenticity,* op. cit., pp. 16–17.

8. Ibid., pp. 17–18.

9. Allan Bloom, *The Closing of the American Mind,* op. cit., p. 84. Bloom is opposing here the "a-political" post-1960s generation to the 1960s generation, known for its political engagement, and clearly seems to prefer the second. However, Albert Hirschman considers both as part of a "normal" historical sequence in which private and public concerns alternate: " . . . some movement back and forth between the public and private life can be wholesome for individuals as well as for society as a whole." (Albert O. Hirschman, *Shifting Involvements—Private Interest and Public Action,* op. cit., p. 132).

10. Charles Taylor, *The Ethics of Authenticity,* op. cit., p. 94.

11. Charles Taylor, *Das Unbehagen an der Moderne,* (Frankfurt am Main: Suhrkamp Verlag, 1995), p. 51.

12. Hartmut Rosa, *Resonanz—Eine Soziologie der Weltbeziehung,* op. cit., p. 42. (Emphasis in the originial, MHVH).

13. Alan Gewirth drew attention to the moral shallowness of the "authenticity" concept when it is disconnected from external value criteria, writing that "this ideal [of 'authenticity,' MHVH] may be characterized in at least two different ways. One way, which reflects the influence of Romanticism, is self-oriented. . . . The agent here appeals to no values except his own vehement desires or aspirations. This position rests on a certain conception of autonomy whereby one sets one's own rules without consideration of any external criteria for their adequacy. Such a conception should be faulted for its arbitrariness in upholding the self's aspirations as the sole basis of action and value. . . . A second interpretation of the 'authentic' pursuit of eminence is object-oriented. Here the agent regards himself as acting not simply as a matter of self-affirmation but rather as affirming also the supreme value of the objects of his pursuit." (Alan Gewirth, *Self-Fulfillment,* op. cit., pp. 104–105).

14. Theodore Zeldin, "How some people have acquired an immunity to loneliness," in Theodore Zeldin, *An Intimate History of Humanity,* (London: Sinclair-Stevenson, 1994), p. 60.

15. Ibid., p. 66. In recent years loneliness in America has only increased. A national survey conducted in 2018 by Cigna and Ipsos revealed that nearly half of Americans report sometimes or always feeling alone (46 percent) or left out (47 percent), and two in five Americans sometimes or always feel that their relationships are not meaningful (43 percent) and that they are isolated from others. The survey reports that Generation Z (born after 1997) is the loneliest generation. Cf. "New Cigna study reveals loneliness at epidemic levels in America," *Cigna,* May 1, 2018. https://www.cigna .com/newsroom/news-releases/2018/new-cigna-study-reveals-loneliness-at-epidemic -levels-in-america.

16. Christopher Lasch, *The Culture of Narcissism—American Life in An Age of Diminishing Expectations,* op. cit., p. 385.

17. Ibid., p. 288.

18. Richard Sennett, *The Culture of the New Capitalism,* (New Haven and London: Yale University Press, 2006), p. 123.

19. Carl Cederström, *The Happiness Fantasy,* (Cambridge: Polity Press, 2018), p. 2.

20. Ibid., p. 7.

21. Julia de Funès, *Développement (im)personnel—Le succès d'une imposture,* (Paris, Éditions de l'Observatoire, 2019), p. 45.

22. Stuart Schneiderman, *Saving Face—America and the Politics of Shame,* (New York: Alfred A. Knopf, 1995), pp. 287–88.

23. Ibid., p. 288.

PART II

Narcissistic Individualism and the Rise of the Modern Shame Society

Chapter 8

How Expressive Individualism Morphed into Narcissism

The new "expressive individualism" of the "Me Decade," in search of the "true self" and "authenticity," was increasingly met with critique. A French author wrote: "In politically correct France one is against individualism like one is against racism or for peace."[1] "It is as if . . . increasingly conversions have taken place to a pronounced and aggressive anti-individualism."[2] This anti-individualism could also be observed elsewhere. In a book, titled *The End of Individualism—The Culture of the West Destroys Itself*, two German authors rang the alarm bell. They wrote that individualism had led to a situation in which " . . . social ties are loosening. Communities are disintegrating. Social institutions are collapsing."[3] And they added: "In many cases lifelong commitments are consciously avoided. The lack of emotional bonds is considered . . . a condition for the development of one's own personality."[4]

THE ATTACK ON "RAMPANT INDIVIDUALISM"

In the same vein Amitai Etzioni attacked the myth of the American Frontier as the cradle of American individualism.

The migration to the American West, for example is usually thought of as a time when individuals were free to venture forth and carve out a life of their own in the Great Plains. . . . Mining towns and trading posts, however, in which rampant individualism often did prevail, were places of much chicanery. . . . In many ways these frontier settlements—with their washed-out social bonds, loose morals, and unbridled greed—were the forerunners of Wall Street in the 1980s. The Street became a "den of thieves," thick with knaves who held that anything went as long as you made millions more than the next guy. Moreover, the mood of self-centered "making it" of the me generation spilled over into large segments of society. It was celebrated by the White House and many in

Congress, who saw in an unfettered pursuit of self-interest the social force that revitalizes economies and societies.[5]

Etzioni attacked both economic individualism and 19th century individualism as a lifestyle. A few years later, Etzioni's attack on America's "rampant individualism" seemed to receive the support of empirical evidence, when Robert Putnam published his bestselling study *Bowling Alone*.

> The dominant theme [of this study] is simple. For the first two-thirds of the twentieth century a powerful tide bore Americans into ever deeper engagement in the life of their communities, but a few decades ago—silently, without warning—that tide reversed and we were overtaken by a treacherous rip current. Without at first noticing, we have been pulled apart from one another and from our communities over the last third of the century.[6]

Not only could a sharp decline in Americans' participation in voluntary organizations be observed, but also a sharp decline in the practice of social visiting: "our centuries-old practice of entertaining friends at home might entirely disappear from American life in less than a generation."[7] This trend would be particularly visible in the younger generation: "The young worker thinks primarily of himself. We are experiencing the cult of the individual. . . . "[8] The younger generation would also be less interested in politics: "The post-baby boom generations—roughly speaking, men and women who were born after 1964 and thus came of age in the 1980s and 1990s—are substantially less knowledgeable about public affairs, despite the proliferation of sources of information."[9]

"Rampant individualism" was considered to be the major cause of the growth of loneliness. In 2017 Vivek Murphy, America's former surgeon general, declared an "epidemic of loneliness."[10] This loneliness epidemic was not confined to the US. In the UK the "Campaign to End Loneliness," founded in 2011, stated on its website that "over 9 million people in the UK across all adult ages—more than the population of London—are either always or often lonely."[11] A parliamentary Loneliness Commission was set up, led by MP Jo Cox, which lobbied for the creation of a special government minister position. The initiative was crowned with success in 2018, when Prime Minister Theresa May appointed Britain's first "Minister for Loneliness." The attack on individualism lumped many things together: egoism, self-centeredness, loss of societal bonds, a declining interest in politics, and loneliness. As such, these attacks on individualism were not new. They were evident right from the very moment that the concept emerged. The French conservative writer Joseph de Maistre (1753–1821), for instance, wrote already that "sects and the spirit of individualism are multiplying in a frightening manner."[12] For him the growth of individualism was already "frightening." Critics of individualism associated it mainly with its negative aspects, neglecting its important positive qualities, such as enhanced personal freedom, the defense of human rights, and providing the philosophical basis of liberal democracy.

THE NARCISSISM EXPLOSION

In the 1970s a completely new kind of critique of individualism emerged, with the theory that individualism had morphed into a new form of social pathology: narcissism. Individualism, from a societal and moral problem, became a psychological problem. This idea had already been popularized by Christopher Lasch in his bestselling book *The Culture of Narcissism*, published in 1979. The book was an immediate success—probably because it offered a new and original explanation for the feelings of malaise that pervaded American society. Lasch wrote that "the culture of competitive individualism" was "a way of life that is dying" and had given way to "the dead end of a narcissistic preoccupation with the self."[13] The narcissist was a person who was "haunted not by guilt but by anxiety. He seeks not to inflict his own certainties on others but to find a meaning in life . . . superficially tolerant, he . . . regards everyone as a rival for the favors conferred by a paternalistic state."[14] Narcissism provided a psychological explanation for the emergence of the new character type, who was searching for his "real self." Otto Kernberg gave the following incisive clinical description of the narcissistic personality:

These patients present an unusual degree of self-reference in their interactions with other people, a great need to be loved and admired by others, and a curious apparent contradiction between a very inflated concept of themselves and an inordinate need for tribute from others. Their emotional life is shallow. They experience little empathy for the feelings of others, they obtain very little enjoyment from life other than from the tributes they receive from others or from their own grandiose fantasies, and they feel restless and bored when external glitter wears off and no new sources feed their self-regard. They envy others, tend to idealize some people from whom they expect narcissistic supplies, and to depreciate and treat with contempt those from whom they do not expect anything (often their former idols). In general, their relationships with other people are clearly exploitative and sometimes parasitic. It is as if they feel they have the right to control and possess others and to exploit them *without guilt feelings*—and behind a surface which very often is charming and engaging, one senses coldness and ruthlessness. Very often such patients are considered to be "dependent" because they need so much tribute and adoration from others, but on a deeper level they are completely unable really to depend on anybody because of their deep distrust and depreciation of others.[15]

The narcissist is a far cry from the independent individualist loner, celebrated in the nineteenth century. Instead of delaying the gratification of his needs in order to reach higher goals in life, he is a consumer who wants instant gratification. Self-reliance, the defining characteristic of the nineteenth century individual, is unknown to him. On the contrary, unable to help himself he turns to experts to explore his inner self. And for his self-esteem he is equally dependent on the opinion of others. At first sight this dependence on others seems to make him more social than the nineteenth century loner or the competitive economic individualist, so that Etzioni's and Putnam's critiques of the loss of social bonds didn't seem to apply. However, social bonds, to the extent that these existed, were subservient to his self-aggrandizement. "For all his inner suffering," wrote Lasch, "the narcissist has many traits that make for success in bureaucratic institutions, which put a premium on the manipulation of interpersonal relations, discourage the formation of deep personal attachments, and at the same time provide the narcissist with the approval he needs in order to validate his self-esteem."[16]

Lasch's book was brilliant. He was among the first to discover and describe a new trend in American popular psychology. From the moment of its publication his book was widely praised. "Like a biblical prophet," wrote *Time* magazine, "Christopher Lasch appears at the gates of our culture with dire pronouncements."[17] And in the same vein Frank Kermode wrote in the *New York Times:* "So here we have a civilized hellfire sermon, with little promise of salvation."[18] The way Lasch was characterized—as a "biblical prophet" with a "hellfire sermon"—he seemed to be a twentieth century reincarnation of the early American puritan prophets. But did his "hellfire sermon" give a realistic picture of the situation? To answer this more empirical evidence was needed. Two scientists who tried to provide this evidence were Jean Twenge and Keith Campbell. In their book *The Narcissism Epidemic,* published in 2009—thirty years after Lasch's book—they wrote that "Christopher Lasch's 1979 bestselling book, *The Culture of Narcissism,* though fascinating, was written before any serious research explored the personality and behavior of narcissists."[19] They rightly emphasized that "empirical research is the place to begin."[20] The research results they presented confirmed not only the trend, described thirty years earlier by Lasch, but also the fact that this trend was deepening.

In data from 37,000 college students, narcissistic personality traits rose just as fast as obesity from the 1980s to the present, with the shift especially pronounced for women. The rise in narcissism is accelerating, with scores rising faster in the 2000s than in previous decades.[21]

The authors also quoted another study which compared more than 11,000 teens aged 14 to 16 who filled out long questionnaires in either 1951 or 1989. "Out of more than 400 items, the one that showed the largest change over time was 'I am an important person.' Only 12% of teens agreed with this statement in the 1950s, but by the late '80s more than 80% of girls and 77% of boys said they were important."[22] The narcissism syndrome is characterized by an exaggerated sense of self-importance and fantasies of superiority and grandiosity. Narcissists believe that they are entitled to the admiration of others, because they are 'special'—a quality that they tend to deny to others. On the contrary, they have an instrumental attitude vis-à-vis other people, who—at best—are considered as an applauding audience. On the whole, however, they have feelings of distrust towards other people. Not only because these could be possible competitors for glory, but also because they could spread negative opinions, which is the greatest fear of the narcissist. How could this narcissism wave be explained? Researchers pointed—again—to changes in the early socialization of children. "Narcissism was predicted by parental overvaluation. . . . Thus, children seem to acquire narcissism, in part, by internalizing parents" inflated views of them (e.g., 'I am superior to others' and 'I am entitled to privileges').[23]

HOW NARCISSISM WAS
BOOSTED BY THE SOCIAL MEDIA

However, this narcissism explosion was caused not only by changes in the early socialization of children. In the first decade of the twenty-first century two new technological inventions, the social media and the smartphone, gave an enormous boost to this trend. In February 2004 Mark Zuckerberg and his associates had created Facebook. In February 2005 this example was followed by Chad Hurley, Steve Chen, and Jawed Karim, who created YouTube, a video-sharing platform. In 2006 Twitter would follow. It was the beginning of a new era, the era of Web 2.0. From a one-way street the Internet became a two-way street: users were no longer exclusively recipients of information, they could become active providers. *Time* magazine couldn't hide its enthusiasm about this democratization of the World Wide Web. The choice for its "Person of the Year" for 2006 was not a specific personality as was the custom, but "YOU"—because everyone was supposedly gaining from this digital revolution.

In today's wired world, you have the chance to change everything. . . . It's a tool for bringing together the small contributions of millions of people and making them matter. Silicon Valley consultants call it Web 2.0, as if it were a new version of some old software. But it's really a revolution. We're looking at an explosion of productivity and innovation, and it's getting started, as millions of minds that would otherwise have drowned in obscurity get backhauled into the global economy.[24]

However, Grossman's euphoria was not unlimited. His message was accompanied by a warning. "Sure," he wrote, "it's a mistake to romanticize all this any more than strictly necessary. Web 2.0 harnesses the stupidity of crowds as well as its wisdom. Some of the comments on YouTube make you weep for the future of humanity just for the spelling alone, never mind the obscenity and the naked hatred."[25] But despite these warnings optimism prevailed. The new social media: YouTube, Facebook, Twitter, Instagram, were expected to "democratize" the information sphere: suddenly everyone could become a journalist and disseminate news—children included, because even thirteen-year-olds could open a Facebook account.

The advent of the social media was accompanied by another new invention: the smartphone. With a smartphone one could not only make phone calls or send an SMS, but one could also use it as a photo camera, a video camera, as well as for sending and receiving email messages, accessing the Internet, managing one's bank account, ordering a meal, calling a taxi, buying theater tickets, etcetera. It was a magic scepter adapted to the twenty-first century, which could fulfill almost any wish. It was no surprise that the smartphone became the favorite toy of young adolescents, because it had one additional feature: it gave direct access to social media. The narcissistic feelings of omnipotence and grandiosity, already present in this generation, were enhanced by these new media. In 2006, *Time* magazine had chosen "YOU" as Person of the Year. The internet-savvy young generation had given this unspecified, general "YOU" a more specific, particularistic meaning, namely: "ME." About what should these adolescents write if not themselves? Social media and the smartphone were the instruments of choice for the "Me Generation," enabling them to disseminate positive narratives about themselves in the wider world. Personal experiences were not valuable per se, but gained importance only if they were shared on the social media. This could even include trivial things, such as meals in restaurants which were photographed at the very moment they were served and immediately put on social media to let other people know what one was eating. In 2013, seven years after *Time* magazine had chosen "YOU" as Person of the Year, the magazine published an article by Joel Stein, entitled "Millennials: The Me

Me Me Generation." The hopeful "You" of 2006 had become a worrying "Me Me Me."

> Here's the cold, hard data. The incidence of narcissistic personality disorder is nearly three times as high for people in their twenties as for the generation that's now 65 or older. . . . 58% more college students scored higher on a narcissism scale in 2009 than in 1982. . . . They are fame-obsessed. . . . They're so convinced of their own greatness that the National Study of Youth and Religion found the guiding morality of 60% of millennials in any situation is that they'll just be able to feel what's right.[26]

However, self-aggrandizement was only one aspect of the use of social media. There was another, less innocent aspect, to which Lev Grossman had already referred in his 2006 Person of the Year article: the dissemination of obscenity and naked hatred. Because social media weren't only instruments to show off and display the aggrandized self, they were equally a place where one could elevate oneself by humiliating others. In recent years practices of "online shaming" and cyber harassment have become increasingly common among adolescents and had led to a growing number of suicides. Current research suggests that suicide ideation and attempts among adolescents have nearly doubled in the United States in the period 2008–2018, making suicide the second leading cause of death for individuals 10–34 years.[27] "The increase in adolescent MDE [Major Depressive Episodes]," another study claims, "began in 2011 concurrent with the increased ownership of smartphones and a concomitant increase in digital media time in this age group."[28] Social media, which were touted as vehicles which would bring new friends and strengthen existing social ties had become instruments of shaming and humiliation. "In less than ten years," writes Éric Sadin, "a 'humiliation culture' has been established, which not only rejoices in someone else's misfortune, but celebrates those who exhibit such behavior, making them . . . the insolent heroes of a contemporary iconoclasm."[29]

DONALD TRUMP: THE NARCISSISTIC PRESIDENT

In 2016 the narcissism epidemic led to an apotheosis, when Americans elected Donald Trump, a narcissistic president. His autobiographical book *How to Get Rich* reads as a manual for narcissists. Referring to his encounter with Mark Burnett, who recommended him for the central figure of the reality show *The Apprentice,* he wrote: "He made sure he established a connection with me. He did this telling me that I'm a genius. Some people may consider such flattery excessive, but when you're on the receiving end, it's usually okay."[30] Trump refers also to a meeting with Burnett's father. "After meeting me, he said, "You're much more handsome in person than I would have thought."[31] Trump wallows in self-admiration. "It's funny, the reaction I get from people when I walk down the street and get recognized . . . often it's a wave and a familiar and friendly 'Hi, Donald!' from total strangers."

Self-admiration is only the "soft side" of the narcissist. Because there is also a hard side. "When somebody hurts you," Trump writes, "just go after them as viciously and as violently as you can. Like it says in the Bible, an eye for an eye. Be paranoid. I know this observation doesn't make any of us sound very good, but let's face the fact that it's possible that even your best friend wants to steal your spouse and your money."[32] It is telling that Trump's greatest fear is that a friend will steal his spouse and his money. For the narcissist a spouse is—like money—primarily an object of possession and a status symbol. Narcissists marry "trophy partners"—models, mannequins, movie stars, or media celebrities—whose beauty and elegance not only make them feel good, but are also a sign of their *own* attractiveness. In another book Trump boasted: "I have a wonderful and beautiful wife. I've got billions of dollars. My children are highly intelligent and accomplished executives who work with me. I've got a pile of potentially huge projects sitting on my desk."[33] He praised also his father. "What he left me . . . ," he bragged, "were the best 'genes' that anybody could get,"[34] claiming a kind of eugenic superiority. Trump's presidency seemed, therefore, the perfect incarnation of the new narcissistic age.

What can we conclude? We can conclude that the narcissism epidemic confirmed and strengthened an already existing trend, which was first observed by Riesman and his colleagues, namely that inner-directed persons were increasingly replaced by other-directed persons. This other-directedness didn't mean an increased sociability. On the contrary, the narcissist is a self-centered, lonely individual, who craves for the admiration and affection of others, without being able to form lasting societal bonds. Rather than feeling guilty he is prone to feeling shame. This trend was compounded by the advent of the social media, which became important instruments for shaming others, as well as for being shamed.

NOTES

1. Alain Laurent, *De l'individualisme—Enquête sur le retour de l'individu,* (Paris: Presses Universitaires de France, 1985), p. 20.

2. Ibid., p. 21.

3. Meinhard Miegel and Stefanie Wahl, *Das Ende des Individualismus—Die Kultur des Westens zerstört sich selbst,* (Munich: Verlag Bonn Aktuell, 1993), p. 143.

4. Ibid., p. 38.

5. Amitai Etzioni, *The Spirit of Community—Rights, Responsibilities and the Communitarian Agenda,* (London: Fontana Press, 1995), p. 118.

6. Robert D. Putnam, *Bowling Alone—The Collapse and Revival of the American Community,* (New York and London: Simon & Schuster, 2000), p. 27.

7. Ibid., p. 100.

8. Ibid., p. 82.

9. Ibid., p. 36. This tendency could be observed not only in the United States, but also in Germany, where "according to results published in 2009, 37 percent of students are interested in politics, while this was still 54 percent in 1983. Increasingly fewer students self-identify as 'left' or 'right,' . . . They are not interested in parties, [and] not at all . . . in political action groups." (Cf. Christiane Florin, *Warum unsere Studenten so angepasst sind,* [Reinbek bei Hamburg: Rowohlt, 2014], p. 19).

10. "All the lonely people," *The Economist,* May 2, 2020.

11. David Vincent, *A History of Solitude,* (London: Polity, 2020), p. 221.

12. Joseph de Maistre, "The Pope," in Joseph de Maistre, *The Works of Joseph de Maistre,* Selected, translated, and introduced by Jack Lively, with a new foreword by Robert Nisbet, (New York: Schocken Books, 1971), p. 146.

13. Christopher Lasch, *The Culture of Narcissism—American Life in An Age of Diminishing Expectations,* op. cit., p. 21.

14. Ibid., p. 22.

15. Otto F. Kernberg, *Borderline Conditions and Pathological Narcissism,* (New York: Jason Aronson, Inc., 1976), p. 17. (My emphasis, MHVH). The incapacity to experience guilt is for Kernberg a major characteristic of the narcissistic personality. See also Kernberg, op. cit., pp. 35–37.

16. Christopher Lasch, *The Culture of Narcissism—American Life in An Age of Diminishing Expectations,* op. cit., p. 91.

17. R. Z. Sheppard, "Books: The Pursuit of Happiness," *Time Magazine,* January 8, 1979.

18. Frank Kermode, "The Way We Live Now," *The New York Times,* January 14, 1979. https://www.nytimes.com/1979/01/14/archives/the-way-we-live-now-narcissism.html.

19. Jean M. Twenge and W. Keith Campbell, *The Narcissism Epidemic—Living in the Age of Entitlement,* (New York and London: Free Press, 2009), p. 3.

20. Ibid.

21. Ibid., p. 2.

22. Ibid., p. 34.

23. Eddie Brummelman, Sander Thomaes, Stefanie A. Nelemans, Bram Orobio de Castro, Geertjan Overbeek, and Brad J. Bushman, "Origins of narcissism in children," *Proceedings of the National Academy of Sciences of the United States of America* (PNAS), March 9, 2015. https://www.pnas.org/content/112/12/3659.

24. Lev Grossman, "You—Yes, You—Are TIME's Person of the Year," *Time* magazine, December 25, 2006. http://content.time.com/time/magazine/article/0,9171,1570810,00.html.

25. Ibid.

26. Joel Stein, "Millennials: The Me Me Me Generation," *Time* magazine, May 20, 2013. https://time.com/247/millennials-the-me-me-me-generation/.

27. "Bullying, Cyberbullying, & Suicide Statistics," *Megan Meier Foundation,* no date. https://www.meganmeierfoundation.org/statistics.

28. J. M. Twenge et al., "Age, Period, and Cohort Trends in Mood Disorder Indicators and Suicide-Related Outcomes in a Nationally Representative Dataset, 2005–2017," *Journal of Abnormal Psychology,* 2019, Vol. 128, No. 3. https://www.apa.org/pubs/journals/releases/abn-abn0000410.pdf.

29. Éric Sadin, *L'ère de l'individu tyran,* (Paris: Bernard Grasset, 2020), pp. 248–249.

30. Donald J. Trump, *How to Get Rich,* op. cit., p. 254.

31. Ibid., p. 258.

32. Ibid., pp. 162–163.

33. Donald J. Trump, *Great Again—How to Fix Our Crippled America,* (New York and London: Threshold Editions, 2015), pp. 12–13.

34. Ibid., p. 99.

Chapter 9

The Narcissist's Pursuit
of the Perfect Body

The narcissist is named after the Greek mythological figure Narcissus, who saw his reflection in the water of a pool and fell in love with himself. When he became aware that he hadn't seen another person, but only his own reflection, he committed suicide, because his love could not materialize. The modern narcissist shares with Narcissus his self-love, but he doesn't share Narcissus's deep despair. When he looks in the mirror, he is fully aware that he sees himself and he seems to be satisfied with his own image. However, narcissists—despite the arrogance, self-assurance, and confidence they exhibit—may harbor doubts as to whether they meet all the prevailing masculine and feminine beauty standards. This question becomes for them even more serious, because—unlike the self-reliant individualist who distinguished himself mainly through his work and his activities—the narcissist's self-admiration is to a large extent based on his looks. And good looks are a gift of nature: they are simply there or they aren't, and, as such, they are the narcissist's Achilles' heel and a possible source of uncertainty.

THE PERFECT BODY: DREAM OR REALITY?

It is, therefore, not surprising that the emergence of the narcissistic personality was accompanied by a boom in plastic surgery. The early beginnings of this trend can be traced back to the 1950s when David Riesman was one of the first to observe the new lifestyle of the American executive and his desire "to stay young." This personality type was clearly a forerunner of the modern narcissist. "We all know the type of American executive or professional man, he wrote, who does not allow himself to age, but by what appears almost sheer will keeps himself 'well-preserved' . . . he lacks inner aliveness. . . . Their outward appearance of aliveness may mask inner sterility."[1] At the beginning of the 1950s Riesman had already observed a development in America, which, in the second part of the twentieth century, would grow into a worldwide trend: body improvement. While in the beginning the emphasis was put particularly on diet, health, and fitness, beauty aspirations would soon expand beyond this realm to realize the narcissist's ultimate dream: the perfect body. With the emergence of plastic surgery the narcissist's dream of a perfect body seemed to come within reach. The first adepts of this trend were mainly women, the so-called fairer sex, many of whom felt that being beautiful was what society expected from them. According to Twenge and Campbell, "the narcissism epidemic seems to have hit girls especially hard. Who knows—by the time our daughters graduate from high school, one of the most common graduation presents might be a breast augmentation. (We're not kidding; the number of teens getting breast augmentation jumped 55% in just one year from 2006 to 2007, and some parents do indeed pay for them as graduation gifts)."[2]

The plastic surgery business was booming and it was particularly women who let themselves be "remodeled" by surgeons who, as omnipotent modern magicians, promised their female clientele the perfect body they always wanted.

> Far more women than men have plastic surgery for cosmetic purposes. In some cases they take the risk of a general anaesthetic and other possible complications such as potentially fatal post-operative blood clots, in order to enlarge breasts, change the shape of their noses or the lie of their ears, remove folds of tissue under eyes or chins, 'lift' and tighten facial skin to smooth out wrinkles, change the shape of stomachs ('tummy-tucks': the names of the procedures are so beguilingly innocent and positive) and buttocks; and more.[3]

Grayling added: "It is an oddity that the type of woman portrayed in magazines for women, and those portrayed in magazines for men, are sharply different; in the former women are tall and thin, in the latter curvaceous and fuller in body. The latter shapes, typically shown nude in these magazines, are more attractive to men."[4]

This is one of the paradoxes of the new trend: women's desire to be beautiful did not take into account the sensual and sexual wishes of the opposite sex, but adapted itself rather to the body image of mannequins and models of the fashion world. It was devoid of what Freud calls "object libido." The female libido remained entirely focused on the self, on one's own Ego, which corresponds with Freud's definition of narcissism. Freud speaks, for instance, about "original narcissism in which the childish Ego feels self-sufficient,"[5] and he suggests that the concept of narcissism, "is the insight that the Ego itself is charged with libido, [that it is] even its original source and in a certain sense remains its headquarters."[6]

NAOMI WOLF AND THE WEIGHT-LOSS
CULT OF WOMEN: A MALE CONSPIRACY?

Weight loss was an integral part of the "perfect body" cult. There are different explanations for the women's attraction to the cult of weight loss. Naomi Wolf, for instance, gives an explanation which comes close to a conspiracy theory.

> Until seventy-five years ago, in the male artistic tradition of the West, women's natural amplitude was their beauty; representations of the female nude reveled in women's lush fertility. Various distributions of sexual fat were emphasized according to fashion—big, ripe bellies from the fifteenth to the seventeenth centuries, plump faces and shoulders in the early nineteenth, progressively generous dimpled buttocks and thighs until the twentieth—but never, until women's emancipation entered law, this absolute negation of the female state. . . .[7]

Why did this complete inversion of the image of female beauty happen?

> Dieting and thinness began to be female preoccupations when Western women received the vote around 1920; between 1918 and 1925, "the rapidity with which the new, linear form replaced the more curvaceous one is startling." In the regressive 1950s, women's natural fullness could be briefly enjoyed once more because their minds were occupied in domestic seclusion. But when women came en masse into male spheres, that pleasure had to be overridden by an urgent social expedient that would make women's bodies into the prisons that their homes no longer were.[8]

The extremely thin female model Twiggy, who appeared in the magazine *Vogue* in 1965, "was shocking at the time," writes Naomi Wolf, but was "reassuring men with her suggestion of female weakness, asexuality, and hunger."[9] It is not clear to me how a woman's *asexuality* or *hunger* could be "reassuring men." But it is part of Naomi Wolf's explanation that the hunger-cult of Western women is deep down a male conspiracy. It is, in her opinion, no coincidence that this cult appeared for the first time after the first feminist wave and the introduction of women's suffrage in the beginning of the twentieth century and that it regained strength again after the second feminist wave of the 1970s. Wolf even speaks about a "sex war" in which the goal is to create a "distinctive [female] personality whose traits are 'passivity, anxiety and emotionality.'"[10] And she continues (the next sentence is emphasized in the original): *"It is those traits, and not thinness for its own sake, that the domi-nant culture wants to create in the private sense of self of recently liberated women in order to cancel out the dangers of their liberation."*

However, Naomi Wolf seems to forget that "the dominant culture" of a country is a *shared* culture of the men *and* women who live in that country and thus her conclusion that the cult of thinness to which women subject themselves was more or less a plot by the male population to maintain or re-establish its domination is not only far-fetched, but also sociological non-sense. Naomi Wolf is not the only author to develop such a conspiracy theory. A female German author writes in the same vein: "It is no coincidence that it is precisely today, when women have more influence, self-determination and money than ever before, that they should also be thinner than ever before."[11] She adds that "the present beauty ideal is also a symbol of the place women should occupy in society: as before, a small place. Women still have much less social power than men, power that is based on something other than their looks and the 'weapons of a woman.' Female corporeality is, as before, controlled predominantly by men. . . . Women often feel that they are reduced to their body."[12] Like Naomi Wolf this author offers a feminist reinterpreta-tion of Marx's famous formulation that the ruling ideas of a society are the ideas of its ruling class—replacing in this case the capitalist ruling class by the male sex. It is a simplification of the complex and intricate ways ideas and ideals—including beauty ideals—are formed. Because the main ques-tion is: if these beauty ideals are imposed by men, why do women *en masse* accept and internalize these ideals? And, secondly—more importantly—why do *men* also submit to these new—insane—beauty standards? Rather than a male conspiracy, another explanation would seem more plausible: that of the emergence of the new psychological profile of the narcissistic personality, a profile which is shared by *both* men and women.

We should also not forget that the female hunger cult is only one aspect of the search for the ideal body. In effect, *any* part of the body can be considered for possible improvement: breasts can be enlarged, ears and noses remodeled, lips 'plumped,' early baldness reversed by hair transplants, birth marks and warts removed, and so on. Even the smallest details of the human body don't escape—such as, for instance, teeth. "Today," write Twenge and Campbell, "if you don't get your teeth whitened, everyone thinks you are either poor or an espresso-drinking, cigarette-smoking European."[13] They observe that "as recently as the 1990s, no one really cared if your teeth were a little yellow. Now that's a clear sign that you've let yourself go or can't afford teeth whit-ening at the dentist."[14] The urge to have one's teeth whitened is shared by men and women and cannot, therefore, be attributed to a patriarchal conspiracy. However, there are more reasons to reject this theory, as we will see in the next paragraph: because men, no less than women, are equally victims of the new beauty trend.

INSANE BODYBUILDERS IN THE #METOO WORLD

While women may have internalized the ideal image of the thin, anorexic model, men also have their own ideal body image which has become a real "male obsession": the image of the bodybuilder. This image of the broad-shouldered male, 'ripped' (with an 'eight-pack' of muscles), which is presented in lifestyle magazines and in TV reality shows, has become the new norm for genuine masculinity.

> It used to be women who were battered with dieting advice and who were flogged endless piles of self-help books. . . . Nowadays, male self-improvement is all the rage and men are now almost as boring about their appearance as women. Bodybuilding, not so long ago a peculiar pursuit, has become a very ordinary hobby and the market for protein products is enormous and swelling. . . . The idea that the male body should be purged and perfected has become a mainstream one.[15]

"So why are these young men turning into narcissists? What's with the almost religious zeal?" asks Prendergast. Her answer: "It can't be a coincidence that the rise in lean, ethical dieting has come during the era of the #MeToo movement. Men are being led to believe that their masculinity is a problem. Their rapacious pursuit of pleasure has damaged the world around them, they are told—and it's up to them to curb their appetites. Women have had enough."[16]

While Naomi Wolf explained the cult of thinness amongst women as a masculine plot to maintain their dominance, Prendergast explains the bodybuilding cult and dieting of men to the influence of the #MeToo movement. In the first case the explanation is a "patriarchal" plot, in the second case the explanation is that women have succeeded in taming and 'disciplining' the male, including his sexual greed. While the first has "bad" connotations, the second, on the contrary, has "good" connotations. In reality, however, neither men, nor the #MeToo movement should be blamed, or commended, for these new body cults. Both body cults are equally insane and caused by the same syndrome: the narcissism epidemic.

Apart from professional bodybuilders, who are able to spend many hours a week in a gym, the ideal body is for the average male not easy to attain. However, there's no need for despair, because there are plenty of ways to speed up the process. According to *The Guardian,* "up to 1 million people in the UK are taking anabolic steroids and other image- and performance-enhancing drugs (IPEDs) to change the way they look. . . . This ranges from teenagers seeking the perfect physique to elderly men hoping to hang on to youthful looks. Research suggests that appearance rather than sporting performance is the reason for the majority of those now using anabolic steroids and other IPEDs."[17] The problem is that the use of anabolic steroids is not harmless. It leads to drug dependency and also has unwanted side effects, such as mood swings and an increase in irritability and aggressiveness. Additionally, the user runs the risk of a reduced sperm count, infertility, testicular atrophy, and reduced sex drive, due to a loss of libido. The desired 'supermale' body leads to a paradoxical result: a diminished sexual libido and performance. However, this is apparently not important, because the bodybuilder is not primarily interested in sex, nor in social bonding: his primary interest is himself. As in the case of the female ideal of thinness, the bodybuilder is not driven by object libido, but by narcissistic, self-directed libido. "The more insignificant he feels on the inside," writes Alan Klein, "the more significant the bodybuilder strives to appear on the outside."[18] Everything revolves around the Ego's desire for power and grandiosity. "What makes this narcissistic is that the need to present themselves in exaggerated terms to themselves and to have others reflect this back to them is excessive."[19]

THE "METROSEXUAL": THE
BODYBUILDER'S FORERUNNER

The "bodybuilder" syndrome is only the most recent ideal image for the modern male narcissist. In 1994 Mark Simpson coined the word "metrosexual." According to him "the metrosexual man contradicts the basic premise of traditional heterosexuality—that only women are looked at and only men do the looking. Metrosexual man might prefer women, he might prefer men, but when all's said and done, nothing becomes between him and his reflection."[20] The metrosexual man was the forerunner of the modern narcissist. But between the metrosexual and the modern narcissist there was a difference: the center of the metrosexual's attention was not (yet) his body, but rather fashionable clothes and accessories to embellish his appearance.

> Metrosexual man wears Davidoff 'Cool Water' aftershave (the one with the naked bodybuilder on the beach), Paul Smith jackets (Ryan Giggs wears them), corduroy shirts (Elvis wore them), chinos (Steve McQueen wore them), motorcycle boots (Marlon Brando wore them), Calvin Klein underwear (Marky Mark wears nothing else). Metrosexual man is a commodity fetishist: a collector of phantasies about the male sold to him by advertising.[21]

In the twenty-first-century "metrosexual man"—with his interest in fashion suits, beautiful shirts, expensive aftershave, and perfumed body lotion—would increasingly lose ground to a new narcissistic model: the bodybuilder. In a study which compared the narcissism levels of bodybuilders before and after anabolic steroid treatment, an increase in narcissism levels was observed after the treatment. "It can be said that after anabolic steroid cure, athletes more liked their body and physical characteristics."[22] The female thinness cult and the male bodybuilding cult are both expressions of the new narcissist personality disorder and are closely related to the newly emerging shame culture. Because not complying with these beauty standards didn't cause guilt feelings, but rather shame. We will see in the next chapter how the pursuit of the perfect body, which started in the United States, became a global movement.

NOTES

1. David Riesman, "Some Clinical and Cultural Aspects of the Aging Process," in David Riesman, *Individualism Reconsidered,* op. cit., p. 167.

2. Jean M. Twenge and W. Keith Campbell, *The Narcissism Epidemic—Living in the Age of Entitlement,* op. cit., p. 8.

3. A. C. Grayling, "Plastic Surgery—When is it justified to be doubtful about the value of plastic surgery?" in A. C. Grayling, *Thinking of Answers—Questions in the Philosophy of Everyday Life,* (London, Berlin, New York: Bloomsbury, 2010), p. 182.

4. Ibid., p. 183.

5. Sigmund Freud, "Massenpsychologie und Ichanalyse," in Sigmund Freud, *Studienausgabe,* Volume IX, *Fragen der Gesellschaft, Ursprünge der Religion,* (Frankfurt am Main: S. Fischer Verlag, 1974), p. 102.

6. Sigmund Freud, "Das Unbehagen in der Kultur," in Sigmund Freud, *Studienausgabe* Volume IX, *Fragen der Gesellschaft, Ursprünge der Religion,* op. cit., p. 246.

7. Naomi Wolf, *The Beauty Myth—How Images of Beauty Are Used Against Women,* (London: Vintage Books, 1991), p. 184.

8. Ibid.

9. Ibid.

10. Ibid., p. 188.

11. Ibid.

11. Waltraud Posch, "Zwischen Schönheit und Schönheitswahn," in Peter Kemper and Ulrich Sonnenschein, (eds), *Globalisierung im Alltag,* (Frankfurt am Main: Suhrkamp Verlag, 2002), pp. 220–221.

12. Ibid., p. 231.

13. Jean M. Twenge and W. Keith Campbell, *The Narcissism Epidemic—Living in the Age of Entitlement,* op. cit., p. 38.

14. Ibid., p. 143.

15. Lara Prendergast, "The New Narcissism," *The Spectator,* August 11, 2018. https://www.spectator.co.uk/article/the-new-narcissism.

16. Ibid.

17. Steven Morris, "Up to a million Britons use steroids for looks not sport," *The Guardian,* January 21, 2018. https://www.theguardian.com/society/2018/jan/21/up-to -a-million-britons-use-steroids-for-looks-not-sport.

18. Alan M. Klein, "Life's Too Short to Die Small—Steroid Use Among Male Bodybuilders," in Donald Sabo and David F. Gordon, (eds), *Men's Health and Illness—Gender, Power, and the Body,* (Thousand Oaks, London, New Delhi: SAGE, 1995), p. 114.

19. Ibid., p. 117.

20. Mark Simpson, "Here Come the Mirror Men: Why the Future Is Metrosexual," *The Independent,* November 15, 1994. https://marksimpson.com/here-come-the -mirror-men/.

21. Ibid.

Chapter 10

Narcissism Goes Global

Narcissists cannot only be found in the United States—or Europe. They are everywhere—even in places where you might never expect them. Twenge and Campbell observed that "the rest of the world is starting to follow America's lead."[1] They are right. The reason they give is that "narcissism is the fast food of the soul. It tastes great in the short term, has negative, even dire, consequences in the long run, and yet continues to have widespread appeal. So, will American-style narcissism spread around the world, like the McDonald's that now sits in Tienanmen Square in China?"[2] The authors answer in the affirmative: "Other cultures are increasingly becoming infected with narcissism, becoming hosts for the fast-moving virus of egotism, materialism, celebrity worship, entitlement, and self-centeredness."[3]

BERLUSCONI AND PUTIN:
TWO BOTOXED POLITICIANS

It is, indeed, interesting to observe that at present, narcissism is infecting not only Russia, but even its administrative center, the Kremlin. Soviet leaders have not been known to be much concerned about their looks. Khrushchev was overweight and resembled a Russian *muzhik,* the typical Russian farmer, and Brezhnev and his gerontocratic successors also seemed to have little interest in their body image. Gorbachev's port wine stain on his forehead made him stand out and even became a kind of personal brand. However, in post-Soviet Russia things are different. The friendship between Russian President Vladimir Putin and the Italian politician Silvio Berlusconi is a case in point. As I observed in an earlier book,

Both men liked to show off their virility in ostentatious and often shameless ways that evoked Mussolini's fascist style. In Berlusconi's case it is the virility of the Latin lover and womanizer. In Putin's case the virility of the sportsman, eager to let himself be photographed as a bare-chested horse rider, a pilot in a cockpit, or driving a racing car: always anxious to expose in a narcissistic way his physical strength and audacity. . . . The obsession of both men with their bodies is, indeed, legendary. Berlusconi has "remade" himself with a hair transplant, retouched eyelids, and botox injections. One could expect that it was only a question of time before Putin would follow the lead of his Italian friend, 16 years his senior. In September 2011, Putin made a wrinkle-free appearance at the party conference of United Russia for the first time. . . . According to experts, Putin underwent a facelift which included cheek-fillers, a brow-lift, removal of bags under his eyes and Botox.[4]

At that time not everyone was enthusiastic about the result. Janek Stanek, one of the UK's top cosmetic surgeons commented on Putin's facelift: "Unfortunately, it has made him look a little odd. By lifting the brow so much it has a feminizing effect, which is not what you want."[5] However, in Russia the reactions were more positive: "As a leader who wants to present the ideal body to his countrymen—particularly, but not only, to the female population—Putin elicits equivalent bodily expressions among the population. In Russia female journalism students posed half naked for a 'Putin calendar' while Russian teenage girls published love letters in their blogs, praising 'ideal man' Putin."[6]

THE BODY IMPROVEMENT TREND GOES GLOBAL

The body-improvement wave, therefore, is not restricted to the United States or Europe, but is spreading worldwide. Some years ago, in a hotel in Shanghai, when the author of this book switched on the TV, he was surprised by the many ads for beauty institutes offering eyelid operations to make the upper eyelids more visible and create rounder, more 'European' eyes. According to two researchers beauty standards in China don't deviate much from Western standards. They wrote that "more recent thinking suggests aesthetic judgment may be both more universal and similar across different backgrounds than previously understood. Facial averageness and symmetry are two characteristics demonstrated to be standards of beauty in both Western and non-Western cultures."[7] The result of their research was conclusive: "Both Chinese and non-Chinese observers considered the medium-height upper eyelid crease most attractive. An absent upper eyelid crease was deemed the least attractive."[8] The Chinese beauty market is booming. "In 2014, more than 7 million Chinese people had plastic surgery. . . . Just three years later data, compiled by [the] Shanghai branch of Frost & Sullivan consultants suggested the figure was closer to 16.3 million."[9] The surge would be due to apps like So-Young and GengMei on which one can see "before and after" photos. As concerns the clients of the beauty institutes, "more than half are under the age of 26. . . . To put that into perspective, cosmetic surgery patients under 30 years old make up a mere 6% of the total in the US."[10]

China is only one example, Iran, another. One would not expect that in Iran—a theocracy, led by severe mullahs—cosmetic surgery would be booming. But also in this country men and women are increasingly obsessed with their looks. Iran has become a leading country in a specific branch of cosmetic surgery: rhinoplasty—nose jobs. Why Iran? Because Iranian people are known for their "Persian nose," or large, hooked nose. "It has been estimated that as many as 200,000 Iranians, mostly women, go to cosmetic surgeons each year to reduce the size of their nose."[11] The trend is visible in the streets of Iran, where you can see people walking around with plasters on their noses. Iran is called the "nose job capital of the world." "And because the Iranian mullahs allow women to expose no skin except for their face, the face has become the focus of vanity efforts. Some women are even wearing bandages on their noses just so others will think they had a nose job."[12]

The narcissism epidemic is going global and is spreading fast. And so far we have not yet understood its possible ramifications and consequences. Ulrich Beck, a sociologist, expressed his concern about the possible emergence of a eugenic "planned child mentality," writing that

> we are already seeing future practices of embryonic, pre-embryonic etc. "quality control" in the selection of male and female candidates for sperm donation and surrogacy. A doctor in Essen, who in his practice specializes in artificial insemination, mentions as criteria for the selection of sperm donors i.a. "No protruding ears or hook noses, at least 1.75 meters tall, no 'freakish types,' from a regular background."[13]

Beck asks: "should one increase the power of the mind or of the muscles . . . ?[14] Or, to put it more bluntly: can one still be satisfied with a less than 'ideal' body in a world in which beauty is within the reach of everyone—thanks to sperm selection, DNA engineering, Botox, breast implants, and the surgeon's scalpel?

TO BECOME AS ATTRACTIVE AS ONE'S SELFIE

The new beauty trend is being boosted by at least three developments. In the first place the new psychological profile of the narcissist. Secondly, the availability of cosmetic surgery, which can make one's dreams come true. And, in the third place, new developments in communication media. The importance of this last factor should not be underestimated. Smartphone ownership has become almost universal in the world. Smartphones are telephones. But they are much more. Each smartphone owner also has a camera at his or her disposal. Not only a photo camera, but also a video camera. With the same smartphone you can connect to the Internet, which gives you not only access to search machines, but also to social media, such as Facebook, Instagram, Snapchat, TikTok, or YouTube, where you can publish your pictures or videos. When you give this new magical device to a narcissist, what happens? He or she will immediately jump at the opportunity to spread the gospel of the narcissistic age: the gospel of the Self. It is no coincidence that in recent years the word "selfie" has become omnipresent. In 2013 Oxford Dictionaries chose it as "word of the year." Although the hashtag #selfie was already being used from 2004 on the photosharing website Flickr, its usage only became widespread around 2012, when the frequency of its usage increased by 17,000 percent.[15] The selfie was defined as "a photograph that one has taken of oneself, typically with a smartphone or webcam and uploaded to a social media website." In 2020 the word "selfie" got 1,380,000,000 hits on Google. To put this in perspective: another word that has gone viral in recent years is "populism." However, for "populism" Google claimed only 25,800,000 hits, which means that the frequency of "selfie" is 53 times higher.[16] Selfies don't need to be exact reproductions of our faces. They can be *improved.* Jia Tolentino, a journalist of the *New Yorker,* described the role played by social media, such as Snapchat, FaceTune, and Instagram, in boosting this trend.

> Snapchat, which launched in 2011 and was originally known as a purveyor of disappearing messages, has maintained its user base in large part by providing photo filters, some of which allow you to become intimately familiar with what your face would look like if it were ten-per-cent more conventionally attractive—if it were thinner, or had smoother skin, larger eyes, fuller lips. Instagram has added an array of flattering selfie filters to its Stories feature. FaceTune, which was released in 2013 and promised to help you "wow your friends with every selfie," enables even more precision.[17]

The result of all this, she wrote, was "the gradual emergence, among professionally beautiful women, of a single, cyborgian face. It's a young face, of course, with poreless skin and plump, high cheekbones. It has catlike eyes and long, cartoonish lashes; it has a small, neat nose and full, lush lips."[18] It is, particularly, the younger generation which is attracted to this new trend. Eva Illouz observed that on dating sites the body profile of participants should conform to current beauty standards; the psychological profile, however, should be original and "authentic."[19]

FROM THE SELFIE TO THE SCALPEL

Virtually improved selfies lead to the desire to have this improved picture of oneself being realized in real life. In a video, "Women get Photoshopped Into Their Ideal Bodies," which went viral on Youtube, a participant can be heard to exclaim that this "makes people feel bad about themselves."[20] These "improved" selfies function, therefore, as a marketing tool for cosmetic surgeons. In an article in *Le Monde,* tellingly titled "From the selfie to the scalpel," one can, for instance, read that in 2019 in France the 18 to 34 age group had for the first time more cosmetic operations than the 50 to 60 age group.[21] This age group comprises not only millennials (born in the 1980s and early 1990s), but also the so-called iGeneration or Generation Z, the generation born in 1995 and later. It is this generation in particular which is attracted to this new trend. "Born in 1995 and later, they grew up with cell phones, had an Instagram page before they started high school, and do not remember a time before the Internet. . . . "[22] This generation is preeminently *the* Internet generation. "iGen is distinct from every previous generation," writes Twenge, "in how its members spend their time, how they behave, and their attitudes toward religion, sexuality, and politics."[23] She observes a great difference between this generation and the generation of millennials that preceded it.

> Millennials quickly gained a reputation for overconfidence and unrealistically high expectations. . . . Those trends tapered off with iGen'ers. . . . iGen'ers score lower in narcissism and have lower expectations, suggesting that the outsize entitlement displayed by some Millennials might be on its way out.[24]

Twenge's conclusion that iGen's score lower in narcissism seems to me to be premature. Because there are *different* forms of narcissism and we may be simply watching the transformation of one kind of narcissism into another kind, in the same way as flu viruses mutate when they are spreading across the globe. A group of researchers, for instance, has established a connection between two kinds of narcissism: "grandiose narcissism" on the one hand and "vulnerable narcissism" on the other. Both would appear to have a common foundation.[25] While "grandiose narcissism" is characterized by overt expressions of feelings of superiority and entitlement, "vulnerable narcissism" is characterized by hypersensitivity and introversive self-absorbedness. According to Dr. Craig Malkin, an expert, vulnerable narcissists "are just as convinced that they're better than others as any other narcissist, but they fear criticism so viscerally that they shy away from, and even seem panicked by, people and attention."[26] These individuals may behave in less arrogant and boastful ways, but—behind a more modest and introvert façade—they can still think that they are superior. Grandiose narcissists and vulnerable narcissists, however, share the same anxiety—a fear which has only increased in recent years after the advent of social media—namely to be shamed by others.

NOTES

1. Jean M. Twenge and W. Keith Campbell, *The Narcissism Epidemic—Living in the Age of Entitlement,* op. cit., p. 17.

2. Ibid., pp. 259–260.

3. Ibid., p. 260.

4. Marcel H. Van Herpen, *Putinism—The Slow Rise of a Radical Right Regime in Russia,* (Houndmills, Basingstoke, and New York: Palgrave Macmillan, 2013), p. 190.

5. Ibid.

6. Ibid., p. 191.

7. Harry S. Hwang and Jeffrey H. Spiegel, "The Effect of 'Single' vs 'Double' Eyelids on the Perceived Attractiveness of Chinese Women," *Aesthetic Surgery Journal,* 2014, Vol. 34 (3), p. 374.

8. Ibid.

9. Julie Zaugg, "China cosmetic surgery apps: Swipe to buy a new face," *CNN,* March 3, 2020. https://edition.cnn.com/style/article/cosmetic-surgery-apps-china-intl -hnk/index.html.

10. Ibid.

11. Kamaljit Kaur Sandhu, "Nose job rage in Iran," *India Today,* November 16, 2019. https://www.indiatoday.in/world/story/nose-job-iran-plastic-surgery-1619523 -2019-11-16.

12. Jean M. Twenge and W. Keith Campbell, *The Narcissism Epidemic—Living in the Age of Entitlement,* op. cit., p. 265.

13. Ulrich Beck, *Gegengifte—Die organisierte Unverantwortlichkeit,* (Frankfurt am Main: Suhrkamp Verlag, 1988), pp. 55–56.

14. Ibid., p. 59.

15. "Selfie is Oxford Dictionaries' word of the year," *The Guardian,* November 19, 2013. https://www.theguardian.com/books/2013/nov/19/selfie-word-of-the-year -oed-olinguito-twerk.

16. Data retrieved on April 3, 2020.

17. Jia Tolentino, "The Age of Instagram Face—How social media, FaceTune, and plastic surgery created a single, cyborgian look," *New Yorker,* December 12, 2019. https://www.newyorker.com/culture/decade-in-review/the-age-of-instagram-face.

18. Ibid.

19. Eva Illouz, *Gefühle in Zeiten des Kapitalismus,* (Frankfurt am Main: Suhrkamp Verlag, 2006), p. 123.

20. "Women Get Photoshopped Into Their Ideal Bodies," *YouTube,* April 9, 2017. https://www.youtube.com/watch?v=C0w6770vky0.

21. Séverine Pierron, "Du selfie au bistouri," *Le Monde,* January 19–20, 2020.

22. Jean M. Twenge, *iGen: Why Today's Super-Connected Kids Are Growing Up Less Rebellious, More Tolerant, Less Happy—and Completely Unprepared for Adulthood. And What That Means for the Rest of Us,* (New York and London: Atria Books, 2017), p. 2.

23. Ibid.

24. Ibid., p. 94.

25. Emanuel Jauk, Elena Weigle, Konrad Lehmann, Mathias Benedek, Aljoscha Neubauer, "The Relationship between Grandiose and Vulnerable (Hypersensitive) Narcissism," *Frontiers in Psychology,* 8:1600, September 13, 2017. https://www.frontiersin.org/articles/10.3389/fpsyg.2017.01600/full.

26. Quoted in Berit Brogaard, "Vulnerable vs Grandiose Narcissism: Which Is More Harmful?" *Psychology Today,* June 23, 2019.

Chapter 11

The Happiness Revolution

In the preceding chapters we have seen how from the middle of the twentieth century the life goals of individuals changed. While in the post–World War II boom period people indulged in the material comforts offered by the newly emerging consumer society, they soon experienced feelings of emptiness and alienation. From the 1970s they began to turn their attention inward, in search of their "real self." In this period "authenticity" became the new keyword. Only when one knew one's "authentic, real self," it was thought, could one follow one's unique path to self-actualization. However, the paradox was that, in order to reach one's full potential, people needed the help of experts and real or self-appointed life coaches, including charlatans and gurus. In the same period a new psychological profile developed: that of the narcissistic personality. The narcissist, being convinced that he was unique and possessed extraordinary talents, was less interested in discovering his hidden psychological and spiritual attributes. These unique qualities were for him self-evident. Living in a world in which attractiveness and physical beauty had become the most important norm, the life goal of these individuals became the achievement of an ideal body. Women subjected themselves to the thinness cult, men sculpted their bodies, and both sexes increasingly went under the knife of cosmetic surgeons to remodel parts of their physique. However, as with consumerism, satisfaction with the results was often only temporary. Cosmetic surgeons often had "eternal clients," who, soon dissatisfied with the last operation, asked for another improvement. The process was never ending, because the patient/client was left with painful feelings of emptiness and senselessness and the question was how to fill the inner void. One did not have to wait for long, because already a new keyword was emerging: that new keyword was "happiness."

THE NEW IDEAL: HAPPINESS

Happiness became the new ideal. At first sight there was nothing new under the sun. Happiness is, of course, an old ideal. Maybe as old as humanity. The ancient Greeks spoke about εὐδαιμονία (*eudaimonia*)—happiness or the "good life"—and gave it a prominent place in their philosophy. So did the Romans. Cicero's book *De Finibus Bonorum et Malorum,* translated in English as *On Ends,* is one long discussion of the principle of happiness. In modern political philosophy happiness has also played a major role. Thomas Jefferson, the author of the American Declaration of Independence, mentioned "Life, Liberty and the pursuit of Happiness" as unalienable human rights. Jefferson had borrowed this expression from John Locke, who, in his *Essay Concerning Human Understanding,* called "the necessity of pursuing true happiness the foundation of liberty."[1] Both John Locke and Thomas Jefferson were prudent enough not to call happiness *as such* a human right. They only spoke about the *pursuit* of happiness. In this sense they were more realistic than James Madison, who wrote that "a good government implies two things: first, fidelity to the object of government, which is the happiness of the people; secondly, a knowledge of the means by which that object can be best attained."[2] Jefferson was conscious of the fact that happiness had different connotations for different people and that it was up to the individual to realize his own conception of happiness.[3] Therefore, one should not impose a "one fits all" approach, nor was it considered the state's task to make people happy. It was left to the individual to define for himself what exactly "happiness" meant and how he wanted to realize this goal.

The emphasis on the individual's right to the pursuit of happiness fitted well with the prevalent individualist ideology of the young United States. This huge country with its endless plains and an ever-receding Western frontier, was a land of immense hope for the constant flow of immigrants, many of whom had fled hunger, poverty, or political and religious oppression. Each of these immigrants had his own conception of the "American Dream," which was essentially a dream of *happiness.* The new arrivals who disembarked on Ellis Island were called "fortune seekers." The word "fortune" referred to expectations of wealth and money, but not exclusively. It meant also the prospect of living a decent life in a free country as a respected citizen with equal rights. Erik Erikson asked the question:

> Was the happiness guaranteed in the Declaration [of Independence] that of wealth and of technological power or that of an all-human identity such as resides primarily in the free person? Is there any other country which continues to ask itself not only "What will we produce and sell next?" but ever-again "Who are we anyway?" which may well explain this country's hospitality to

such concepts as the identity crisis which, for better or for worse, now seem almost native to it.[4]

Erikson may be mistaken when he writes that "happiness was guaranteed in the Declaration," because it was only the individual *pursuit* of happiness that was mentioned. However, he is right when he emphasizes the utterly endless American preoccupation with the definition of happiness and its relation to questions of identity. This was precisely what was at stake when the "happiness revolution" took place.

HAPPINESS: JUST AN ACT OF WILL?

In 1988, when the "happiness revolution" was taking shape, the British historian Theodore Zeldin called happiness "the world's fastest-growing religion." "It seemed to me," he wrote, "there are fashions in happiness, as in religion, and they pass."[5] He was right. In the same vein Edgar Cabanas and Eva Illouz wrote in their book *Manufacturing Happy Citizens—How the Science and Industry of Happiness Control our Lives* that "happiness has grown into a fundamental part of our commonsensical understanding of ourselves and the world, a concept so familiar that we take it for granted. It feels and rings so natural today that to call happiness into question is odd if not audacious."[6] These authors observed that it is

> Not only the frequency and pervasiveness with which happiness shows up that have radically changed in the past few decades. The way in which we have come to understand happiness has radically transformed as well. We no longer believe that happiness is somewhat connected to fate or circumstances; the absence of ailment, the valuation of a whole life, or a petty consolation for the foolish. In fact, happiness is now generally seen as a mindset that can be engineered through willpower; the outcome of putting into practice our inner strengths and authentic selves; the only goal that makes life worth living; the standard by which we should measure the worth of our biographies, the size of our successes and failures, and the magnitude of our psychic and emotional development.[7]

In the past happiness used to be viewed through the prism of what the Romans called *fortuna*. Human happiness was seen as dependent on external influences and it was the role of astrologers and fortune tellers to inform their clients about imminent opportunities or imminent perils. Happiness was influenced by "life events," which could be positive or negative—such as marriage, promotion, divorce, illness, death of a relative, or the loss of a job. Even those philosophers who preached that one should remain impassive under the blows of *fortuna*, such as the Stoa, recognized the importance of these external factors. There existed no "right" to be happy, as Sartre reminds us, writing: "No one owes you anything—and above all, you have no rights over your destiny."[8]

However, in the "happiness revolution" these external factors seemed to have been erased or completely forgotten. Happiness became an individual project, a so-called life goal,[9] and its realization became a purely *personal* affair. Happiness became a question of *choice.* Everyone was considered to be responsible for his own happiness or misery. Cabanas and Illouz observed that

> The scientific approach to happiness and the happiness industry that emerges and expands around it contribute significantly to legitimizing the assumption that wealth and poverty, success and failure, health and illness are of our own making. This also lends legitimacy to the idea that there are no structural problems but only psychological shortages; that, in sum, there is no such thing as society but only individuals, to use Margaret Thatcher's phrase inspired by Friedrich Hayek.[10]

Often the results of the happiness revolution are the opposite to what has been promised, because this revolution "produces a new variety of 'happiness seekers' and 'happychondriacs' anxiously fixated with their inner selves, continuously occupied with correcting their psychological flaws, and permanently worried about their own personal transformation and betterment."[11] Cabanas and Illouz concluded that "striving for happiness might damage people's connections and increase both their sense of loneliness and detachment from others. Similarly . . . happiness positively correlates with narcissism, which lies at the core of self-aggrandizement, selfishness, egocentrism, hubristic pride and self-absorption, all of them aspects underlying a vast array of mental disorders."[12]

THE EXPANDING MARKET
FOR "HAPPINESS COACHES"

These authors rightly stressed that the "happiness revolution" is only a new expression of the narcissistic syndrome, because, essentially, it is focused—again—on the self. The search for happiness is related to the narcissist's feelings of omnipotence: happiness is considered to be something within the individual's reach and it would, therefore, only be a question of his own willpower and choices to attain this goal. The same message can be found on the websites of so called "happiness coaches." On one of these one can read the following introduction:

A happiness coach brings your heart and mind together so you can discover true happiness of spirit. *The saying that happiness is a choice is correct*: so a purposeful approach is essential to building inner happiness. This is what your coach does for you.[13]

The various happiness coaches on this website present their services as follows: "Get the life you want and deserve," "I am there to help you reach your goals, dreams, or desires," "Reach your highest potential with coaching." On the website of another happiness coach one can read: "Happiness is here. Learn how to create a ridiculously happier life today. Hi, I'm so glad you're there. I can't wait to get to know you and help you get your happy on!" This coach presents herself as follows: "Choosing and practicing happiness daily has changed my life so profoundly that I feel a strong desire to help you too." She is reassuring her potential clients, emphasizing that "happiness is a choice."[14]

The importance and sanctity of "free choice" is firmly entrenched in the American ideology. Alan Ehrenhalt wrote: "Most of us believe a few simple propositions that seem so clear and self-evident they scarcely need to be said. Choice is a good thing in life, and the more of it we have, the happier we are."[15] This seems even more pertinent when happiness is the object of one's choice. But is this so self-evident? Can "choice" be in itself "a prime value, irrespective of what it is a choice between, or in what domain?"[16] In February 2013 Nataly Kogan, founder and CEO of Happier Inc., launched a phone app encouraging users to reflect upon and share pleasant everyday moments, a practice which would, she believed, boost the happiness of its users.[17] On her website one can read: "What if you could be happier right now, without radically changing your life? You can! We'll help you practice your Happier Skills so you can find more joy in everyday moments and handle the difficult ones with resilience."[18]

Happiness coaches not only purport to enhance their clients' happiness, clearly their own happiness also is at stake. Nataly Kogan, for instance, said she believed her business could one day be worth $1 bn.[19] In 2016 the average salary of a coach was $61,900 in North America and $55,300 in Western Europe. In the same year the average fee for a one-hour coaching session was $231.[20] The happiness coach claims to have expert knowledge. This is not only a question of diplomas, but also of having shared the potential client's negative experiences. "You're fed up of the negative voice in your head telling you 'you can't' or 'you shouldn't,'" it says on the website of a coach who calls herself the "happyologist." "That's where I come in," she writes. "I've been exactly where you have, and I've climbed out of there."[21] The happiness coach presents herself as a "soul sister," who has not only shared the same negative experiences as the client, but who has managed to "climb out" of the negative situation. Therefore she knows better than anyone else what to do. A life coach told the *New York Times* that she was as bewildered by her success as anyone else:

> Everything I've ever taught in terms of self-help boils down to this—I cannot believe people keep paying me to say this—if something feels really good for you, you might want to do it. And if it feels really horrible, you might want to consider not doing it. Thank you, give me my $150.[22]

The role of the happiness coach seems to be that of a personal *cheerleader,* with the only difference that he or she is not supporting and motivating a team, but an individual client.

A NEW FUNCTION: "CHIEF HAPPINESS OFFICER"

We may ask ourselves: is happiness really just a question of choice as these new happiness prophets want us to believe? Obviously not. Much unhappiness is the result of an individual's family history, health status, social background, and life accidents. Being born in a poor neighborhood does not automatically predestine one to be unhappy, but it restricts one's life chances and professional prospects. Happiness researchers have developed a "happiness formula." This formula takes the form of

$$H = S + C + V$$

in which (H)—the level of happiness—is determined by three factors: a biological set point (S)—this is the individual's inborn "mood" of optimism/pessimism[23]—plus the conditions of one's life (C), plus the voluntary activities (V).[24] Happiness coaches concentrate on the (V) factor: the voluntary activities which depend on the individual's choices and willpower. However, one's level of happiness depends also on the biological setpoint (S) and conditions of life (C). The first is given and the second is partly given (race, family background, health, intelligence, etcetera) and partly changeable. Most of these conditions of life, however, cannot be changed by the individual, but only by collective action. An African American citizen, a person with a disability, or a LGBTQ person, they all tend to suffer from discrimination, but they are unable to change their situation individually. They can do so by collective action and political pressure. This fact is often forgotten in the "happiness revolution." One reason for this could be that the majority of clients of happiness coaches come from a privileged background. They are mostly white middle-class women, and many of them are college-educated professionals.

The "happiness revolution" has been warmly embraced by CEOs and human resources managers, who invite the happiness coaches to lead in-company seminars. A new phenomenon is the creation of *Chief Happiness Officers* (CHOs) in companies. No, this is no joke: the company takes care of your happiness. The CHO encourage you to socialize with colleagues by organizing 'happy hours' or 'beers on the rooftops.' You may bring your child to the company's nursery, improve your fitness in the company's gym, play Ping-Pong in the breakroom, or bring your dog with you to work. At Amazon's Seattle-based headquarters, for instance, employees share their workspace with approximately 6,000 dogs on any given day.[25] An international recruitment consultancy describes the role of Chief Happiness Officer as having a psychological side and a "fun" side. For the "fun" side the following examples are given: "CHO may plan group movie outings, bartending shows, massage sessions, game rooms, tasting of oriental dishes, cosmetic treatments, coffee barista courses, Japanese tea ceremonies, etc."[26] Certainly, this may be "fun" (although even this may be questionable), but does it increase employees' happiness?

This is, indeed, the real question: do these trendy innovations really boost workers' happiness? Duena Blomstrom, a columnist for *Forbes,* is not convinced. "We seem to have collectively resigned to the fact that it is the norm to be unhappy to a degree or another in the workplace in particular in large companies," she writes, "and we neither demand or expect it to change. . . . When entrepreneurs enter corporate environments they are stunned to see a culture where the disrespect towards the workers is so great it's not uncommon for them to feel like they deserve nothing and to have forgotten that work is meant to be a meaningful exchange, not an exercise in flagellation."[27] The hidden function of the "happiness revolution" is to make employees feel happier without calling into question the power structure and the workings of the modern capitalist market economy. The role of happiness coaches and in particular of Chief Happiness Officers is to adapt workers to an economic system which in recent years has become much more anxiogenic and stressful. "Worldwide there is an increase in stress," writes Richard Layard, " . . . more and more people are saying 'Yes,' when asked 'Did you experience a lot of stress yesterday?'"[28] Layard emphasizes that "the general rise in stress . . . derives from an over-competitive society targeted too heavily on personal success."[29] Richard Sennett has pointed to the fact that "in work, the traditional career progressing step by step through the corridors of one or two institutions is withering; so is the deployment of a single set of skills through the course of a working life. Today, a young American with at least two years of college can expect to change jobs at least eleven times in the course of working, and change his or her skill base at least three times during those forty years of labor."[30] The "long term" order which characterized the post–World War II period has given way to short-term solutions: "Corporations have also farmed out many of the tasks they once did permanently in-house to small firms and to individuals employed on short-term contracts. The fastest-growing sector of the American labor force, for instance, is people who work for temporary job agencies."[31] "No long term," writes Sennett, "disorients action over the long term, loosens bonds of trust and commitment, and divorces will from behavior."[32]

How might the individual cope with an economic system that has become more stressful? He has the choice to adapt and become a "flexible, disposable worker" or to resist dehumanizing changes. However, changing this system to make it more humane belongs to the (C) factor of conditions of life and, as such, falls outside the scope of the happiness coaches. One might, therefore, compare the function of these coaches with that of the early clergy, who kept people happy with the promise of happiness in the afterlife. The difference is that happiness coaches don't promise happiness in an afterlife, but happiness "here and now" for immediate, "instant consumption," as one can read on their websites: "Happiness is here," "You could be happier right now." It is a message for an individualist society in which collective action has atrophied.

HAPPINESS AND COLLECTIVE ACTION

It is, maybe, no coincidence, that the early manifestations of the "happiness revolution" began in the period after the student revolts of the 1960s and early 1970s. This worldwide youth rebellion was the culmination of a period of collective action. However, the subsequent generation, called "Generation X," seemed less interested in politics and turned its attention inward. Albert O. Hirschman, who analyzed this phenomenon in his book *Shifting Involvements*, wrote:

> An important ingredient of the "spirit of 1968" was a sudden and overwhelming concern with public issues—of war and peace, of greater equality, of participation in decision-making. This concern rose after a long period of individual economic improvement and apparent full dedication thereto on the part of large masses of people in all of the countries where these "puzzling" outbreaks occurred. While poorly understood at the time they took place, those outbreaks are today classed as abnormal and quixotic episodes, in the course of the seventies, people returned to worry primarily about their private interests. . . .[33]

"Thus," he continued, "the change from the fifties to the sixties and then to the seventies and other such alternations in earlier periods raise the question whether our societies are in some way predisposed toward oscillations between periods of intense preoccupation with public issues and of almost total concentration on individual improvement and private welfare goals."[34] Hirschman answered this question in the affirmative. According to him the student rebellion was the result of disappointment with the consumer society. It is interesting that the same conclusion had already been reached in 1966 by the Dutch novelist Harry Mulisch in a book on the Provo Movement, a youth rebellion which shook The Netherlands in 1965 and which was a precursor to the French May 1968 movement.[35] Mulisch observed a values rift between parents, born before World War II, who were fully submerged in the new consumer society, and their postmaterialist offspring, born after World War II, writing: "While their parents, sitting on their refrigerators and washing machines, were watching TV with their left eye, with their right eye on THE CAR outside the front door, in one hand the FOOD MIXER, in the other De Telegraaf (a conservative daily, MHVH), on Saturday evening the children were going to the Spui (where the Provo happenings were)."[36]

Collective action is not only a means to changing the (C) factor of the conditions of life and, consequently, promoting the happiness of the individual, but it is also in itself an element of happiness. Moritz Schlick already pointed to the important role of enthusiasm for experiencing feelings of happiness. "Enthusiasm, "he wrote, "is the highest possible satisfaction for man. To be enthusiastic about something means to experience the highest joy when imagining it."[37] In the same vein Hirschman observed: "There is no such clear distinction at all between the pursuit of public happiness and the attainment of it. . . . Indeed, the very act of striving for public happiness is often the *next best thing* to actually *having* that happiness (and sometimes not just the next best thing, but much the best thing of the whole process . . .)."[38] Participants in public action experience happiness and satisfaction as a result of their activities, because "public-oriented action belongs, in this as in other respects, to a group of human activities that includes the search for community, beauty, knowledge, and salvation. All these activities 'carry their own reward,' . . . "[39] This is a message that seems to have been lost in an epoch of increasing self-oriented narcissism.

THE GROWTH OF THE "INDIVIDUALISM TRANSFORMATION TREE"

We can represent the different phases of modern individualism we have analyzed in Part I and Part II graphically in an "Individualism Transformation
Tree" (Figure 11.1).

We present the different development phases of individualism through a
cross section of a tree. Why? For this there are two reasons. The first reason
is that the different phases follow one other over time. However, this does
not mean that when a new type of individualism emerges a former type
disappears. A former type can become less prominent, but in most cases it
persists even while a new type is developing. In this sense the development of
modern individualism resembles the growth of a tree trunk which adds new,
annual rings (though the time intervals of the "rings" of the "Individualism
Transformation Tree" are, of course, much longer). A second reason to opt

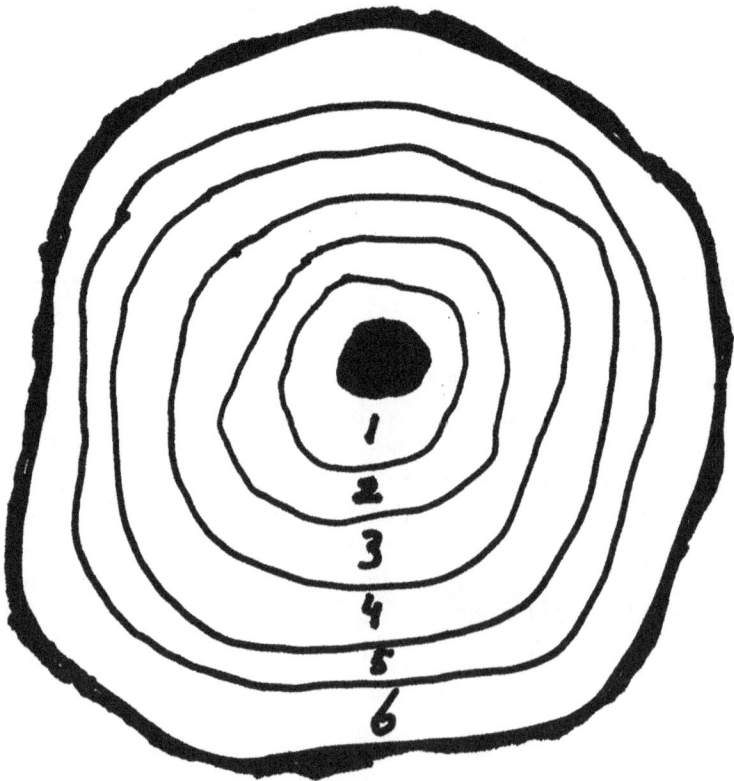

**Figure 11.1 The Growth of the "Individualism Transformation Tree": A Cross-Section of
the Development of Modern Individualism. Source: Author**

for a cross-section of a tree is that the "annual rings" of a tree vary: some are thinner, others are thicker, depending on the amount of sunshine and rainfall in the particular periods. A dry period will lead to a thin annual ring, a rainy period will lead to a thick annual ring. In an analogous way some forms of modern individualism will be "thinner" than others and have less impact, while others are "thicker" and have more impact. The influence of religious individualism, for instance, although not completely disappearing, has certainly diminished over the years. The same is true of the nineteenth-century individualistic lifestyle. However, the influence of economic individualism, instead of declining, got a boost at the end of the twentieth century with the advent of neo-liberalism.

The different rings around the core of the "Individualism Transformation Tree" are presented in Table 11.1.

Of course, the indicated periods in which the different kinds of individualism emerge are approximate and should be treated with a certain degree of caution. In the "Individualism Transformation Tree" religious individualism is the starting point of modern individualism. Martin Luther's Theses made a major contribution to the emergence of a guilt society by emphasizing man's autonomy and the moral role of the individual conscience. The first ring is reserved for philosophical individualism. The revolutionary event here was Descartes' *cogito,* which made the individual mind the bedrock of modern philosophy. Radical protestant sects, which were oppressed by the authorities,

Table 11.1 The Core and 6 "Rings" of the "Individualism Transformation Tree"

Core and Rings	Emerges in	Keywords
The Core: Religious Individualism	16th century	individual autonomy/conscience/guilt feelings
Ring 1: Philosophical individualism	17th century	thinking starts with the individual
Ring 2: Political individualism	17th/18th centuries	the state is created by individuals, for individuals
Ring 3: Individualism as a lifestyle	19th century	idealization of the "loner"/creative artist
Ring 4: Economic individualism	19th century	competition between individuals/maximum freedom for entrepreneur/minimal state
Ring 5: Expressive individualism	20th century	individual seeks "authentic self"
Ring 6: Narcissistic individualism	20th/21st centuries	individual seeks narcissistic gratification/other-directed person/emergence of a shame society

preached the right of the people to revolt, and would lay the foundation for the subsequent "ring" of political individualism, for which John Locke would become the most important spokesman and theorist. This religious core and the first two rings fit well together. All three emphasized human autonomy, the right of people to think for themselves, and egalitarianism, leading to demands for democratic self-determination. The undisputed moral bedrock of this early individualism was the individual conscience. Guilt feelings reminded one that the interests of others should be taken into account. Political individualism—despite its emphasis on the individual—was not an individual, but a *collective* project of people who founded modern liberal democracy, a political system characterized by negotiation, compromise, give and take, in order to find a consensus.

The third ring: individualism as a lifestyle, is different. The "loner" avoids the company of others. He seeks the freedom of vast, empty spaces, and is not really interested in politics. His European counterparts—creative artists and bohemians—seem not very much interested in politics either. The fourth "ring" of economic individualism represents a real break. The economic individualist, of whom the American "robber baron" is the prototypical incarnation, is not that concerned about his fellow creatures. He is rather a social Darwinist, who is not unduly tortured by guilt feelings. Living and working in an extremely competitive environment he is focused mainly on his own interests and doesn't shy away from exploiting others or from making the state subordinate to his interests. However, this economic individualism creates an affluent welfare state and in its wake modern consumerism, which in its turn generates a new kind of individualism: "expressive individualism." This is the fifth ring. Dissatisfied with the consumerism and affluence of the modern welfare state people begin to search for their "authentic self." This solipsistic inward turn leads to much navel gazing, but is morally neutral. In this period a new character type emerges, the "other-directed person," described by David Riesman and his colleagues. This "other-directed person" is guided less by the "inner compass" of conscience than by the opinions of the peer group, which means that he is much more susceptible to experiencing shame and to being shamed. The emergence of this new character type marks the gradual transition from a guilt society to a shame society. The sixth ring: "narcissistic individualism" is, as yet, the culmination of this development. The narcissist falls in love with himself and harbors grandiose ideas of power, beauty, and happiness. His narcissism finds an outlet in the search for the perfect body and the pursuit of individual happiness. However, much more than the "inner-directed person" the narcissist is dependent on the applause and approval of others. Despite his grandiose ambitions he is extremely vulnerable to shame.

NOTES

1. John Locke, *An Essay Concerning Human Understanding: Complete and Unabridged in One Volume,* (Milwaukee: WLC Books, 2009), p. 180.

2. James Madison, "Paper No. 62" in Alexander Hamilton, James Madison, John Jay, *The Federalist Papers,* op. cit., p. 380. This emphasis on happiness as a human goal is a modern phenomenon. In traditional Christianity supreme happiness could only be realized in the afterlife. Arthur Schopenhauer, known as a misanthrope, wrote: "There is only *one* innate mistake and it is that we are there to be happy." (Arthur Schopenhauer, "Die Welt als Wille und Vorstellung," Volume 2, in Arthur Schopenhauer, *Sämtliche Werke,* Volume 3, [Wiesbaden: F. A. Brockhaus, 1972], p. 729).

3. This idea, that happiness has many different meanings, could already be found in Aristotle, who wrote: "But what constitutes happiness is a matter of dispute; and the popular account of it is not the same as that given by philosophers. Ordinary people identify it with some obvious and visible good, such as pleasure or wealth or honour—some say one thing and some another, indeed very often the same man says different things at different times: when he falls sick he thinks health is happiness, when he is poor, wealth." (Aristotle, *The Nicomachean Ethics,* Aristotle in Twenty-Three Volumes, XIX, Loeb Classical Library, with an English translation by H. Rackham, [Cambridge, MA: Harvard University Press, 1975], p. 11).

4. Erik Erikson, *Dimensions of a New Identity: The Jefferson Lectures in the Humanities,* (New York: W. W. Norton & Company, 1974), p. 60.

5. Theodore Zeldin, "On the Subject of Happiness," *The London Review of Books,* Vol. 10, No. 13, October 1988.

6. Edgar Cabanas and Eva Illouz, *Manufacturing Happy Citizens—How the Science and Industry of Happiness Control our Lives,* (Cambridge: Polity, 2019), p. 3.

7. Ibid.

8. Jean-Paul Sartre, *Carnets de la drôle de guerre—Septembre 1939—mars 1940,* (Paris: Gallimard, 1995), p. 297.

9. The concept "life goal" gets 1,770,000,000 hits on Google (retrieved on April 15, 2020)—a sign of how important the concept "life goal" has become.

10. Edgar Cabanas and Eva Illouz, *Manufacturing Happy Citizens—How the Science and Industry of Happiness Control our Lives,* op. cit., p. 9.

11. Ibid., p. 10.

12. Ibid., p. 70.

13. Lifecoachhub. https://www.lifecoachhub.com/happiness-coach (My emphasis, MHVH).

14. https://www.myhappinesscoach.ca/.

15. Quoted in Charles Taylor, *A Secular Age,* op cit., p. 479.

16. Ibid., p. 478. Anthony Giddens presents the increasing number of choices, available to an individual in modern society, as a kind of fatality. "Modernity," he writes, "confronts the individual with a complex diversity of choices and, because it is non-foundational, at the same time offers little help as to which options should be selected." (Anthony Giddens, *Modernity and Self-Identity—Self and Society in*

the Late Modern Age, (Stanford, CA: Stanford University Press, 1991), p. 80. He—fatalistically—concludes: " . . . We have no choice but to choose." (p. 81).

17. Will Henley, "The tech startups that believe happiness can be found in an app," *The Guardian,* July 29, 2013. https://www.theguardian.com/sustainable-business/technology-happiness-found-in-app.

18. https://www.happier.com/.

19. Will Henley, "The tech startups that believe happiness can be found in an app," op. cit.

20. Universal Coach Institute. https://www.universalcoachinstitute.com/life-coach-salary/.

21. https://happyologist.co.uk/happyologist_coaching/.

22. Taffy Brodesser-Aknar, "The Merchant of Just Be Happy," *New York Times,* December 28, 2013. https://www.nytimes.com/2013/12/29/business/the-merchant-of-just-be-happy.html.

23. This individual innate "mood" has been perfectly described by William James: "The sanguine and healthy-minded live habitually on the sunny side of their misery-line, the depressed and melancholy live beyond it, in darkness and apprehension. There are men who seem to have started in life with a bottle or two of champagne inscribed to their credit; whilst others seem to have been born close to the pain-threshold, which the slightest irritants fatally send them over." (William James, *The Varieties of Religious Experience—A Study in Human Nature,* [New York and London: Penguin Books, 1985], p. 135). James emphasizes that "in many persons, happiness is congenital and irreclaimable." (p. 79). James's observations are confirmed by recent research. Carol Graham, who conducted international surveys on happiness, writes, for instance, that "a person's disposition or personality is assuredly one of the determinants of their level of reported happiness, so we would expect a person with a generally sunnier disposition to report a higher level of happiness than a person who is identical in every other respect but has a gloomier outlook." (Carol Graham, *Happiness around the world—The paradox of happy peasants and miserable millionaires,* [Oxford and New York: Oxford University Press, 2009], p. 98).

24. Jonathan Haidt, *The Happiness Hypothesis—Putting Ancient Wisdom and Philosophy to the Test of Modern Science,* (London: Arrow Books, 2006), p. 91.

25. Ruth Umoh, "More than 6,000 dogs 'work' at Amazon, where every day is 'take Your Dog to Work Day,'" *CNBC,* June 22, 2018. https://www.cnbc.com/2018/06/22/at-amazon-every-day-is-take-your-dog-to-work-day.html.

26. "Don't worry, be happy—Chief Happiness Officer will show you how," *Sowelo Consulting,* February 6, 2019. https://sowelo.eu/chief-happiness-officer/.

27. Duena Blomstrom, "Do You Have a Chief Happiness Officer?" *Forbes,* January 24, 2019. https://www.forbes.com/sites/duenablomstrom1/2019/01/24/do-you-have-a-chief-happiness-officer/#1c8a92e35256.

28. Richard Layard with George Ward, *Can We Be Happier? Evidence and Ethics,* (London: Pelican, 2020), p. 54.

29. Ibid., p. 247.

30. Richard Sennett, *The Corrosion of Character—The Personal Consequences of Work in the New Capitalism,* (New York and London: W. W. Norton & Company, 1999), p. 22.

31. Ibid.

32. Ibid., p. 31.

33. Albert O. Hirschman, *Shifting Involvements—Private Interest and Public Action,* op. cit., p. 3.

34. Ibid.

35. For an analysis of the Dutch Provo Movement and its relation to May 1968, see my paper "Paris May '68 and Provo Amsterdam '65—Trying to Understand Two Postmodern Youth Revolts," *Cicero Foundation,* May, 2008. https://www.cicerofoundation.org/wp-content/uploads/Marcel_Van_Herpen_May_68_and_Provo_Amsterdam_65.pdf.

36. Harry Mulisch, *Bericht aan de rattenkoning* (Message to the Rat King), (Amsterdam: De Bezige Bij, 1966), p. 62.

37. Moritz Schlick, *Fragen der Ethik,* (Suhrkamp Verlag: Frankfurt am Main, 1984), p. 85.

38. Albert O. Hirschman, *Shifting Involvements—Private Interest and Public Action,* op. cit., p. 85.

39. Ibid.

PART III

The Development of a New Dialectic: "Old Shame" versus "New Shame"

Chapter 12

De-Shaming Processes I

Is Racial Shame Becoming "Old Shame"?

Shame in the United States and other Western societies is on the rise. This rise is like a groundswell which affects society as a whole. The question is: is this a fatality or can we do something to reverse this trend? I think we can. In society there are some groups which had to cope with this problem a long time before it became a problem for society as a whole. These were groups that were shamed and of which the members experienced shame before this became a general trend. These groups, such as African Americans, the LGBTQ community, and people with a handicap, have developed strategies to fight back. And some of these de-shaming strategies were met with success. The rise of a shame society is, therefore, a nuanced process, because there are segments of society which are less affected and segments that are more affected. There are even groups in society, which—going against the general trend—are involved in de-shaming processes, while other groups, on the contrary, are hit doubly hard. Shaming is, therefore, not a one-dimensional, but a dialectical process.

Shame is one of the basic human emotions. Although bodily expressions are the same, the reasons for an individual to feel ashamed will vary according to the culture and the epoch in which he is living. What is a reason for shame in one society need not be so in another. Similarly, reasons for shame in the same society will change over time, which allows us to speak of "old shame" and "new shame." An example is how our societies viewed unmarried women who had passed the normal age for getting married. In Anglo-Saxon countries these women, usually over thirty, were called "old maids." In France they were called *vieilles filles,* in Germany *alte Jungfer,* and in the Netherlands *oude vrijster.* In all these languages the noun was preceded by the adjective "old." A girl was "old" if she was thirty and still unmarried. It meant that she was no longer available for the marriage market, or, when she was available, she had only a slight chance of finding a partner. She was considered good for staying at home and taking care of her parents or becoming a nun.

Being an "old maid" was clearly a shameful situation. However, this was different for her male counterpart, the unmarried man of over thirty. Called a "bachelor" he was considered to be someone who fully profited from life, had plenty of erotic adventures and was available for the marriage market— although reluctantly, because he wouldn't let himself be "caught" so easily. In Germany his name was *Junggeselle* and in the Netherlands *vrijgezel,* names which emphasized respectively that he was *young* and *free.* However, in the modern, metropolitan, urbanized world a de-shaming process took place. Unmarried women over thirty lost the stigma that they were "left-overs" from the marriage market. Instead these often highly educated, independent women claimed the same status as the bachelor: far from being victims, they presented their situation as the result of free choice and emphasized that they were certainly not lost to the marriage market, but that an eventual partner had to fulfill a number of conditions. The word "old maid" became obsolete and with it the stigma of being an unmarried woman.

Over the past fifty years one can observe that in Western societies some other forms of "old shame" have also diminished, while forms of "new shame" have emerged. Forms of "old shame" which have diminished (without, however, completely disappearing) concern shame caused by discrimination on the basis of race, disability, or sexual orientation. This process of "de-shaming" has two sides: the "receiving side," which is the target group of shaming practices, and the "shaming side," which is "society" or, rather, *sections* of society, because not everyone will participate in these shaming practices. While emancipation movements of the victims have played an important role in de-shaming strategies, one should not underestimate the role of society, because de-shaming is only possible if society displays increased receptivity to the demands of discriminated groups and a growing willingness to end open forms of discrimination. Although modern societies seem to have become more tolerant, processes of "de-shaming" are, as a rule, painstakingly slow. And one should not forget that under the cover of official and legal "de-shaming" policies, often more hidden and subtle practices of discrimination and "micro-aggressions" tend to live on.

TONI MORRISON'S *THE BLUEST EYE*

How deep racial shame affects the individual one can read in Toni Morrison's brilliant novel *The Bluest Eye*. Morrison describes, for instance, what happens at the moment when a black girl enters a shop to buy candies.

> [The storekeeper] senses that he need not waste the effort of a glance. He does not see her, because for him there is nothing to see. How can a fifty-two-year-old white immigrant storekeeper with the taste of potatoes and beer in his mouth, his mind honed on the doe-eyed Virgin Mary, his sensibilities blunted by a permanent awareness of loss, *see* a little black girl? Nothing in his life even suggested that the feat was possible, not to say desirable or necessary. . . . She does not know what keeps his glance suspended. Perhaps because he is grown, or a man, and she a little girl. But she has seen interest, disgust, even anger in grown male eyes. Yet this vacuum is not new to her. It has an edge; somewhere in the bottom lid is the distaste. She has seen it lurking in the eyes of all white people. So. The distaste must be for her, her blackness. All things in her are flux and anticipation. But her blackness is static and dread. And it is the blackness that accounts for, that creates, the vacuum edged with distaste in white eyes.[1]

Morrison describes the humiliation experienced by the black girl. For the white storekeeper "there is nothing to see," she is a *non-person* and the only reason for this is that she has a black skin. "In American history the closest approximation of having 'no face' is being black in America," wrote Stuart Schneiderman. "The most eloquent presentation of this condition can be found in the writings of James Baldwin. The title of one of his books, *Nobody Knows My Name,* renders well the sense of having no face. Roughly speaking, if you have no face you will either be ignored, treated as though you are not there, or else taken to be a threat by your mere presence."[2] The white shopkeeper in Morrison's novel didn't look the girl in the eyes, because this would in some way mean that he acknowledges her existence as a human being.[3] But that is not the whole story. Morrison describes also how the main character is harassed by black boys. The boys are yelling: "Black e mo," [sic] attacking her for the color of her skin. "That they themselves were black . . . ," writes Morrison, "was irrelevant. It was their contempt for their own blackness. . . . "[4] The boys had internalized the contempt of the racist white population and shame became intermingled with self-hate.

WHITE AND BLACK DOLLS

In the 1940s Kenneth B. Clark and Mamie Phipps Clark, a couple of African American social psychologists, conducted experiments in which they presented white and brown dolls to black children, aged three to seven years. The children were asked: "Give me the doll that you like to play with . . . the doll that is a nice doll . . . the doll that looks bad. . . . "[5] The majority of the children rejected the brown doll. "The rejection of the brown doll and the preference for the white doll," wrote the researchers, "when explained at all, were explained in rather simple, concrete terms: for white-doll preference— ''cause he's pretty' or ''cause he's white'; for rejecting of the brown doll— ''cause he's ugly' or ''cause it don't look pretty' or ''cause him black' or 'got black on him.'"[6] When asked: "Give me the doll that looks like you," the children gave the brown doll. This was a crucial moment. "Some of the children who were free and relaxed in the beginning of the experiment," wrote the researchers, "broke down and cried or became somewhat negativistic during the latter part when they were required to make self-identifications."[7] This experiment played an important role in the Supreme Court's landmark ruling *Brown v. Board of Education* of 1954 on racial integration of American public schools. Erik Erikson wrote that "the Negro's unavoidable identification with the dominant race, and the need of the master race to protect its own identity . . . established in both groups an association: light—clean— clever—white, and dark—dirty—dumb—nigger."[8] "The result," he wrote, "especially in those Negroes who left the poor haven of their Southern homes, was often a violently sudden and cruel cleanliness training, as attested to in the autobiographies of Negro writers. It is as if by cleansing a whiter identity could be achieved."[9] Small black children preferred white dolls. Other black children preferred white heroes. Black Panther leader Stokely Carmichael, for instance, wrote:

> I remember that when I was a boy, I used to go to see Tarzan movies on Saturday. White Tarzan used to beat up the black natives. I would sit there yelling, "Kill the beasts, kill the savages, kill 'em!" I was saying: Kill *me*. It was as if a Jewish boy watched Nazis taking Jews off to concentration camps and cheered them on. Today I want the chief to beat hell out of Tarzan and send him back to Europe.[10]

In his book *Soul on Ice,* published in 1968, Eldridge Cleaver, another leader of the Black Panther Party, tells how he was interned in prison and decided to get himself a pin-up girl to paste on the wall of his cell. It was a white pin-up. When the guard came, he removed it and tore it to pieces. "Get yourself a colored girl for a pinup," he said, "no white women—and I'll let it stay up."[11] "The disturbing part about the whole incident," wrote Cleaver, "was that a terrible feeling of guilt came over me as I realized that I had chosen the picture of the white girl over the available pictures of black girls. . . . Was it true, did I really prefer white girls over black? The conclusion was clear and inescapable: I did. I decided to check out my friends on this point and it was easy to determine, from listening to their general conversation, that the white woman occupied a peculiarly prominent place in all our frames of reference."[12]

THREE DE-SHAMING STRATEGIES

For a discriminated group there are different de-shaming strategies. I would like to mention three. In the first place one has to conquer the self-hate. This can be done by directing this hate toward its real cause, which is not oneself, but the racist community which is discriminating. In the books of Toni Morrison and Eldridge Cleaver we find examples of this. When the girl in Morrison's novel received for Christmas a pink-colored doll with blue eyes, she was "physically revolted," notwithstanding the fact that "adults, older girls, shops, magazines, newspapers, window signs—all the world had agreed that a blue-eyed, yellow-haired, pink-skinned doll was what every girl child treasured."[13] The reaction of the girl: "I had only one desire: to dismember it."[14] We find a similar turning outward of self-hate in Eldridge Cleaver's book, where he describes how feeling attracted by white women became an act of rebellion and revenge. "I became a rapist," he wrote.[15] And he tells how he "sought out white prey." "Rape was an insurrectionary act. It delighted me that I was defying and trampling upon the white man's law, upon his system of values, and that I was defiling his women—and this point, I believe, was the most satisfying to me, because I was very resentful over the historical fact of how the white man has used the black woman. I felt I was getting revenge."[16] The same feelings of revenge we find in Frantz Fanon, a psychiatrist and philosopher from French Martinique, who wrote that the first idea of people from the West Indies, arriving in France, "was to sleep with a white woman."[17] Fanon equally attributed this to "a need for revenge."[18]

Apart from turning one's self-hate against those who caused the shame, a second de-shaming strategy consists of what the German philosopher Peter Sloterdijk has called *Umwertungskämpfe*—"re-evaluation struggles."[19] This happens when a victim refuses to see himself any longer through the eyes of the oppressor, but turns the contempt upside down and expresses his contempt for the values and beauty standards of the other side. "In this second contempt a preceding contempt is turned against itself and re-evaluated."[20] Movements, like *Black is beautiful* fit into this strategy. Being beautiful is no longer the privilege of white people, was the message, Black people can equally lay claim to it. These de-shaming practices could go far—sometimes, apparently, a bit too far, as Arthur Schlesinger explains. He wrote about a Task Force on Minorities, which, in 1989, published a report to foster the "multiculturalization" of the New York State history curriculum. The report of the Task Force opened as follows: "African Americans, Asian-Americans, Puerto Ricans/Latinos and Native Americans have all been the victims of an intellectual and educational oppression that has characterized the culture and institutions of the United States and the European American world for centuries."[21] One of the consultants of the Task Force, wrote Schlesinger, was Dr. Leonard Jeffries, who "describes Europeans as cold, individualistic, materialistic, and aggressive 'ice people' who grew up in caves and have brought the world the three D's, 'domination, destruction, and death,' whereas Africans grew up in sunlight, with the intellectual and physical superiority provided by melanin, are warm, humanistic, and communitarian 'sun people.'"[22]

To the re-evaluation strategies of the victims of discrimination there also belongs the practice of claiming negative nicknames as a badge of honor. A case in point is the word "nigger." "Nigger" comes from the Latin word *niger,* what means "black." The English noun: "to denigrate" comes from *de-nigrare,* which means "blackening." This "blackening" can concern someone else's status or reputation. There exists, therefore, a long tradition of using the word "black" for negative phenomena. This was all the more a reason for the Black community to appropriate this term. In the 1990s, the word 'nigger' became popular in the hip-hop movement. The Black comedian Richard Pryor said:

> When we say "nigger" now, it's very positive. Now all white kids who buy into hip-hop culture call each other "nigger" because they have no history with the word other than something positive. . . . When black kids call each other "a real nigger" or "my nigger": it means you walk a certain way . . . have your own culture that you invent so you don't have to buy into the U.S. culture that you're not really part of. *It means you're special.* We have our own language.[23]

Pryor claimed: "Saying it changed me, yes it did. It gave me strength, let me rise above. . . . "[24] The same phenomenon can be observed in the de-shaming strategies of gay people. In the 1970s, for instance, homosexuals in the Netherlands began to claim the negative word *flikker* (fagot) for themselves and published their own paper, titled *Flikkerkrant* (Fagot Paper).

A third, and more important de-shaming strategy consists of civil and political action. Morrison's novel *The Bluest Eye* was published in 1970, two years after the assassination of Martin Luther King, at the culmination of the civil rights movement. Thirty-seven years earlier the African American sociologist William Du Bois had published his essay "On Being Ashamed of Oneself: An Essay on Race Pride." Du Bois deplored "the fact that we are still ashamed of ourselves and are thus stopped from valid objection when white folks are ashamed to call us human."[25] Du Bois observed that the African American had a "sense of always looking at one's self through the eyes of others, of measuring one's soul by the tape of a world that looks on in amused contempt and pity. One ever feels his two-ness—an American, a Negro; two souls, two thoughts, two unreconciled strivings."[26] Du Bois was conscious of the fact that ending racial shame ultimately depended on the decision and the will of black Americans to organize themselves: "American Negroes will be beaten into submission and degradation if they merely wait unorganized to find some place voluntarily given them in the new reconstruction of the economic world."[27] African Americans *did* organize and thanks to the civil rights movement official discrimination decreased. The election of Barack Obama as forty-fourth President of the United States, the first African American to occupy this high position, was the culmination of this process of de-shaming.

"RACIAL BLURRING"

However, for a process of de-shaming to be successful *both* sides have to move: not only the discriminated group, but also society as a whole. The question is why racism in the United States has been diminishing. Have white Americans suddenly lost their prejudices and become more tolerant? Maybe. However, Morrison points to the fact that so-called liberal white Americans are ambiguous allies because they prefer not to talk about race. In their effort not to embarrass the other, they pretend to ignore the race problem, because " . . . ignoring race is understood to be a graceful, liberal, even generous habit. To notice is to recognize an already discredited difference; to maintain its invisibility through silence is to allow the black body a shadowless participation in the dominant cultural body."[28] Samuel Huntington has tried to give a different answer to the question why racism has decreased. He has pointed to the demographic and social changes underlying these changes of attitude. According to him "a slow process of racial blurring is occurring both biologically from intermarriage and symbolically and attitudinally, with individual multiracialism becoming a more widely accepted norm. Americans approve of their country moving from a multiracial society of racial groups to a non-racial society of multiracial individuals."[29] Huntington emphasized that "to a small but growing extent, intermarriage is blurring the lines between races. Much more importantly, race and racial distinctions are losing significance in people's thinking."[30] "In the 1960s," he wrote, "the slogan was "Black is beautiful." By the 1990s, the equivalent slogan would be "Biracial (or multiracial) is beautiful."[31] Public figures, such as the golf champion Tiger Woods, began to boast of their mixed-race heritage. Woods, for instance, called himself 'Cablinasian,' a blend of Caucasian, black, Indian, and Asian.[32] The trend in the United States of people identifying as multiracial got a boost with the 2000 Census, which allowed respondents for the first time to select more than one race. However, racial blurring is not confined to the United States. It is also taking place elsewhere. "The number of Britons who say they have a mixed-ethnic background almost doubled between the census of 2001 and 2011, to about 1.2m, or slightly more than 2% of the overall population," wrote *The Economist,* adding that "that figure is probably an undercount . . . and the true figure could be three times as high."[33]

Huntington concluded that "racial perceptions and racial prejudices are and will remain facts of life in America. Yet the salience of race in people's perceptions and attitudes is clearly declining."[34] The importance of race in people's perceptions is declining not only in America. A longitudinal survey conducted by a French human rights commission concluded that tolerance toward minorities in France was increasing. Between 2013 and 2019 the Longitudinal Tolerance Index progressed from 53 to 66 points on a 0 to 100 scale. Tolerance toward black people reached 79 points, which was one of the highest scores. "The French are becoming more and more tolerant overall," wrote the authors.[35] They observed with satisfaction that "each generation is more tolerant than the one before it." A factor which could play a role here is what the Dutch sociologist Abram de Swaan has called "expanding circles of identification." This is the fact that in the course of history the groups with which individuals identify become less exclusive and more inclusive. "For the majority of the history of their existence on earth," writes De Swaan, "people have lived in small groups of blood relatives. Their circle of identification must have consisted of at least a few dozen fellow men and at most a few hundred. . . . It's only been since a few hundred generations, some five to ten thousand years, that another principle of social organization has developed: close proximity."[36] Group identifications with family and neighbors expanded to encompass nation, class, or race. "However," writes De Swaan, "there is one form of identification which differs from all others in one important aspect: worldwide identification, with mankind as a whole, is all encompassing and no people are now excluded from this."[37] The same idea is formulated by Norbert Elias, who writes in the same vein that "there are clear signs that people are beginning to identify beyond state borders, their we-group identity is shifting to the plane of humankind."[38] These de-shaming practices are therefore signs of a changing mentality and one can agree with Robert Nozick who writes, that "after all, we hope that recent gains in moral sensitivity to issues such as women's equality, homosexual rights, racial equality, and minority relations will not be the last."[39]

However, despite these signs of progress, race discrimination and shaming practices tend to be stubborn. Although bureaucratic and legal forms of discrimination are diminishing, it is too early to declare victory. When, for instance, in the summer of 2005, Hurricane Katrina hit New Orleans, a city in which two-thirds of the population is black,

> Many, primarily white, Americans have been unable or unwilling to relate to or empathize with these relatively poor black New Orleanians. This social distance became apparent at the onset of the disaster. During a trip to a Houston arena shelter, Barbara Bush, the former First Lady, made a comment that reflected a lack of empathy for the hardest-hit hurricane victims and the stark social distance separating whites from blacks generally: "So many of the people in the arena here, you know, were underprivileged anyway, so this—this [she chuckles slightly] is working well for them." Such out-of-touch white women and men somehow believed that poor, African American evacuees, without even the resources to afford a hotel room, were *better off* after the hurricane than before. This kind of flippant reaction to suffering by thousands reveals the deeper dynamic of *alienating* racist relations, in which a white-racist framing and ideology deny any white agency in creating black poverty and impede empathy, understanding, and solidarity across the US color line.[40]

"COLORISM": A NEW DISCRIMINATION?

There is yet another problem: it is called "colorism." "Colorism" is a new kind of discrimination, associated with a growing number of mixed marriages, which has led to an increase in lighter-skinned black Americans. "Colorism," writes Robert Reece, "is the process by which people of color with phenotypic features more closely associated with whiteness—such as lighter eyes, thinner noses and lips, straighter hair, and particularly lighter skin tones—are offered social and economic advantages relative to their counterparts with more 'ethnic' phenotypic features—darker eyes, thicker noses and lips, curly hair, and darker skin."[41] Research showed that a lighter skin tone had a positive effect on income and social acceptance—particularly in the case of men. "In addition to wages and income, relative to darker skinned black Americans, lighter skinned black Americans have been shown to enjoy better mental and physical health, experience fewer negative encounters with the criminal justice system, are punished less and less harshly in schools, and are viewed as more attractive."[42] This phenomenon has, apparently, led to a "desolidarization" among the black population, because "recent studies suggest darker skinned black Americans are more liberal and less likely to embrace racial stereotypes about black people; whereas lighter skinned black Americans are less supportive of liberal social policies and tend to embrace more racial stereotypes about black people."[43] Lighter-skinned black Americans could become some kind of a black "aristocracy," welcomed as equal partners by the white population, while the darker-skinned remain the victims of ongoing discrimination. One author observed that in recent years in the United States. "Onscreen, there are more Black and brown characters . . . but even the non-white leads often have light skin. . . . Some 80 percent of Black female lead roles in family films have 'light' or 'medium' skin tone. . . . "[44] A survey of Latinos, conducted in 2021, concluded that "Hispanics with darker skin are more likely to have experienced at least one discrimination incident than Hispanics with lighter skin color."[45] The problem was that these incidents were not only caused by white people, but equally by members of their own group. If this trend would be confirmed, racism, although diminishing, would give way to another kind of discrimination: "colorism."

The *Black Lives Matter* (BLM) movement also is a sign that—despite some progress—it is still too early to declare discrimination and shaming practices founded on race "old shame." The movement was launched in 2013 by Patrisse Cullors, Alicia Garza, and Opal Tometi, after the acquittal of the man who killed a seventeen-year-old African American boy, Trayvon Martin, in Florida. In 2014 the movement became nationwide after a police officer in Ferguson, Missouri, shot Michael Brown, an eighteen-year-old African American boy. Recent cases of police brutality against African Americans, such as the murders of George Floyd and Jacob Blake in 2020, make it clear that much has yet to be done. "The past half century has seen visible progress," wrote *The Economist*. "The ceiling white society once imposed on black opportunity and ambition has started to lift."[46] However, "the incarceration rate for black men and women more than tripled from 1960 to 2010. One in three African-American men born in 2001 can expect to be imprisoned at some point in his life, compared with one in 17 white boys."[47] Segregation in poverty-stricken neighborhoods, unstable families, unemployment, and bad education are the causes of this dire situation which can only be improved by adopting drastic measures to lift the black population out of poverty.

Even the French report on the fight against racism, which hailed the fact that in 2018 "black people were one of the most accepted minorities in France," draws attention to the fact that "they are also among the most discriminated against. Whether it concerns access to housing, employment or even work, differences in treatment are very clear. Victims must fight against inferior treatment due to the colour of their skin."[48] The report mentions that "a black person is 32% less likely to find housing," and "49.9% of black people report having experienced discrimination in the workplace."[49] This kind of discrimination is often referred to as some kind of residual, "systemic racism," but systems are not racist, people are. Only when people change and give up their prejudices will governments, housing agencies, and companies change. The authors of the French report seemed to have understood this. They pleaded for "an increased awareness of the phenomenon. This requires a reversal of perspectives . . . white people should work on understanding the experiences black people endure and put an end to a process that they themselves, sometimes inadvertently, are instrumental in."[50]

MICROAGGRESSIONS ARE AGGRESSIONS

That an increase in the white population's empathy is more than overdue became clear from testimonies about "microaggressions," collected in July 2020 by the French paper *Le Monde*. Examples mentioned in the report include a white woman touching the hair of a black girl without asking her permission and exclaiming: "Oh, that's weird, you'd think it's cotton!" Another example was a black girl waiting on an underground platform when behind her back some white teens start humming: "cho—cho—cho—chocolate." In another, a black boy quits a party when someone's leather bag goes missing. One of the others turns to the boy, roaring with laughter, "Come on, we know that it is you, give the bag back." The boy says nothing, but is not amused. "'Ordinary racism,' 'invisible racism,' 'microaggressions' or 'microracism' . . . whatever name one gives these remarks, these jokes, these allusions," wrote the paper, "it is the same story: minorities forever being reminded of their origins or the color of their skin." Alice Hasters, a German woman with a German father and an African American mother tells how people often ask her: "Where do you come from?" or speak English to her. "What is behind this question is the idea that someone who is black cannot be German," she said.[51] She explained that when she is accompanied by white friends, "the world seems to be friendlier. I feel this, for instance, in a museum, in a theater, in hotels. Otherwise what I experience often is a nonverbal 'Are you sure you should be here?' These brief moments are like mosquito bites—I call them microaggressions—taken individually you can put up with it, but taken together the pain is unbearable."[52]

The prefix "micro" in the word "microaggression" suggests that it is only minor offenses, small "pinpricks" that are often made by ignorant people who are unconscious of the pain they cause. But these "microaggressions" are, indeed, not as innocent as they are presented: deep down they are classifying people as second-class citizens. "I do not use 'microaggression' any more," writes Ibram Kendi. "I detest the post-racial platform that supported its sudden popularity. I detest its component parts—'micro' and 'aggression.' A persistent daily low hum of racist abuse is not minor. I use the term 'abuse' because aggression is not as exacting a term. Abuse accurately describes the action and its effects on people: distress, anger, worry, depression, anxiety, pain, fatigue, and suicide."[53]

A stress survey, conducted in 2015 by the American Psychological Association, found that people from racial and ethnic minorities who reported experiences of day-to-day discrimination, rate their stress levels higher on average, than those who say they have not experienced discrimination. Chronic stress was reported to be linked to health problems, such as anxiety, obesity, depression, high blood pressure, and substance abuse. In particular so-called microaggressions were also claimed here to play a role: "receiving poorer service at stores and restaurants, being treated with less courtesy and respect, or being treated as less intelligent or less trustworthy—may be more common than major discrimination."[54] However, the report continued: "People who are on the receiving end of day-to-day discrimination often feel they're in a state of constant vigilance, on the lookout for being a target of discrimination. That heightened watchfulness is a recipe for chronic stress."[55] When, in 2019, a young black woman, pregnant and unwed, arrived at her clinic, she "felt judged for not being married, and dismissed because she was African-American. Her doctor, she said, would not look her in the eye and did a poor job answering her questions."[56] Like the girl in Morrison's novel, the white doctor didn't look the woman in the eye. She was treated as a "non-person." It is not surprising, then that happiness surveys come to the conclusion that "blacks are less happy than other races in the United States. . . . "[57]

However, there are also signs for hope. When in May 2020 George Floyd was killed in Minneapolis by a police officer, there followed worldwide protests. The massive participation in these rallies of young whites, who expressed their solidarity with the black community, was a new and hopeful phenomenon. The Reverend Al Sharpton who delivered the eulogy at Floyd's funeral drew attention to this fact. "They never thought they'd see young whites marching like they marching now," he said. "All over the world, I seen grandchildren of slave masters, tearing down slave master statue over in England, and put it in the river. . . . I've seen whites walking past curfews saying, 'Black lives matter. No justice. No peace.'"[58] Patrisse Cullors, one of the founders of the Black Lives Matter movement, "described the current uprisings as 'a watershed moment' in U.S. and global history. 'The entire world is saying, 'Black lives matter,'" she said."[59] The same thoughts were expressed by the author Ta-Nehisi Coates. When asked for his commentary on the worldwide protests following the murder of George Floyd, he said:

> I can't believe I'm gonna say this, but I see hope. I see progress right now, at this moment. I had an interesting call on Saturday with my dad, who was born in 1946, grew up dirt poor in Philadelphia, lived in a truck, went off to Vietnam, came back, joined the Panther Party, and was in Baltimore for the 1968 riots. . . . I asked him if he could compare what he saw in 1968 to what he was seeing

now. And what he said to me was there was no comparison—that this is much more sophisticated. And I say, well, what do you mean? He said it would have been like if somebody from the turn of the 20th century could see the March on Washington. The idea that black folks in their struggle against the way the law is enforced in their neighborhoods would resonate with white folks in Des Moines, Iowa, in Salt Lake City, in Berlin, in London—that was unfathomable to him in '68, when it was mostly black folks in their own communities registering their anger and great pain. I don't want to overstate this, but there are significant swaths of people and communities that are not black, that to some extent have some perception of what that pain and that suffering is. I think that's different.[60]

Another African American author, John McWhorter, wrote in the same vein:

As I write this in 2021, America has become conscious of racism, within just a year, to a degree so extreme, so sustained, and so sincere that history offers no parallel, either in this country or any other."[61] "Confederate statues are coming down not just one at a time but in droves. The Associated Press has decided to capitalize the word *Black*. . . . Suddenly the entire nation is aware of, and help-ing black America to celebrate, the holiday Juneteenth, with many cities giving black people the day off as a paid holiday. In many of the protests in the wake of George Floyd's murder, so many of the faces are white that you'd think the movement was sponsored by Greenpeace.[62]

Kurt Streeter, an African American reporter, jogging with his nine-year-old son through the mostly white Seattle neighborhood where he lives, saw with amazement Black Lives Matter signs popping up everywhere: on front lawns, displayed in windows, attached to trees, stapled to telephone poles. Looking at this incredible burst of support he told his son: "Never in a million years would I have thought we'd see this. . . . Never." And he wrote: "I noticed how the show of support had changed me. I felt safer, as free as I've felt on any run."[63]

The Trump Presidency, which followed Obama's Presidency, could be interpreted as a "revenge of beleaguered racist whites." The "war on shame" is, therefore, certainly not yet won. Open racism may be decreasing, but there is still a long way to go before it can definitively be called "old shame."

NOTES

1. Toni Morrison, *The Bluest Eye,* (London: Vintage, 2016), pp. 46–47.

2. Stuart Schneiderman, *Saving Face—America and the Politics of Shame,* op. cit., pp. 124–125.

3. "Perhaps the classic type of a non-person in our society," writes Erving Goffman, "is the servant . . . in certain ways he is defined . . . as someone who isn't there."

(Erving Goffman, *The Presentation of Self in Everyday Life,* op. cit., pp. 150–51). Goffman quotes a book by Mrs. Trollope, *Domestic Manners of the Americans,* published in 1832, in which she writes: "I had, indeed, frequent opportunities of observing this habitual indifference to the presence of their slaves. They talk of them, of their condition, of their faculties, of their conduct, exactly as if they were incapable of hearing." Goffman comments: "It would seem that the role of non-person usually carries with it some subordination and disrespect . . . " (Ibid., pp. 151–52). To call the treatment of a "non-person" as implying "*some* subordination and disrespect" sounds like an understatement.

4. Toni Morrison, *The Bluest Eye,* op. cit., p. 63.

5. Kenneth B. Clark and Mamie P. Clark, "Racial Identification and Preference in Negro Children," no date. Available at https://i2.cdn.turner.com/cnn/2010/images/05/13/doll.study.1947.pdf.

6. Ibid.

7. Ibid.

8. Erik H. Erikson, *Childhood and Society,* (London: Vintage, 1995), pp. 217–218.

9. Ibid., p. 218.

10. Stokely Carmichael, "What We Want," *The New York Review of Books,* September 22, 1966.

11. Eldridge Cleaver, *Soul on Ice,* (New York: Delta Books, 1992), pp. 26–27.

12. Ibid., p. 27.

13. Toni Morrison, *The Bluest Eye,* op. cit., p. 18.

14. Ibid.

15. Eldridge Cleaver, *Soul on Ice,* op. cit., p. 33.

16. Ibid.

17. Frantz Fanon, *Peau noire, masques blancs,* (Paris: Éditions du Seuil, 1952), p. 58.

18. Ibid., p. 59.

19. Peter Sloterdijk, *Die Verachtung der Massen—Versuch über Kulturkämpfe in der modernen Gesellschaft,* (Frankfurt am Main: Suhrkamp Verlag, 2000), p. 57.

20. Ibid., p. 56.

21. Quoted in Arthur M. Schlesinger, Jr., *The Disuniting of America—Reflections on a Multicultural Society,* (New York and London: W. W. Norton & Company, 1998), p. 72.

22. Ibid., p. 73.

23. Derrick Z. Jackson, "The N-word and Richard Pryor," *The New York Times,* December 15, 2005. (My emphasis, MHVH). https://www.nytimes.com/2005/12/15/opinion/the-nwordand-richard-pryor.html Ibram X. Kendi gives a different explanation. "While hip-hop artists recast 'nigga' as an endearing term," he wrote, "'nigger' remained a derisive term outside and inside Black mouths." (Ibram X. Kendi, *How To Be An Antiracist,* [London: The Bodley Head, 2019], p. 137).

24. Ibid.

25. W. E. B. Du Bois, "On Being Ashamed of Oneself: An Essay on Race Pride," *The Crisis,* 1933.

26. Ibid.

27. Ibid.

28. Toni Morrison, "Black Matter(s)," in Toni Morrison, *The Source of Self-Regard— Selected Essays, Speeches, and Meditations,* (New York: Alfred A. Knopf, 2019), p. 142.

29. Samuel P. Huntington, *Who Are We? The Challenges to America's National Identity,* (New York and London: Simon & Schuster, 2005), p. 304.

30. Ibid., p. 305.

31. Ibid., pp. 306–7.

32. "Tiger Woods describes himself as 'Cablinasian,'" *AP News,* April 23, 1997.

33. "Not black and white," *The Economist,* October 3, 2020.

34. Samuel P. Huntington, *Who Are We? The Challenges to America's National Identity,* op. cit., p. 308.

35. Report on the Fight against Racism, Anti-Semitism and Xenophobia 2019, *Commission Nationale Consultative des Droits de l'Homme,* Paris, 2019, p. 9. https://www.cncdh.fr/sites/default/files/essentiels_rapport_racisme_2019_format_a4 _anglais.pdf.

36. Abram de Swaan, "Identificatie in uitdijende kring," in Abram de Swaan, *De draagbare De Swaan,* (Amsterdam: Prometheus, 1999), p. 214.

37. Ibid., p. 224.

38. Norbert Elias, "Wandlungen der Wir-Ich-Balance," in Norbert Elias, *Die Gesellschaft der Individuen,* (Frankfurt am Main: Suhrkamp Verlag, 1991), p. 308.

39. Robert Nozick, *The Examined Life—Philosophical Meditations,* (New York: Touchstone, 1989), p. 111.

40. Kristen Lavelle and Joe Feagin, "Hard Truth in the Big Easy: Race and Class in New Orleans, Pre-and Post-Katrina," in Michael D. Yates, (ed.), *More Unequal— Aspects of Class in the United States,* (New York: Monthly Review Press, 2007), pp. 89–90. (Emphasis in the original, MHVH).

41. Robert L. Reece, "The Gender of Colorism: Understanding the Intersection of Skin Tone and Gender Inequality," *Journal of Economics, Race, and Policy,* (2020), March 11, 2020. https://link.springer.com/article/10.1007/s41996-020-00054-1.

42. Ibid.

43. Ibid.

44. Wajahat Ali, "Teaching my daughter to love her skin," *New York Times,* November 16, 2021.

45. Luis Noe-Bustamante, Ana Gonzalez-Barrera, Khadija Edwards, Lauren Mora and Mark Hugo Lopez, "Majority of Latinos Say Skin Color Impacts Opportunity in America and Shapes Daily Life," *Pew Research Center,* November 4, 2021. https://www.pewresearch.org/hispanic/2021/11/04/majority-of-latinos-say-skin-color -impacts-opportunity-in-america-and-shapes-daily-life/.

46. "Staying apart," *The Economist,* July 11, 2020.

47. Ibid.

48. Report on the Fight against Racism, Anti-Semitism and Xenophobia 2019, op. cit., p. 14.

49. Ibid., p. 15.

50. Ibid., p. 14.

51. Christine Holch, "Als ob mein Deutschsein nicht echt wäre," *Chrismon,* September 2020.

52. Ibid.

53. Ibram X. Kendi, *How To Be An Antiracist,* op. cit., p. 47.

54. "Discrimination: What it is, and how to cope," *American Psychological Association,* no date. https://www.apa.org/helpcenter/discrimination.

55. Ibid.

56. Catherine Richert, "For black mothers and babies, prejudice is a stubborn health risk," *MPR News,* August 19, 2019. https://www.mprnews.org/story/2019/08 /19/for-black-mothers-and-babies-prejudice-is-a-stubborn-health-risk.

57. Carol Graham, *Happiness around the world—The paradox of happy peasants and miserable millionaires,* op. cit., p. 56.

58. The Reverend Al Sharpton, Eulogy at the funeral of George Floyd, June 9, 2020. https://www.rev.com/blog/transcripts/reverend-al-sharpton-george-floyd -funeral-eulogy-transcript-june-9.

59. Quoted in Keisha N. Blain, "Civil Rights International—The Fight Against Racism Has Always Been Global," *Foreign Affairs,* Volume 99, No. 5, September/ October 2020, p. 181.

60. Ezra Klein, "Why Ta-Nehisi Coates is hopeful," *Vox,* June 5, 2020.

61. John McWhorter, *Woke Racism—How a New Religion Has Betrayed Black America,* (New York: Portfolio/Penguin, 2021), p. 37.

62. Ibid., p. 38.

63. Kurt Streeter, "For Black joggers, signs of fragile progress," *The New York Times,* November 25, 2020. In the same vein the singer Harry Belafonte wrote "that we have never had so many white allies, willing to stand together for freedom, for honor, for a justice that will free us all in the end . . . " (Harry Belafonte, "Trump has been standing in the way of Black Americans," *New York Times,* November 4, 2020).

Chapter 13

De-Shaming Processes II

De-Shaming of LGBTQI People and People with a Disability

Another example of a group which successfully has fought shame is LGBTQI people. Still in 1963 Erving Goffman could classify homosexuals in his book *Stigma* as "social deviants," a group which, according to him, consisted of "prostitutes, drug addicts, delinquents, criminals, jazz musicians, bohemians, gypsies, carnival workers, hobos, winos, show people, full-time gamblers, beach dwellers, homosexuals, and the urban unrepentant poor. . . . "[1] Goffman put homosexuals in the same category as delinquents and criminals and other deviants, such as prostitutes, drug addicts, winos, and gamblers (while the reader may well ask why others, such as jazz musicians and the urban *unrepentant (!)* poor, are part of this group). However, since the 1970s homosexuality has gradually lost its stigma, due to a "de-shaming" process. This started with de-shaming strategies, used by the gay community. Until the 1960s being gay was a cause of opprobrium and public disgrace. Many homosexuals preferred to hide their orientation and even married partners of the opposite sex. "Coming out of the closet" was rare.

FROM ANDRÉ GIDE'S "COMING OUT" TO THE STONEWALL RIOTS

A famous exception was the French novelist and Nobel Prize for Literature Laureate André Gide. Although he was married to Madeleine, a cousin, he had the courage to openly confess his attraction to the same sex in four dialogues, published under the title *Corydon* (1920–1924). In his *Journals* Gide wrote that "the sexual question . . . ceased to harass me from the day when I made up my mind to look it squarely in the face, really to pay attention

145

to it. *Corydon,* far from being evidence of an obsession . . . is the token of a release. And who can tell the number of those whom that little book has, likewise, *released*?"[2] In 1954 in the UK Peter Wildeblood (1923–1999), a British-Canadian journalist and playwright, was sent to jail on charges relating to "indecency between males." It led to a public outcry and to the Wolfenden Report on Homosexual Offences and Prostitution (1957) which called for the decriminalization of gay sex for over twenty-one-year-olds. It would take another ten years, before, in 1967, the law was actually changed.[3] Wildeblood famously said he was "no more proud of my condition than I would be of having a glass eye or a hare lip."[4]

As in the case of African Americans, we can distinguish the same three de-shaming strategies. Directing the self-hate outward took a special form. In the gay liberation movement the "Stonewall riots" of June 1969 have become an iconic event. They refer to a raid by the New York police on the "Stonewall Inn" in Greenwich Village, a meeting place for local homosexuals, which led to violent resistance by the gay community. Because gay people were not only the victims of discrimination, but were also physically attacked by "queer bashers," they began to take boxing lessons to defend themselves. One year after the Stonewall riots this event was commemorated by marches in New York, San Francisco, and Los Angeles. These marches would become a tradition and developed into Gay Pride Parades, which were organized worldwide. The Gay Pride movement was part of the second strategy: a re-evaluation movement. Being gay was no longer considered a fact to be ashamed of, but a source of pride.

Gay and lesbian people soon started developing the third strategy, formulating political demands under the LGBTQI banner—a banner which included also bisexual, transgender, queer, and intersex people. In particular, these demands were concerned with ending discrimination on the housing and labor markets, the right to a civil marriage, and the right for gay couples to adopt children. These actions led to increasing acceptance of homosexuals. In this acceptance the Netherlands was a frontrunner. In the World Values surveys of 1990 it was the least homophobic country with only 10 percent of the Dutch public unwilling to have homosexuals as neighbors, compared with 38 percent of Americans.[5] The actions of gay people for equal rights were relatively successful. In 2019 thirty countries had enacted laws allowing gay and lesbian people to marry. The first country to grant the right to marry and to adopt children was the Netherlands in 2000. In the first decade of the twenty-first century the Dutch example was followed by Sweden, Norway, South Africa, Spain, Canada, and Belgium.[6] The second decade brought a major breakthrough, when twenty-three countries enacted legislation allowing gay marriage. In 2003, Massachusetts was the first American state to allow same-sex marriage, followed by Connecticut in 2008 and the District of Columbia, Vermont, and New York in 2009. In 2015 the US Supreme Court ruled that all state bans on same-sex marriage were unconstitutional.[7] *The Economist* spoke of "a dramatic softening of public attitudes towards same-sex relationships. In 1987, more than half of Americans thought gay sex should be illegal, according to Gallup; nearly three-quarters now approve that it is legal."[8] Gay and lesbian people were not only successful in extending their legal rights. Capitals and major cities, such as Paris, Berlin, Houston, Chicago, and Bogotá elected openly gay mayors, while Ireland and Serbia respectively got a gay and a lesbian prime minister. Even more telling was the US 2019–2020 Democratic nomination, where Pete Buttigieg became the first openly gay person to present himself as a candidate in a primary for an American presidential election. In 2020 the International Lesbian, Gay, Bisexual, Trans and Intersex Association (ILGA) had 1697 member organizations in 164 countries.[9]

GAY LIBERATION: A WESTERN PHENOMENON?

However, this emancipation wave remained confined mainly to Western countries. In seventy-two countries gay relationships are still considered criminal offenses and in Iran, Qatar, Sudan, and Saudi Arabia, an offender can get the death penalty.[10] However, there are also some bright spots. In Turkey, an Islamic country, "as recently as 2012, a whopping 85% of Turks said they did not want to have a gay neighbor. In a new poll [in 2020], that had fallen to 47%."[11] A special case is Russia, which has made homophobia a pillar of its political identity. In January 2020, relying on the homophobic teachings of the Russian Orthodox Church,[12] President Putin proposed a revision of the Constitution. One of the amendments was to define marriage as a contract between a man and a woman, banning gay marriage by making it "unconstitutional."[13] Eastern European countries did not follow the Western trend either. In the first months of 2020, for instance, a hundred Polish municipalities—taking in around a third of the country—declared themselves "LGBTQI-free zones": an openly homophobic action which was condemned by the European Commission.[14] Even in the United States the number of Americans aged 18 to 34 who are comfortable interacting with LGBTQI people slipped from 63 percent in 2016 to 53 percent in 2017, and to 45 percent in 2018, results which were called "alarming."[15] It is a reminder that "de-shaming" processes need not be definitive and irreversible. However, the increasing acceptance of homosexuality in Western countries over the last few decades is undeniable. Is it enough to speak of "old shame"? As was the case with discrimination on the basis of race it is too early to give a positive answer. It would be advisable to remain cautious and to speak only of "decreasing shame."

DE-SHAMING OF PEOPLE WITH A DISABILITY

According to the World Health Organization about one billion people in the world have a disability.[16] This is 13 percent of the world population. There are many different disabilities. People can have intellectual, physical, and sensory impairments. There are blind people, deaf people, people with a spinal cord injury, who need a wheelchair, and many others. The WHO gives the following definition of "disabilities": "Disabilities is an umbrella term, covering impairments, activity limitations, and participation restrictions." The WHO emphasizes that it is not just a health problem: "It is a complex phenomenon, reflecting the interaction between features of a person's body and features of society."[17] This is, indeed, important to bear in mind: a disability is not just a physical phenomenon, a dysfunction of (parts of) the body, but it involves also the way in which society—the "normal" environment—interacts with it. The way society reacts—whether it rejects or accepts the disabled person—has a major impact on his or her self-image.

> The relative position of disabled people has changed little through the present century. They endure levels of economic and social deprivation rarely encountered by other sections of the population. Exclusionary practices in the labour market lead to poverty and reliance on the charity of others. The resulting feelings of dependency and "lack of worth" are deeply embedded.[18]

The impact of the social environment on a disabled person was analyzed by four Brazilian researchers. They published a case study, based on oral reports regarding the life trajectory of Laila (her name was changed), a physically disabled woman. The narrative was "a means of understanding how one's environment builds an identity and produces emancipatory metamorphoses."[19] When Laila was three months old, she got polio, and since then has relied on a wheelchair. In Laila's life story we recognize two of the three above-mentioned strategies: from self-hate to a positive re-evaluation of the shameful identity, leading ultimately to political action. Until she was about twenty-five years old, Laila avoided relationships with disabled people:

> *I was prejudiced. I would not accept another wheelchair user near me . . . when someone said to me, "Look there's a wheelchair user there!" I would reply: "Don't even tell me, 'cause I don't want to go near them."*[20]

Later this changed. Laila joined a community association, where she was welcomed by a man who had been in a wheelchair for four months. Under his influence her attitude changed. *"This man was really my master, so I often tell him 'You are my inspiring muse!' My life started changing radically."*[21] Laila began to participate in political actions. She developed a project in which city councilors were invited to move around public spaces using wheelchairs. "The project intended to subject councilors to a practical experience. That would lead them to take a stand against architectural barriers, creating projects in favor of accessibility. During the experience, the councilors complained a lot about the discomfort in the chair, pain in the arms, and difficulties to climb ramps."[22] Her political activities led to a positive re-evaluation of her identity. She no longer describes herself as someone who is a pathetic person, a person without self-worth, dependent on the help of others, but she describes herself as a "warrior" or a "soldier." However, the researchers conclude that despite her struggles, Laila "is still unable to count on social recognition. Her struggle is slow, silent, lonely. . . . "[23]

Another example is Judith Heumann, an American woman who got polio when she was eighteen months old. She became paralyzed and dependent on a wheelchair. Heumann became one of America's most prominent disability rights activists. President Obama appointed her as the first Special Advisor for International Disability Rights at the US Department of State, where she served from 2010 to 2017. Despite her disability Heumann wrote in her autobiography: "I never wished I didn't have a disability."[24] This didn't mean that she felt no anger. "We had the right to feel angry," she said in an interview, "but we needed to take this anger and work on the changes we wanted."[25] Heumann told that her mother, who as a Jewish child was sent to America to escape from the Nazis, "was an optimist. And a fighter." She adds: "And so am I."[26] We see here the same self-definition as in the case of Laila, who defined herself as a "warrior" and a "soldier." The life-stories of both women seem to confirm Goffman's observation that "social deviants often feel that they are not merely equal to but better than normal, and that the life they lead is better than that lived by the persons they would otherwise be."[27]

Emancipation actions and de-shaming strategies by disabled people are hindered by two facts. In the first place by the fact that there are many *different* categories of disabled people, which have their own associations and fight for their own, specific demands. Creating a unity was, therefore, a first imperative. "We had to be able to come together and jump across the silos represented by our different types of disability," said Heumann. "There are thousands of different disabilities, and they impact people in different ways and at different times in people's lives. As a community, though, we had to be unified and agree that we would throw no one under the bus."[28] A second obstacle was the fact that the physical limitations of people with a disability often restrict their capacity to organize rallies. A rally by wheelchair users is more difficult to organize than a protest meeting by able-bodied people. Despite these obstacles campaigns for equality led to an expansion of self-help organizations. In the United States the first initiatives began during the cultural revolution of the 1960s and early 1970s, when disabled persons started the Independent Living Movement (ILM).

THE INDEPENDENT LIVING MOVEMENT

The protest movements of the 1960s and early 1970 were a fertile breeding ground for people with disabilities who sought to emancipate themselves from patronizing authorities. "Anti-authoritarianism," "autonomy," and "self-reliance" were the keywords of these movements. It is, therefore, no surprise, that the first initiatives were taken at the University of Berkeley, California, one of the hotbeds of the protest movement.

> The group of students with significant physical disabilities eventually began calling themselves the Rolling Squads. . . . They could not get around Berkeley because there were no curb-cuts for them to roll on. Wheelchair accessible buses were yet to be a dream in most people's worlds. If they could have solved their transportation needs, they still would not have been able to live in the community because there were no houses that were adapted for their needs. The Berkeley pioneers did not wait for the revolution; they instigated it. With friends and allies they took to the streets of Berkeley in mid-morning hours and poured tar and concrete and made their own makeshift ramps from the streets to the sidewalks. Those ramps still exist.[29]

In 1972 this group founded the first Center for Independent Living (CIL) in Berkeley. "Core services comprised peer counselling, the provision of information on organizing personal assistant schemes, accessible housing, welfare benefits and advocacy."[30] "At its peak the Berkeley CIL controlled a budget of $3.2 million and employed over two hundred staff."[31] The initiative led to the setting up of over five hundred CILs in the United States. Its success was undeniable: people with disabilities felt that they were increasingly integrated into the everyday community.

A key event took place in 1977, when about 150 disabled people occupied the federal building in San Francisco with the aim of forcing the government to enact the first civil rights legislation for disabled people in US history, in particular their right to an education. "For 26 days, around 150 disabled people lived in a single floor of an office building . . . most participants didn't have any bedding or a change of clothes with them. Many participants required attendant care for eating, using the bathroom. . . . "[32] The protesters were fighting for the implementation of *Section 504* of the Rehabilitation Act of 1973 which made it illegal for entities receiving federal funding to discriminate on the basis of disability.

These grassroots initiatives were followed up by broader political action. The American Coalition of Citizens with Disabilities campaigned successfully for federal legislation affecting persons with disabilities. On July 26, 1990, President George H. W. Bush signed the Americans with Disabilities Act (ADA), which was an important step forward. The ADA was an extension of the Civil Rights Act of 1964. On the occasion of the signing President Bush said: "Let the shameful walls of exclusion finally come tumbling down."[33] Note that the word "shameful" did not refer to the shame of the disabled people, but to the shame of society which had neglected their rights. The new law prohibited discrimination against people with disabilities in employment, public services, public accomodation, and telecommunications. National organizations of people with a disability also began to organize themselves internationally. However, one of the problems was that these organizations employed people without disabilities, who often occupied the leading managerial positions. At the World Congress of "Rehabilitation International," organized in 1980 in Winnipeg, Canada, this led to open conflict. Members proposed, in a motion, that people with a disability should occupy 50 percent of the seats on the executive board. When this motion was rejected, it led to a scission and the subsequent foundation of the "Disabled People's International" (DPI), which, in 1981, organized its first World Congress with 400 delegates from 53 countries.[34]

THE IMPORTANCE OF INTERNATIONAL TREATIES

The United Nations also joined the equal rights movement. In 1976 the General Assembly proclaimed 1981 as the International Year of Disabled Persons (IYDP). The theme of the International Year was "full participation and equality."[35] The UN called for a plan of action at national, regional, and international levels. In 1982 this led to the formulation of a "World Program of Action Concerning Disabled Persons." The decade 1983–1992 was proclaimed the "United Nations Decade of Disabled People." However, progress was slow. It would still take more than twenty years before the United Nations Convention on the Rights of Persons with Disabilities (UN CRPD) would see the light.[36] The Convention was adopted by the General Assembly on 13 December 2006 and came into force on 3 May 2008. The objective of the Convention was "to promote, protect and ensure the full and equal enjoyment of all human rights and fundamental freedoms by all persons with disabilities and to promote respect for their inherent dignity." In 2020 the Convention had 181 signatories. The European Union became a party as of 21 January 2011. The Convention aimed to remove barriers concerning access to buildings, guarantee equal opportunities and access to the labor market, and ensure the personal mobility of people with a disability. What was new was the focus on making electronic media—PCs, tablets, smartphones, as well as e-commerce and electronic communication—accessible to people with a disability.

Compared to the 1980s, therefore, a lot of progress has been made. The Dean of Leiden University in the Netherlands, for instance, could proudly announce that in 2020 10 percent of the students of his university were students with a disability.[37] According to the Dean, "a major reason that studying with a disability has become easier over the last decades . . . is the international treaties to which Leiden University, like many Dutch colleges and universities, adhered. An example is the UN Convention on the Rights of Persons with Disabilities, which on July 7, 2016, came into force in the Netherlands, although it still has to be implemented."[38] Are these improvements enough to talk about "old shame"? Certainly not. The success-story to which the Dutch university dean refers, is, maybe, valid for people with disabilities of average or above average intelligence. But what about people with cognitive impairments? Martha Nussbaum points to the special position of this group:

> More, even, than people with many physical disabilities, children with cognitive impairments have been shunned and stigmatized. Many of them have been relegated to institutions that make no effort to develop their potential. And they are persistently treated as if they have no right to "live in the world." In the congressional hearings prior to the passage of the ADA, many examples of this shunning were cited, including that of children with Down syndrome who were denied admission to a zoo so as not to upset the chimpanzee.[39]

However, here too attitudes are changing. One example is the "Café Joyeux" on the Paris' Champs Élysées, which in March 2020 was opened by French President Emmanuel Macron. The café, the third of its kind, employs 19 people with psychological or cognitive impairments, such as autism and Down syndrome.[40] There are projects to open similar cafés in seven other French cities.[41] "De-shaming" is, therefore, a process with different speeds for different groups of disabled people. But undoubtedly the increasing acceptance of people with disabilities and the recognition of their equal rights has set a process in motion which has made it easier for many disabled people to accept themselves and to occupy a place in society that fits their potentialities. In a decent society no one should feel ashamed of what he or she is. An important observation made by Goffman is that the world of people with disabilities and the world of so-called able-bodied people are not completely separate, as many assume. "The most fortunate of normal," he writes, "is likely to have his half-hidden failing, and for every little failing there is a social occasion when it will loom large, creating a shameful gap between the virtual and actual social identity. Therefore the occasionally precarious and the constantly precarious form a single continuum, their situation in life analysable by the same framework."[42] Not only does every individual have his "half-hidden failing," but in the course of his life—due to ill-health or an accident—an able-bodied person can end up becoming a member of the world he fears most: the world of the disabled. Behind the self-confidence and self-assurance displayed by the so-called able-bodied persons one can find a hidden vulnerability and fragility. Goffman wrote that "there is only one complete unblushing male in America: a young, married, white, urban, northern, heterosexual Protestant father of college education, fully employed, of good complexion, weight and height, and a decent record in sports."[43] He adds that "any male who fails to qualify in any of these ways is likely to view himself—during moments at least—as unworthy, incomplete and inferior. . . ."[44] And he concluded that "the general identity values of a society may be fully entrenched nowhere. . . . "[45]

NOTES

1. Erving Goffman, *Stigma—Notes on the Management of Spoiled Identity,* (Harmondsworth: Penguin Books, 1976), p. 170.

2. André Gide, *Journals,* Volume 3, 1928–1939, op. cit., p. 252. (Diary entry of December 29, 1932). (Emphasis in the original, MHVH).

3. Patrick Thursfield, "Peter Wildeblood," *The Guardian,* November 16, 1999.

4. "The world comes out," *The Economist,* August 8, 2020.

5. Ronald Inglehart, *Modernization and Postmodernization—Cultural, Economic, and Political Change in 43 Societies* (Princeton, NJ: Princeton University Press, 1997), p. 157.

6. David Masci, Elizabeth Sciupac, Michael Lipka, "Same-Sex Marriage Around the World," *Pew Research Center,* October 28, 2019. https://www.pewforum.org/fact-sheet/gay-marriage-around-the-world/.

7. "Same-Sex Marriage, State by State," *Pew Research Center,* June 26, 2015. https://www.pewforum.org/2015/06/26/same-sex-marriage-state-by-state/.

8. "Queer, there and everywhere," *The Economist,* August 8, 2020.

9. The International Lesbian, Gay, Bisexual, Trans and Intersex Association (ILGA), https://ilga.org/.

10. Pamela Duncan, "Gay relationships are still criminalised in 72 countries, report finds," *The Guardian,* July 27, 2017. https://www.theguardian.com/world/2017/jul/27/gay-relationships-still-criminalised-countries-report.

11. "Istanbully," *The Economist,* May 9, 2020.

12. In the "Bases of the Social Concept of the Russian Orthodox Church," an official document published in 2000, one can read that homosexuality is a "sinful distortion of human nature" and that "homosexual desires, just as other passions torturing fallen man, are healed by the Sacraments, prayer, fasting, repentance, reading of Holy Scriptures and patristic writings, as well as Christian fellowship with believers who are ready to give spiritual support." (Quoted in Marcel H. Van Herpen, *Putin's Propaganda Machine—Soft Power and Russian Foreign Policy,* [Lanham and London: Rowman & Littlefield, 2016], p. 145).

13. Andrew E. Kramer, "Putin Proposes Constitutional Ban on Gay Marriage," *New York Times,* March 3, 2020. https://www.nytimes.com/2020/03/03/world/europe/putin-proposes-constitutional-ban-on-gay-marriage.html.

14. Cf. Nikolaj Nielsen, "Polish 'LGBTI-free zones' not ok, says EU commission," *EU Observer,* February 5, 2020. https://euobserver.com/justice/147362.

15. Susan Miller, "The young are regarded as the most tolerant generation. That's why results of this LGBTQ survey are 'alarming,'" *USA Today,* June 24, 2019. https://eu.usatoday.com/story/news/nation/2019/06/24/lgbtq-acceptance-millennials-decline-glaad-survey/1503758001/.

16. Cf. "Better health for people with disabilities," *World Health Organization.* https://www.who.int/disabilities/facts/Infographic_en_pdf.pdf?ua=1.

17. "Disabilities," *World Health Organization.* https://www.who.int/topics/disabilities/en/.

18. Colin Barnes and Geof Mercer, "Disability: Emancipation, Community Participation and Disabled People," in Gary Craig and Marjorie Mayo (eds), *Community Empowerment,* (London and New Jersey: Zed Books, 2004), pp. 33–34.

19. Vadilene Wagner; Lucas França Garcia; Tiago Franklin Rodrigues Lucena; Leonardo Pestillo de Oliveira, "The identity-metamorphosis-emancipation syntagm in people with disabilities," *Revista Bioética,* Vol. 28, No. 1, January/March 2020. https://www.scielo.br/scielo.php?script=sci_arttext&pid=S1983-80422020000100024&lng=en&nrm=iso&tlng=en.

20. This kind of "desolidarization" is typical for members of stigmatized groups. French researchers found, for instance, that social benefit receivers wanted to distance themselves from others: "I am not like them!" The social benefit receiver is "confronted with a double identity conflict: 1. He must be different from the person he is, which means different from those who are like him, the group to which he belongs. Indeed, how could he identify himself—which means recognize oneself—with those who provoke disgust, rejection and stigmatization? . . . 2. This leads to him having to identify himself with the others who represent the norm, power, success, but that means accepting the judgments which stigmatize, which justify the contempt for which he is the object, and desolidarizing himself from those whose condition he shares. On the one hand he is ashamed to be like them, on the other hand he

is ashamed of wanting to distance himself from them." (Vincent de Gaulejac, *Les sources de la honte,* [Paris: Desclée de Brouwer, 1996], p. 289).

21. Vadilene Wagner; Lucas França Garcia; Tiago Franklin Rodrigues Lucena; Leonardo Pestillo de Oliveira, "The identity-metamorphosis-emancipation syntagm in people with disabilities," op. cit.

22. Ibid.

23. Ibid.

24. Judith Heumann with Kristen Joiner, *Being Heumann—An Unrepentant Memoir of a Disability Rights Activist,* (Boston: Beacon Press, 2020), p. xi.

25. Marc Climaco, "Confronting shame—and accepting my disability—with Judy Heumann," *Ford Foundation,* February 25, 2020. https://www.fordfoundation.org/ideas/equals-change-blog/posts/confronting-shame-and-accepting-my-disability-with -judy-heumann/.

26. Judith Heumann with Kristen Joiner, *Being Heumann—An Unrepentant Memoir of a Disability Rights Activist,* op. cit., p. xiii.

27. Erving Goffman, *Stigma—Notes on the Management of Spoiled Identity,* op. cit., p. 172.

28. Marc Climaco, "Confronting shame—and accepting my disability—with Judy Heumann," op. cit.

29. Steven E. Brown, "I Was Born (in a Hospital Bed)—When I Was Thirty-One Years Old," *Disability and Society,* 1995. https://www.independentliving.org/docs3/ brown95c.html.

30. Colin Barnes and Geof Mercer, "Disability: Emancipation, Community Participation and Disabled People," op. cit., p. 35.

31. Ibid.

32. Katie Murphy, "Fighting Shame with History," *Paul K. Longmore Institute on Disability,* no date. https://longmoreinstitute.sfsu.edu/fighting-shame-history.

33. Cf. Chris Sparks, "The Emancipation Proclamation for the Disability Community," *ANCOR,* August 1, 2015. https://www.ancor.org/resources/publications/links/ emancipation-proclamation-disability-community.

34. Colin Barnes and Geof Mercer, "Disability: Emancipation, Community Participation and Disabled People," op. cit., p. 41.

35. "The International Year of Disabled Persons 1981," General Assembly resolution 31/123, *United Nations.* https://www.un.org/development/desa/disabilities/the -international-year-of-disabled-persons-1981.html.

36. "Convention on the Rights of Persons with Disabilities," *United Nations.* https: //www.un.org/development/desa/disabilities/convention-on-the-rights-of-persons -with-disabilities.html.

37. Wessel de Cock, "Studeren met een beperking in 2020: interview met Marcel Melchers, decaan aan de Universiteit van Leiden," *Rethinking Disabilities,* no date. http://rethinkingdisability.net/studeren-met-een-beperking-in-2020-interview-met -marcel-melchers-decaan-aan-de-universiteit-van-leiden/.

38. Ibid.

39. Martha C. Nussbaum, *Hiding from Humanity—Disgust, Shame, and the Law,* op. cit., p. 313.

40. "Handicap: Macron inaugure un Café Joyeux des Champs Élysées," *Le Figaro,* March 9, 2020. https://www.lefigaro.fr/flash-actu/handicap-macron-inaugure-un-cafe-joyeux-des-champs-elysees-20200309.

41. On the website of Café Joyeux one can read that "Café Joyeux wants to place persons with a psychological or cognitive impairment in the center of our cities and our lives." https://www.cafejoyeux.com/.

42. Erving Goffman, *Stigma—Notes on the Management of Spoiled Identity,* op. cit., p. 152.

43. Ibid., p. 153.

44. Ibid.

45. Ibid.

Chapter 14

The Emergence of New Shame I

Fat Shaming

The central thesis of this book is that the United States—and, in a lesser degree, Europe also—are being transformed from guilt cultures into shame cultures. This is a general trend which affects the majority of the population. However, this does not exclude that some minority groups in society, which were traditionally exposed to shaming practices, may succeed in overcoming old shame. In the preceding chapters we have seen some examples. We have analyzed how for these groups old forms of shame were diminishing due to a range of factors, such as civil rights actions by the groups concerned, demographic developments, government programs, international treaties, and—last but not least—changes of attitude amongst the general population. As concerns these attitudes, a consensus seems to be developing, which Anthony Grayling summarized as follows: "So the rule is this: never asperse people for what they physically cannot help being."[1] The application of this rule could be considered a part of what Norbert Elias has called a "civilizing process." Elias was focusing on the development of etiquette and table manners. Obviously, it is clear that the art of not hurting the feelings of others unnecessarily is more important. "As children we have to learn gradually not only to express what we feel," wrote Thomas Nagel, "but to keep many thoughts and feelings to ourselves in order to maintain relations with other people on an even kneel . . . one avoids showing that one has noticed the failings of others, in order to allow them to carry on without having to respond to one's reactions of amusement or alarm."[2] However, this civilizing process cannot be taken for granted. Thomas Nagel observed, for instance, that "these forms of tact are conspicuously absent in childhood, whose social brutality we can all remember."[3] For this reason education should play a major role in this civilizing process. We have also to take into account that while for some groups old forms of shame are gradually decreasing, simultaneously for other groups *new* forms of shame may emerge and develop.

FAT SHAMING: THE OBESE AS FAIR
GAME FOR RIDICULE AND REJECTION

One of these forms of new shame is *fat shaming*. Being overweight or obese has become a social disgrace. A person is overweight when his Body Mass Index (BMI) is between 25 and 30, he is obese when his BMI is between 30 and 40, and he is severely obese with a BMI of over 40.[4] In two decades (from 1999–2000 through 2017–2018) obesity in the United States increased from 30.5 percent of the adult population to 42.4 percent. In the same period the number of severely obese people almost doubled from 4.9 percent to 9.2 percent.[5] Although Europe is lagging behind, here too the same upward trend could be observed. One of the most dramatic increases took place in the United Kingdom, where in 2017 28.7 percent of the adult population was obese—almost *twice* the percentage in 1993, when it was 15 percent.[6] In other European countries the increase has been smaller, but still significant. In 2017 16 percent of the German adult population was obese.[7] In 2019 this was the case for 17 percent of the French[8] and 14.7 percent of the Dutch.[9] One might have expected the increase in the numbers of obese people to have led to an increasing tolerance. However, the contrary is true. A study by the Yale Rudd Center for Food Policy and Obesity found that over a ten-year period, between 1995 and 2005, reports of weight discrimination had increased by 66 percent. The researchers found that weight discrimination is common among Americans. Women especially were the victims of weight discrimination or *weightism,* which was even more widespread than racial discrimination.[10] The fact that women particularly were targeted was sad, because, as the Dutch psychiatrist Joost Baneke explained in his book *Why Women Are More Ashamed than Men,* women are more shame-prone than men because "girls and women feel themselves often uncertain about their body and especially their physical attractiveness for boys and men."[11]

In Europe the situation was scarcely better. The French sociologist Jean-François Amadieu wrote that in France "physical appearance has important effects because French society has always been obsessed by [people's] looks." Therefore, he wrote, "it is for one half of the French acceptable to refuse to hire a candidate because of his weight or a lack of physical attractiveness. . . . Even when employers have problems in finding employees, they still eliminate those who are overweight or senior."[12] Two other French authors wrote: "Today, 60% of female adolescents say they are too fat and only 20% is satisfied with their bodies. At the age of fourteen one third has already followed a diet. Between fourteen and twenty-three, when self-esteem is generally increasing for the boys, it is diminishing among girls."[13] The fact that obese people have become fair game for ridicule and shaming practices has also been observed by Stuart Schneiderman, who wrote that in the United States "obnoxious and insulting behavior became acceptable. Infatuated with their rights to free speech, people believed it acceptable to walk up to someone who was overweight and berate him for being disgusting and repellent."[14] Research in Sweden among school-aged children revealed that "children associate obesity with a number of undesirable traits and prefer to associate themselves with nonobese peers. Overweight children are more likely to be victims or perpetrators of bullying behavior than other children are, and there are observations to suggest that obesity may influence college-admission rates negatively."[15] In the Netherlands it is equally the younger generation for whom being overweight is taboo: 24 percent of the age cohort of 18–34 years said they would feel ashamed if they were overweight, for people 35 years and older the percentage was 17.[16] However, being lean and thin is not and has never been a universal beauty standard. Ruth Benedict, for instance, writing about puberty rites, mentions

> The institution of the fatting-house for girls in central Africa. In the region where feminine beauty is all but identified with obesity, the girl at puberty is segregated, sometimes for years, fed with sweet and fatty foods, allowed no activity, and her body rubbed assiduously with oils. She is taught during this time her future duties, and her seclusion ends with a parade of her corpulence that is followed by her marriage to her proud bridegroom.[17]

Also the fat and pot-bellied statues of Buddha and the paintings of Rubens are a reminder that lean and meager was not always considered beautiful. "The opulent fleshy beauty of Rubens's women probably made the leaner ladies of his day frown when they patted their own meager stomachs," wrote Anne Hollander, "and wish they could compete in the big leagues. Yet today the very name of Rubens is apt to produce a reaction of disgust. Those puffy knees, those bumps and hilts of flesh have never had less fashionable appeal than right now. . . . "[18] And she continued: "Fatness and softness—status symbols for centuries—have become thoroughly déclassé in two generations. They are now in fact accepted signs of mental slavery—weakness of will, neurosis or bondage to ethnic traditions that are dependent on starchy foods as a staple of diet."[19]

IS OBESITY A QUESTION OF CHOICE AND FREE WILL?

Hollander pointed here to an important reason why bullying and discriminating fat persons has become acceptable: the fat person is considered to suffer from *a weakness of will,* which means that his or her obesity is *not* something "what they physically cannot help being" (and for which they should not be attacked an discriminated), but something for which they are personally responsible—either by being self-indulgent, eating too much, or, if they fight against their obesity, by a lack of discipline to stick to a healthy diet. "Fatness in the United States 'means' excess of desire, of bodily urges not controlled, of immoral, lazy, and sinful habits," wrote Amy Farrell.[20] "What is clear . . . is that the connotations of fatness and of the fat person—lazy, gluttonous, greedy, immoral, uncontrolled, stupid, ugly, and lacking in willpower—preceded and then were intertwined with explicit concern about health issues."[21] Research showed that obesity stigma varies according to the perceived cause of obesity. "In general, women and minority racial groups are found to be more likely to identify causes over which individuals have little control and place responsibility on societal factors than men and Whites. People in higher income categories are found to be more likely to identify individual responsibility for obesity."[22]

It is mostly men, whites, and middle class people, who regard obesity as the result of *choice,* particularly of *bad* choice. Martha Nussbaum observed that "in America . . . the sense of the omnipotence of the will is especially sharp. . . . "[23] It is an integral part of the individualist ideology of the autonomous and self-reliant person who is the master of his own life and proudly makes his independent choices. Because of this a supposed lack of willpower is considered a major character flaw. In this social context ridiculing and stigmatizing fat people, instead of being morally reprehensible, becomes legitimate and can even be attributed a positive function: either as a deserved sanction for poor choice, or as an incentive for the obese person to change his behavior. It is clear that as long as this prejudice prevails, discrimination against obese people and the practice of fat shaming will continue. This prejudice can even be observed in the text of the Americans with Disabilities Act, which "leaves out some pervasive sources of stigma: obesity, for example, is not covered unless the person is 100 percent above desirable weight."[24]

BLACK PEOPLE AND OBESITY: MULTIPLE STIGMAS?

The problem is that the obesity pandemic cannot be reduced to a question of individual choice and weakness of will, because it is in fact a complex—and still not fully understood—phenomenon, caused by multiple factors. This was a reason for the American Medical Association (AMA) to recognize obesity as a disease in 2013.

Research has provided a deeper understanding of the genetic, metabolic, environmental, and behavioral factors that contribute to obesity. [This evidence] challenges the dominant public understanding of obesity as a revertible condition resulting primarily from dietary and lifestyle choices that reflect ignorance or limited motivation.[25]

Robert Putnam pointed to the importance of social class.

In the 1990s . . . as the obesity epidemic raged across the country, obesity increased at similar rates for all adolescents, but in the past decade or so obesity has begun to diminish among kids from college-educated homes while continuing to expand among kids from high-school-educated homes. Thus, the class gap in adolescent obesity has widened significantly.[26]

"Why this growing gap?" asks Putnam.

Part of the explanation is probably that public health messages were quicker to reach upper class kids, precisely because those kids are embedded in much richer transmission networks for such messages. Conversely, the relative isolation of poor kids leaves them more vulnerable to all sorts of threats. Neighborhood quality is another likely explanation for this growing gap, since the obesity disparity appears to be due primarily to disparities in physical activity, so differential access to outdoor activities and athletic amenities is a prime suspect.[27]

This may be true, but also Putnam has to admit that this is only "part of the explanation." It is regrettable that in particular those groups which are in a process of emancipating themselves from "old shame," such as African Americans and people with disabilities, are overrepresented in the category of obese people. While gradually losing an old stigma, they acquire a new stigma. Let us just have a look at the figures. In 2017–2018 42.2 percent of (non-Hispanic) American white adults were obese, this was the case for 49.6 percent of African American men and 56.9 percent of African American women.[28] The same phenomenon could be observed in the UK, where, according to a report for Parliament, "people with Black ethnicity have the highest rates of excess weight . . . ," while "among people with disabilities, excess weight is 11 percentage points higher than among those without disabilities."[29]

Obesity is to a great extent a question of poverty, poor health, and unsafe neighborhoods. The poverty and poor health of African Americans is no new phenomenon. In his book *The Philadelphia Negro,* published in 1899, the African American sociologist William Du Bois had already written: "Many things combine to cause the high Negro death rate: poor heredity, neglect of infants, bad dwellings and poor food."[30] And he continued: "Negroes are commonly supposed to eat rather more than necessary. And this perhaps is partially true. The trouble is more in the quality of the food than its quantity,

in the wasteful method of its preparation, and in the irregularity in eating."[31]
It is interesting that Du Bois was already pointing to the dubious quality of
the black population's diet and the irregularity of their meals. Du Bois also
points to the fact that the bad health of the black population was caused
not only by their miserable living conditions, but also by the "superstitious
fear of hospitals prevalent among the lower classes of all people, but especially among Negroes. This must have some foundation in the roughness or
brusqueness of manner prevalent in many hospitals, and the lack of a tender
spirit of sympathy with the unfortunate patients. At any rate, many a Negro
would almost rather die than trust himself to a hospital."[32] Condescending,
if not outright humiliating treatment by white doctors and hospital personnel
discouraged black people from going to hospital, with negative effects on
their health situation. Du Bois concluded that "the main movement for reform
must come from the Negroes themselves, and should start with a crusade for
fresh air, cleanliness, healthfully located homes and *proper food*."[33] In 2020,
more than a century later, the health situation of the black population has not
much improved. According to *The Economist,*

> African-Americans are still the country's poorest, poorest-housed and unhealthi-
> est large group with high incidences of asthma, diabetes, hypertension, cancer
> and obesity. In 1899 infant mortality was almost twice as high among blacks
> as among whites; now it is 2.2 times higher. If anything, African-American
> diets are unhealthier now than the rations of milk, bread and fat pork Du Bois
> described. So-called "food deserts" are a modern phenomenon. The 160,000
> people who live in the District of Columbia's two poorest and overwhelm-
> ingly black wards, 7 and 8, east of the polluted Anacostia river, have only three
> supermarkets. They also have the sparsest health care in the city, with no major
> hospital.[34]

During the COVID-19 pandemic that hit the world from 2020 to 2022 African
Americans were disproportionally exposed, often due to obesity and other
ailments from which they suffered. Black people who got the virus were 2.4
times more likely to die than whites and 2.2 times more likely than Asians
and Latinos.[35]

"WEIGHTISM": THE NEW STIGMA

Obese people are more depressed, are often suicidal, earn less, and have difficulties finding a partner. Being obese is not fun and certainly not a question
of free choice. A Swiss paper wrote that "Studies have shown that fat women
assess their quality of life as being even lower than female cancer patients. It

seems to be psychologically healthier to consider an ailment as one's 'fate' that cannot be influenced than to assume 'guilt' for it—as fat people do. They recognize their lack of willpower and their 'weak personality.'"[36] The prejudice that eating disorders are the result of "choice" and "free will" is a major factor behind fat people often being treated as not quite human. And black women are the main victims of this prejudice.

> While there has been a massive public health campaign urging fat people to eat right, eat less and lose weight, black women have been specifically targeted. This heightened concern about their weight is not new; it reflects the racial stigmatization of black women's bodies. . . . Today the idea that weight is the main problem dogging black women builds on these historically racist ideas and ignores how interrelated social factors impact black women's health . . . many studies show that the stigma associated with body weight, rather than the body weight itself, is responsible for some adverse health consequences blamed on obesity, including increased mortality risk. Regardless of income, black women consistently experience weightism in addition to sexism and racism . . . the stress of these life experiences contributes to higher rates of chronic mental and physical illnesses such as heart disease, diabetes, depression and anxiety . . . the predominant reason black women get sick is not because they eat the wrong things but because their lives are often stressful and their neighborhoods are often polluted.[37]

These authors point to the fact that Black women often suffer from a *cumulative* discrimination—a phenomenon which was already analyzed in 1989 by Kimberle Crenshaw, who coined for this the concept of inter-sectionalism. "Black women," she wrote, " . . . often . . . experience a double-discrimination—the combined effects of practices which discriminate on the basis of race, and on the basis of sex."[38] Fat shaming is an additional cause of discrimination. Even if discrimination on the basis of race and sex is diminishing, this new kind of discrimination is a reason for concern. Not only is the stress caused by fat shaming a cause of the bad health of obese people, but being obese also has, as such, a negative influence on one's health. The problem is that even today—apart from surgery—there doesn't seem to exist a real cure. Since 1969 research has shown that up to 98 percent of attempts to lose weight fail and two-thirds of people who tried, in the end gained more weight than they lost.[39] "Failed attempts to keep weight off have a biological basis. Losing just 3% of your body weight results in a 17% slowdown of your metabolism, and an intense blast of hunger hormones causes you to feel like you are literally starving. This continues until you rise back to your highest weight. This is not the feeling of hunger that reminds you to eat—it is the feeling that you will die if you don't."[40] Marc Ambinder, a former obese person, who tried—in vain—all kinds of diets and exercises and finally took recourse to surgery, attacked the received idea that obesity should be considered a character stigma. He made an appeal "to redirect the stigma that brutally accompanies obesity, away from those who don't deserve it, and toward those who do—like food marketers who deploy psychological deception, or grocers who put sugary cereals where kids are most likely to see them. Those are the people who should feel ashamed."[41] Aubrey Gordon, who writes also under the pseudonym 'Your Fat Friend" tells about her own experience:

> I was in the fourth grade, sitting in a doctor's office, the first time my face flushed with shame. I was, I had just learned, overweight. I will remember the pediatrician's words forever: *It's probably from eating all that pizza and ice cream. It tastes good, doesn't it? But it makes your body big and fat.* I felt my face sear with shame. . . . I learned so much in that one moment: *You're not beautiful. You're indulging too much. Your body is wrong. You must have done it.* I'd failed a test I didn't even know I'd taken, and the sense of failure and self-loathing it inspired planted the seeds of a depression I would live with for many years.[42]

She points to counterproductive government programs, such as the Strong4Life campaign conducted by Georgia in 2012, where billboards targeted fatness in children with texts, such as "WARNING: Fat prevention begins at home," calling it "one of the nation's highest-profile fat-shaming campaigns," a campaign which was "hinged on shame and fear." However, weight stigma and the related stress did not lead to weight loss, but to eating and self-isolation. The problem with dieting is that it leads to yo-yo effects and—in the long run—often not to weight loss, but rather to weight gain. This was a reason for the "anti-diet movement" "to anticipate a future "in which people don't try to change their weight. Instead of relying on weight or body-mass index, this subset of dietitians, nutritionists and other advocates ending diets and placing more emphasis on markers of health such as endurance, sleep and mental well-being."[43]

THE BODY POSITIVE MOVEMENT

As in the case of other stigmatized groups, fat and overweight people began to develop strategies to fight their stigma. This meant in the first place overcoming their self-hatred. An example of this strategy is the organization of alternative beauty contests for overweight women. In France, for instance, since 2008, parallel to the official *Miss France* contest, are organized *Miss Ronde* (chubby girl) contests. Since 2010 overweight girls can also compete in a *Miss Curvy* contest. A condition for participation in both contests is being overweight.[44] In 1996 in the United States, Connie Sobczak and Elizabeth Scott founded The Body Positive Movement. The goal of this movement was "to create a lively, healing community that offers freedom from suffocating societal messages that keep people in a perpetual struggle with their bodies" and "can help people leave body hatred behind."[45] On the Movement's website one can read that "the media is the single greatest contributor to body negativity. . . . The majority of the images that we see in the mainstream media are of young, white, thin, feminine women, (or tall, muscular, masculine men) which sends a clear message to the viewer that this is the ideal, leaving anyone who doesn't identify with this image feeling unpresented and unvalued."[46] The Movement tries to reach its goal through "Fat Activism." "Fat Activism means working to change the way society views fat people and fat, itself. It means shifting the overwhelming belief and perception that fat is bad into one that embraces and accepts body diversity. . . . It is recognizing the micro-aggressions that are inflicted upon people of all sizes everyday, especially fat people, and educating those who knowingly or unknowingly enact them."[47]

The Body Positive Movement was criticized for its maximalist approach. Critics argued that moving people with a negative body image suddenly to a positive body image was unrealistic. In 2015 the term "body neutrality" became viral on the Internet and in the social media. The movement gained popularity in 2016 when Anne Poirier started programs based on this concept. According to members of the "body neutrality" movement the goal of "body positivity" was a bridge too far: it was "kind of a long jump to move there from dissatisfaction. Some people are just going to land in body neutrality, which is the term we utilize here for somewhere in the middle. It's a kind of détente, a white flag, a way station between hating oneself and loving oneself."[48] "Body neutrality" was an intermediate goal. "In short, body neutrality is rooted in acknowledging what your body does, not how it appears. Your body allows you to exercise, travel the world and experience new cultures. Your body gives you the ability to hold hands and hug someone you love. Your body gets you from point A to point B."[49] The "body neutrality" movement changed the focus: instead of emphasizing aesthetics its adherents emphasized the functional utility of the body. However, despite these efforts to fight the shaming and discrimination of fat people, there is, apparently, still a long way to go.

NOTES

1. A. C. Grayling, "Free Speech and Political Correctness," in A. C. Grayling, *Thinking of Answers—Questions in the Philosophy of Everyday Life*, op. cit., p. 176.

2. Thomas Nagel, "Concealment and Exposure," *Philosophy & Public Affairs,* Vol. 27, No. 1, (Winter 1998). http://www.nyu.edu/gsas/dept/philo/faculty/nagel/papers/exposure.html.

3. Ibid.

4. The formula of the Body Mass Index (BMI) is weight (kg) divided by height (in centimeters) squared. A person of 175 centimeters (5.7 feet) has a BMI of 30 (obese) when he weighs 92 kg (202 lb). He has a BMI of 40 (severe obese) when he weighs 123 kg (271 lb).

5. Craig M. Hales, M.D., Margaret D. Carroll, M.S.P.H., Cheryl D. Fryar, M.S.P.H., and Cynthia L. Ogden, Ph.D., "Prevalence of Obesity and Severe Obesity Among Adults: United States, 2017–2018," *NCHS Data Brief No. 360,* February 2020. https://www.cdc.gov/nchs/products/databriefs/db360.htm.

6. Carl Baker, "Obesity Statistics," *House of Commons Library,* Briefing Paper No. 3336, August 6, 2019. https://commonslibrary.parliament.uk/research-briefings/sn03336/.

7. "Mehr als die Hälfte aller Erwachsenen in Deutschland ist übergewichtig," *Aerzteblatt.de,* April 2, 2019. https://www.aerzteblatt.de/nachrichten/102121/Mehr-als-die-Haelfte-aller-Erwachsenen-in-Deutschland-ist-uebergewichtig.

8. "Obésité: prévention et prise en charge," *Ministère des Solidarités et de la Santé,* September 12, 2019. https://solidarites-sante.gouv.fr/systeme-de-sante-et-medico-social/strategie-nationale-de-sante/priorite-prevention-rester-en-bonne-sante-tout-au-long-de-sa-vie-11031/priorite-prevention-les-mesures-phares-detaillees/article/obesite-prevention-et-prise-en-charge.

9. "Overgewicht volwassenen," *Volksgezondheidenzorg.info,* https://www.volksgezondheidenzorg.info/onderwerp/overgewicht/cijfers-context/huidige-situatie#node-overgewicht-volwassenen-naar-leeftijd-en-geslacht.

10. Cf. Rebecca Puhl, PhD, "Weight Discrimination: A Socially Acceptable Injustice," *Obesity Action org.,* Summer 2008. https://www.obesityaction.org/community/article-library/weight-discrimination-a-socially-acceptable-injustice.

11. Joost Baneke, *Waarom vrouwen zich meer schamen dan mannen—Over psychologie, criminaliteit en cultuur,* (Amsterdam: Uitgeverij Bert Bakker, 2009), p. 227.

12. Jean-François Amadieu, "Comment notre apparence physique influe sur notre carrière," *Slate,* June 6, 2020.

13. Christophe André and François Lelord, *L'estime de soi,* (Paris: Odile Jacob, 2019), p. 147.

14. Stuart Schneiderman, *Saving Face—America and the Politics of Shame,* op. cit., p. 124.

15. Richard L. Sjöberg, Kent W. Nilsson, and Jerzy Leppert, "Obesity, Shame and Depression in School-Aged Children: a Population-Based Study," *Pediatrics,* 116(3), September 2005.

16. Marcel Maassen and Frans Oosterwijk, *Taboe—100 gevoelens waar Nederlanders zich voor schamen,* op. cit., p. 99.

17. Ruth Benedict, *Patterns of Culture,* (Boston and New York: Houghton Mifflin Company, 1934), pp. 27–28.

18. Anne Hollander, "When Fat Was in Fashion," *The New York Times,* October 23, 1977. https://www.nytimes.com/1977/10/23/archives/when-fat-was-in-fashion -abundant-flesh-was-a-thing-of-beauty-to.html.

19. Ibid.

20. Amy Erdman Farrell, *Fat Shame: Stigma and the Fat Body in American Culture,* (New York and London: New York University Press, 2011), p. 10.

21. Ibid., p. 4.

22. Cristy Brady, "Decreasing Obesity and Obesity Stigma: Socio-Demographic Differences in Beliefs about Causes of and Responsibility for Obesity," *Social Sciences,* March 2016. https://ideas.repec.org/a/gam/jscscx/v5y2016i1p12-d64926.html.

23. Nussbaum, Martha C., *Hiding from Humanity—Disgust, Shame, and the Law,* op. cit., p. 200.

24. Ibid., p. 309. Michela Marzano equally points to the fact that being overweight is considered a character flaw: "It is by being thin or by any other form of taking care of one's body that one can prove that one is in control of oneself, while by one's size and the lack of attention to one's physical appearance, one shows one's weakness." (Michela Marzano, *Philosophie du corps,* [Paris: Presses Universitaires de France, 2007], p. 21).

25. Theodore K. Kyle, Emily J. Dhurandhar, David B. Allison, "Regarding Obesity as a Disease: Evolving Policies and Their Implications," *Endocrinal Metab Clin North America,* 2016, Sep. 45(3). As concerns the metabolic factors, in recent years researchers have explored the role of microbiota, the microbes that live in the guts of obese persons, which appear to be less diverse than those of thin people. They are exploring the possibility of changing the metabolism of obese people through fecal microbiota transplants (FMT) (in plain English: "poop pills") from thin donors. (Cf. P. F. de Groot, M. N. Frissen, N. C. de Clercq and M. Nieuwendorp, "Fecal microbiota transplantation in metabolic syndrome: History, present and future," *Gut Microbes,* Vol. 8, Issue 3, 2017). https://www.tandfonline.com/doi/full/10.1080/19490976.2017 .1293224.

26. Robert D. Putnam, *Our Kids—The American Dream in Crisis,* (New York and London: Simon & Schuster, 2016), p. 222.

27. Ibid., pp. 222–223.

28. Craig M. Hales, M.D., Margaret D. Carroll, M.S.P.H., Cheryl D. Fryar, M.S.P.H., and Cynthia L. Ogden, Ph.D., "Prevalence of Obesity and Severe Obesity Among Adults: United States, 2017–2018," op. cit.

29. Carl Baker, "Obesity Statistics," *House of Commons Library,* Briefing Paper No. 3336, op. cit.

30. W. E. B. Du Bois, *The Philadelphia Negro—A Social Study,* Introduction by Elijah Anderson, (Philadelphia: University of Pennsylvania Press, 1996), p. 148.

31. Ibid., p. 161.

32. Ibid., p. 162.

33. Ibid., p. 163. (My emphasis, MHVH).

34. Lexington, "Black America in peril," *The Economist,* May 30, 2020.

35. Ibid.

36. "Schutzpanzer aus Fett," *Neue Zürcher Zeitung,* May 27, 2007. https://www .nzz.ch/articleF6DXS-1.365160.

37. Sabrina Strings and Lindo Bacon, "The Racist Roots of Fighting Obesity—Prescribing Weight Loss to Black Women Ignores Barriers to Their Health," *Scientific American,* June 4, 2020. https://www.scientificamerican.com/article/the-racist-roots -of-fighting-obesity/.

38. Kimberle Crenshaw, "Demarginalizing the Intersection of Race and Sex: A Black Feminist Critique of Antidiscrimination Doctrine, Feminist Theory and Antiracist Politics," in *University of Chicago Legal Forum,* Vol. 1989, Issue 1, p. 149.

39. Robin Young, L. C. S. W., Ph.D., "Fat Shame—Being overweight is often not a choice. Being ashamed is," *Psychology Today,* October 31, 2018. https://www .psychologytoday.com/us/blog/contemporary-psychoanalysis-in-action/201810/fat -shame.

40. Ibid.

41. Marc Ambinder, "Beating Obesity," *Atlantic,* May 2010. https://www.theatlantic .com/magazine/archive/2010/05/beating-obesity/308017/.

42. Aubrey Gordon, "Leave fat kids alone," *New York Times,* November 14–15, 2020.

43. Sarah Toy, "The Next 'It' Diet? Not Trying to Lose Weight," *Wall Street Journal,* January 8, 2022.

44. Frédéric Potet, "Concours de beauté," *Le Monde,* December 20–21, 2020.

45. The Body Positive Movement. https://thebodypositive.org/faq/.

46. Ibid.

47. Ibid.

48. "Body Neutrality: A New Way to Relate to Our Bodies," *Columbus Park,* no date. https://columbuspark.com/2017/03/14/body-neutrality-a-new-way-to-relate-to -our-bodies/.

49. Leigh Weingus, "Body Neutrality Is A Body Image Movement That Doesn't Focus On Your Appearance," *Huffington Post,* August 15, 2018. https://www.huffpost .com/entry/what-is-body-neutrality_n_5b61d8f9e4b0de86f49d31b4.

Chapter 15

The Emergence of New Shame II

Hikikomori: The Shameful Hermits

In the 1990s in Japan a new social phenomenon could be observed, called *hikikomori,* which means literally "pulling inward." The word is used as a noun, as well as an adjective, to refer both to the syndrome and to the people affected by it. The phenomenon was defined as "a form of pathological social withdrawal or social isolation whose essential feature is physical isolation in one's home."[1] The phenomenon drew international attention after the publication in 1998 of Tamaki Saito's bestselling book *Hikikomori: Adolescence Without End.* Hikikomori are mainly adolescents and young adults who are living in their parents' home and are characterized by social withdrawal and self-confinement. Their relationships with other family members are shallow, there is an absence of social activity and a refusal to attend school or to find work. In order to qualify as a hikikomori the person must meet the following criteria: social isolation at home for a duration of at least six months, and—in the long term—feelings of distress because of the social isolation. "Patients frequently describe a sense of relief at being able to escape from the painful realities of life outside the boundaries of their home. However, as the duration of social withdrawal gets longer, most people with hikikomori begin endorsing distress, such as feelings of loneliness."[2]

HIKIKOMORI: A JAPANESE PHENOMENON?

Saito described the phenomenon as a specifically Japanese problem, which led to the assumption that it could only be observed in Japan, where, according to one study, the syndrome had taken on "near epidemic proportions."[3] A survey conducted in 2015 by the Cabinet Office revealed that an estimated 541,000 people aged between 15 and 39 were hikikomori. Another survey, conducted in 2018, revealed that in the age group 40 to 64 even more people, an estimated 613,000 suffered from this syndrome—and that 76.6 percent of these were men.[4] This meant that an estimated total of 1,154,000 people between 15 and 64—almost 1 percent of the Japanese population of 127 million—was hikikomori. It was clear that the phenomenon had taken on alarming proportions.

> In serious cases, *hikikomori* almost never leave their rooms other than to use the toilet or shower. Terrified of contact even with other family members, they feed themselves by raiding the fridge at night when everyone else in the house is sleeping. Conversation is nonexistent. One mother lamented that her son had not talked to her since he was 12 years old, so she had never heard his adult voice.[5]

The hikikomori pass their time with sleeping, videogames, watching movies, reading manga, and surfing the Internet. It is an existence of idleness and boredom. Brian O'Connor's category of "existential boredom" would seem to apply here, which he describes as "a mood that leads us to believe that life has nothing of interest to offer us. At the same time, we don't really know what would interest us. We feel no motivation or capacity to find pleasing activities, none of which are, in any case, conceivable from within the perspective we fall into during this type of boredom . . . the very value of life itself can seem doubtful when we are bored in this way."[6] The question is: what are the reasons of this phenomenon? Is it completely new?[7] Or is it just a new expression of an already existing, "old" anxiety disorder, such as, for example, agoraphobia, which is characterized by an irrational fear of open or crowded spaces? This specific kind of anxiety, however, seems absent in the case of the hikikomori. Agoraphobia has always been mainly a "women's disorder": "women constitute 60 to 75 percent of the agoraphobics,"[8] while the majority of the hikikomori are men.

According to Hiroshi, "two key words for understanding social recluses are 'shame' and 'conflict.' *Hikikomori* feel a deep sense of shame that they cannot work at a job like ordinary people. They think of themselves as worthless and unqualified for happiness. . . . Many say that they want to disappear or that they wish they had not been born."[9] Finding oneself worthless and wanting to disappear are symptoms of deep feelings of shame. Many hikikomori one day refused to go to school or work and never returned. For young adolescents the major reason was that at school they were the victims of bullying. In Japan the practice of bullying—in Japanese called *ijime*—is widespread and extremely humiliating for the victims.[10] This practice starts at the beginning of the school year, when a class seeks one or more scapegoats to become the targets of endless abuse and harassment.[11] In the most extreme cases the victims are driven to suicide. A voluntary seclusion at one's home is a less drastic solution for the adolescent in order to escape from those who mock and taunt him. Research by Saito revealed that 90 percent of the hikikomori involved school refusers, who were "mostly excluded in class," which is a clear indication of the importance of bullying in the creation of this group of social outsiders.[12]

HIKIKOMORI AND "NEETS": A GLOBAL EPIDEMIC?

In the early days the Japanese hikikomori epidemic was considered a typically Japanese problem. Hikikomori are mostly motivated by shame. Ruth Benedict had already described Japan as a "shame culture" in her book *The Chrysanthemum and the Sword* (1946). If the Japanese were more prone to feelings of shame wouldn't this mean that the inhabitants of Western countries—considered to be "guilt cultures"—were immune to this kind of shame? However, it soon became clear that the phenomenon was not confined to Japan. It began to acquire a global dimension from which Western societies were not excluded. In 2012 an international study revealed that "hikikomori cases seem to exist not only in Japan but also in other parts of Asia, Australia and the USA."[13]

In the English language an equivalent of the word hikikomori appeared with the abbreviation NEET, which stands for "Not currently engaged in Employment, Education or Training." This abbreviation emphasizes what the person is *not* doing, while its Japanese equivalent emphasizes the person's status as a recluse. This means that both expressions overlap only partially. A NEET is not necessarily a hikikomori. However, society tends to put them in the same basket, because "with . . . the socially withdrawn *hikikomori* and the part-time working *freeters* having been used to highlight a lack of masculinity, work motivation and maturity among young men in particular, it was predictable that the same symbolic meanings would come to be ascribed to NEETs."[14] Being a NEET meant being considered lazy, immature, and not masculine, a condition that was just as shameful as being a hikikomori.

According to a Pew survey, conducted in 2015, there were nearly 10.2 million NEETs aged 16 to 29 in the United States, which is 16.9 percent of that age bracket's total population.[15] In the period January to March 2020 in the UK the number of NEETs, aged 16 to 24 years, was 771,000, which was 11.2 percent of that age bracket.[16] These figures give no information about how many of these are hikikomori, living in seclusion. In Germany one in eight young Germans are reported as suffering from "social phobia," as the phenomenon is called there, but there also the number of the most extreme cases, leading to social seclusion, is unknown.[17] In recent years in France, too, the interest in this phenomenon has been growing. In 2018 a French hikikomori, helped by an editor, even published a book about his experience.[18]

The group of hikikomori in France is estimated at several thousand. Most of them are young men who were confronted with problems at school or work.[19] According to the French pedopsychiatrist Marcel Rufo the prognosis of adolescents with school phobia is unfavorable: "One estimates as a matter of fact that 30% of young people with serious school problems will develop serious psychiatric disorders."[20] Marco Crepaldi, the founder of the Italian association "Hikikomori" estimated the number of hikikomori in Italy at about 100,000 cases.[21] Most young hikikomori start their life as a recluse after refusing to go to school. In an Australian report about school phobia the authors write: "The literature calls it 'school refusal.' We call it 'school can't.' Our children are not refusing to go to school. They are unable to go to school."[22] The report continues:

> It is soul-destroying for families to watch the shell of a person, they once knew to be a happy child, merely exist. In the darkest days, that sometimes lasts for years, the most complex of these children and young people do not leave the house, do not sleep at night, do not shower or brush their teeth, do not engage with other family members and will not engage in health services. They are violent and abusive. They hate themselves. They are guilt-ridden and ashamed. They are non-responsive. They shut down. They talk about dying. Some do more than talk about it. They spend school camps, graduations, Christmases, birthdays in their bedrooms.[23]

An important observation in this report is that the hikikomori do not *refuse* to go to school, because that would imply a free choice. They just *can't*. It is stronger than them. And, once installed in this new life of a hermit, it is extremely difficult for them to go back to normal life. We can see here a similarity with another "new shame" category: the obese. Nobody chooses to be obese. It is stronger than the affected person. And it is equally difficult to go back to normal life—in this case to go back to normal weight. However, the shame experiences of the obese and the hikikomori are different. The obese are shamed *after* becoming obese. The hikikomori are shamed *before* becoming hikikomori. It is these early shame experiences (mostly at school), which trigger the flight reaction, which—in its turn—is a source of shame. Different from the obese, the hikikomori are experiencing *cumulative shame:* first at school, later at home.

SHAME AND DEPRESSION

On July 15, 2010, a community with the title "NEET" (r/NEET) was created on the discussion website Reddit. In 2020 this group had 14,700 members.

One of the themes of this group was: "Is it possible to be bullied so much you have no shame in being NEET?" Below are some of the answers:

- It sucks seeing the people that bullied you become successful.
- The only bad thing about neeting is the fear of it ending.
- I'm tired of being treated like garbage. When you don't have a job people treat you like shit, I'm tired of being treated like shit just because can't get a job, I didn't ask to be here, I'm not strong enough to live in this world, I always felt like I don't belong in this world. . . .
- I always remember the times where I was treated like absolute shit and it pisses me off and ruins my day.
- Being a NEET sucks but being a wage slave is just as bad. I really don't know what to do. As a NEET of 2+ years I'm finding there is very little enjoyment to be had from living most of my life by staying in my bedroom, but I really couldn't care less about being "successful" by society's standard.[24]

Here we can find feelings of jealousy (of former bullies who have become successful), feelings of shame, humiliation, and low self-esteem (tired of being treated like shit; being a NEET sucks), feelings of desperation, seeing no way out (work is no alternative, being a wage slave is just as bad).

THE GROWING IMPACT OF BULLYING

Bullying at school is one of the major causes of the hikikomori phenomenon. This means that we need to have a closer look at the bully, the perpetrator. At first sight the situation seems clear: on the one hand there is the bully and on other hand there is the victim. The aggressive and humiliating treatment of the victim by the bully leads to feelings of anxiety, shame, depression, and low self-esteem in the victim. However, a closer look shows that the situation is more ambiguous. In the first place a victim seldom faces his bully in a one-to-one situation. As a rule bullying takes place in the classroom or in the school playground, which means that there is an audience and the members of this audience can react in different ways. They can actively participate in the bullying, they can passively watch the bullying or look away, or they can intervene to stop the bullying. Research on bullying in the school yard revealed that it occurred regularly, once every seven minutes and was of short duration, 38 seconds. Adults intervened only in 4 percent of the episodes, peers in 11 percent. Boys bullied more than girls and most of the time targeted boys.[25]

Estimates of bullying show that it is on the rise. In a 2008 survey bullies represent approximately 10 percent of school-age children, the victimized children 11 percent.[26] The same percentage of the victimized occurs in a PISA survey of 15-year-old children, conducted in 72 countries, which states that "on average across OECD countries, around 11% of students reported that they are frequently (at least a few times per month) made fun of, 8% reported that they are frequently the object of nasty rumours in school and 7% reported that they are frequently left out of things."[27] However, research in the United States and the UK produced more alarming results. A survey in the USA of students aged 12–18 indicated that 21 percent had been bullied at school during the 2015 school year.[28] Cyberbullying became an integral part of bullying. During the 2013 school year 7 percent of the age group 12–18 indicated that another student had done one or more of the following things to them: posted hurtful information about them on the Internet; purposely shared private information about them on the Internet; threatened or insulted them through instant messaging, text messaging, or e-mail, or excluded them online.[29] This trend seems to be continuing unabated. In the period September 2016–September 2017, 19 percent of American high school students reported that they had been bullied on school property and 7.4 percent had attempted suicide. In a survey[30] conducted in 2019 in the UK, 22 percent of youths reported that they had been victims of bullying in the past 12 months.[31] A German survey concluded that in the school year 2018/2019 more than a third of pupils had been bullied.[32]

Contrary to what one might expect not only the victims are at risk, but also the bullies. However, in their case the risk is different and concerns mostly aggressive and delinquent behaviors, school failure, and dropping out.[33] A special category is the "bully-victim," the victim who, on other occasions, acts as the bully. In this case "bullying might result from activation of a threat schema (e.g., 'Everyone is going to bully me,') which can promote negative self-other beliefs (e.g., 'I'd better ruin her reputation before she ruins mine,') leading the individual to become aggressive in social relationships in order to maintain power and control."[34] These "bully-victims," who play a double role, represent about 6 percent of school-age children.[35] Longitudinal studies revealed that these "bully-victims" almost always start their career as victims: "a pathway from peer victimization to involvement in bullying is more likely than a pathway from bullying perpetration to peer victimization."[36] This category has the broadest range of problems, presenting difficulties common to both bullies and victims.

Of particular interest is the behavior of the peer group—those who are neither bullies, nor victims. According to Craig and Pepler peer bystanders joined the bullies in 21 percent of the episodes and intervened on behalf of the victims in 25 percent of the incidents. However, most often—in 54 percent of the episodes—they watched passively.[37] Bullying can take different forms: physical, verbal, and social. Physical bullying consists of hitting, spitting, kicking, pushing, hazing, as well as hiding, stealing, or breaking things. Verbal bullying consists of insulting, name-calling, sexual comments, and threatening to do harm. Social bullying consists of excluding someone from groups, spreading rumors, embarrassing someone in public, refusing to talk to him or her or telling others not to be their friends. While physical bullying is mostly practiced by boys, verbal and social bullying is practiced more frequently by girls.

CYBERBULLIES

It is clear that bullying is a powerful "shame generator" which can lead to lifelong negative consequences for the victims. Since the emergence of the Internet and the social media, bullying has acquired a new dimension: it is no longer confined to the class room or to the school playground. Bullies can become *cyberbullies* and attack and humiliate their victims online, which means that it is impossible for the victims to escape their tormentors—even at home. They are no longer exposed only when they are at school, but they are exposed 24/7—any day, any time. A report in the UK quotes a fourteen-year-old boy, saying: "I go to school and get bullied. Go home and online and still get bullied. I can't ever escape it."[38] The audience which can witness cyber-bullying is no longer confined to the small group of one's class mates, but can consist of hundreds and even thousands of unknown strangers, which exacerbates the vulnerability and the feelings of shame experienced by the victim. Unlike bullying in the class room, cyberbullying can be done anonymously, which even further increases the vulnerability of the victim. A particular phenomenon is "sexting": adolescents sending nude images of themselves, a trend which is on the increase. In the United States "in 2019, among 12-to 17-year-olds, 14% reported sending nude images, compared with 12% three years earlier; 23% received them, up from 19%."[39] Often this is not the result of free choice. "Things go wrong when teenagers pressure and coerce others, most often girls and younger teenagers, to send nude photos . . . sext-senders are often the victims of harassment."[40]

Bullying is, of course, not a new phenomenon. It existed before. But in the modern school system it has taken on previously unknown proportions—particularly as a consequence of cyberbullying. In many countries this has led to different initiatives. In France, for instance, where bullying affects 700,000 pupils every year (about 10 percent of pupils), a "No to Bullying Day" is organized in schools. In secondary schools pupils can become "ambassadors against bullying" who have the task of making other pupils aware of the issue and act as a reference point for victims. Additionally a helpline has been set up for parents, witnesses, victims, and professionals.[41] France's First Lady, Brigitte Macron, a former literature teacher, is personally engaged in the fight against bullying. In 2018 she accompanied the education minister to speak in a school about the problem.[42] However, it soon became clear that more was needed. In November 2019 the French deputy Erwan Balanant was tasked by Prime Minister Édouard Philippe to write a report and formulate concrete proposals. "We all remember bullying at school," Balanant wrote on the first page of his report. "In the most traumatic scenario as a victim, but equally as a perpetrator, or, in most cases, as a witness."[43] He emphasized that "a quarter of victims have already thought about suicide [and] it is unfortunately not uncommon that they take the step."[44] In his report the parliamentarian mentioned also a subject which was taboo: the role of the teachers. Bullying, he wrote, "isn't exclusively perpetrated by pupils, but can, sometimes, be initiated or nurtured by teachers."[45] He proposed that both the victim and the perpetrator of bullying should be obliged to receive psychological counseling and that bullying at school, like workplace harassment, should be made a criminal offense, punishable by a two-year jail sentence and a fine of 30,000 euros.

In Germany a close cooperation has been established between the schools and the police, based on the application of what is there known as the "Olweus Bullying Prevention Program" (OBBP).[46] Professor Dan Olweus (1931–2020) was a Swedish-Norwegian psychologist at the University of Bergen, who developed the first anti-bullying program in the world after the suicide of three Norwegian boys, who were victims of bullying. The program consists of five elements: engaging adults, setting clear criteria for unacceptable behavior, introducing a consequent sanctions regime, improving surveillance and control, and calling on adults to act as authorities. This program has also been introduced in the United States. A three-year evaluation study, jointly conducted by Clemson University (South Carolina) and the University of Bergen (Norway), which evaluated nearly 70,000 students across 210 elementary, middle, and high schools, found a clear reduction in students' reports of being bullied and bullying others. The researchers found also an increase in students' expressions of empathy.[47] It is clear that fighting bullying is not a task for the parents or the individual teacher, but needs a holistic approach, in which the school and the education system, together with parents, should play a major role. Special attention needs to be paid to the phenomenon of cyberbullying in order to avoid the hikikomori phenomenon growing into a worldwide pandemic.

HOW TO REIN IN THE SOCIAL MEDIA?

However, what about the role of the social media? In September 2021 the *Wall Street Journal* revealed that according to an internal report of Facebook, "Thirty-two percent of teen girls said that when they felt bad about their bodies, Instagram made them feel worse."48 And this was not all. "Among teens who reported suicidal thoughts, 13% of British users and 6% of American users traced the desire to kill themselves to Instagram . . . "49 It is known that suicidal thoughts are shame related. The findings of the internal report were not made public by Facebook, but by Frances Haugen, a whistleblower, who, as a former Facebook employee, participated in the research. Instagram is a photo and video-sharing app, acquired by Facebook in 2012 for $1 billion to boost its access to teen users. Instagram resembles Snapchat, another photo and video-sharing app, but, unlike the latter, which focuses on the face, Instagram focuses on the whole body. Particularly young girls are victims. "We make body image issues worse for one in three girls," said one internal Facebook slide from 2019."50 But boys also are not immune: "14% of boys in the U.S. said Instagram made them feel worse about themselves."51 Feelings of malaise could lead to depression, and—in the worst cases—to suicide or attempted suicide. "Suicide . . . ," wrote Micha Hilgers, "is the consequent and sadistic destruction of the despised sources of shame in the self and of the unbearable stains and defects of one's own person."52

One would think that these revelations would have led to some soul searching at Facebook. However, the contrary seems to be the case. Senators who asked questions did not get clear answers and Facebook refused to make the research results public. Senator Richard Blumenthal (D-CT) said: "Facebook seems to be taking a page from the textbook of Big Tobacco—targeting teens with potentially dangerous products while masking the science in public."53 Also the whistleblower accused Facebook of not willing to protect the public from harm.54 A public debate on the role of the social media is long overdue—even more so because Facebook is working on a controversial new app, called "Instagram Kids," for a target audience of ten- to twelve-year-olds.55 Facebook was temporarily putting a hold on these plans, without, however, abandoning them. Critics called for firm measures, writing that "it is up to the lawmakers to act and act hard, since there is no countervailing power to Facebook except a government."56 Others argued that Instagram should just be for adults, writing that "a 14-year-old has no more constitutional right to use Instagram than she has a constitutional right to purchase a fifth of Hennessy, and strong limits on teenage access to various substances and products are a normal feature of liberal society. . . . "57

Facebook and Instagram are only two among many online "shame genera-tors." Video games are another online circuit where hate groups are active. "A 2020 Anti-Defamation League survey found that 68 percent of online gamers experienced severe harassment. Fifty-three percent of respondents said they were harassed based on 'race/ethnicity, religion, ability status, gender or sexual orientation'; and 51 percent received threats of violence."[58] Another popular medium is the video-sharing platform TikTok, owned by the Chinese firm ByteDance. Since its launch in 2016 it has become a serious competi-tor of Facebook and Instagram. American children aged between 4 and 15 spent in 2020 an average of 87 minutes per day on TikTok, compared with 17 minutes on Facebook.[59] Although TikTok touts its successful protection from harmful content, the reality seems to be different. "Last year the Intercept, a news site, published Chinese moderation documents, revealing a preference to filter out users with "ugly facial looks," "beer belly" and content that risked "endangering . . . national honour and interests," while "teenage girls have been targeted with adverts about intermittent fasting."[60] Not only Instagram reinforces negative thoughts about body image among teenage girls. "A simi-lar culture flourishes on TikTok too. There are currently 8.8bn total views on videos tagged #whatIeatinaday, a viral trend where mostly young girls docu-ment their food diaries, some of which include undereating."[61]

Are the social media able to moderate online content and remove hate speech and misinformation, as they pretend? One may doubt it. According to internal Facebook documents, provided by whistleblower Frances Haugen, "Facebook has actively worked to expand the size of its young adult audi-ence even as internal research suggests its platforms, particularly Instagram, can have a negative effect on their mental health and well-being."[62] And even if they would be willing to moderate, they don't seem to be capable to do so, because, as the French paper *le Monde,* which had access to the docu-ments, wrote: "Many passages from the thousands of pages of the internal documents . . . seem to indicate that Facebook does no longer understand, or badly understands, what their own algorithms do. And that its social net-work has become a machine which is difficult to control."[63] It is, therefore, high time that governments take their responsibility and—together with civil society—take steps to reduce the negative impact of the social media on the young generation.

NOTES

1. Takahiro A. Kato, Shigenobu Kanba, Alan R. Teo, "Defining pathological social withdrawal: proposed diagnostic criteria for hikikomori," *World Psychiatry,* 19:1, February 2020, p. 116. https://onlinelibrary.wiley.com/doi/epdf/10.1002/wps.20705.

2. Ibid.

3. Yuichi Hattori, "Social Withdrawal in Japanese Youth: A Case Study of Thirty-Five Clients," *Journal of Trauma Practice,* Vol. 4, 2006, Issue 3–4.

4. Andrew McKirdy, "The prison inside: Japan's hikikomori lack relationships, not physical spaces," *Japan Times,* June 1, 2019. https://www.japantimes.co.jp/life/2019 /06/01/lifestyle/prison-inside-japans-hikikomori-lack-relationships-not-physical -spaces/#.XvG1lJozbIU.

5. Sekiguchi Hiroshi, "Islands of Solitude: A Psychiatrist's View of the 'Hikikomori'," *Nippon.com,* December 13, 2017. https://www.nippon.com/en/column/ g00455/.

6. Brian O'Connor, *Idleness—A Philosophical Essay,* (Princeton and Oxford: Princeton University Press, 2018), p. 107.

7. The phenomenon, as such, may have existed before. The French artist Christian Boltanski (born in 1944), said, for instance, in an interview that as a child he was "incapable, almost ill, mentally. I left school when I was 12–13 years old and even before I practically never went there, I escaped every time." His parents accepted that he stayed at home. "I went out into the street for the first time when I was 18 years old. I passed my days doing nothing, painting, counting the cars that passed by." Here, too, there is a background of bullying. "At school they called me "little rabbi." (Boltanski had a Jewish Ukrainian father). However, in the 1950s–1960s this behavior was extremely rare. ("Christian Boltanski 'Je ne crois pas beaucoup à la normalité'" Interview with Denis Cosnard, *Le Monde,* January 5–6, 2020).

8. Abram de Swaan, "Uitgaansbeperking en uitgaansangst: over de verschuiving van bevelshuishouding naar onderhandelingshuishouding," in *De Draagbare De Swaan,* op. cit., p. 163.

9. Sekiguchi Hiroshi, "Islands of Solitude: A Psychiatrist's View of the 'Hikikomori'," op. cit.

10. Heinz Kohut writes that "the tendency of the Japanese to react with narcissistic rage, for instance, is attributed by Ruth Benedict (1946) to the Japanese child rearing method which ridicules and threatens with ostracism, as well as to the socio-cultural meaning of upholding decorum." (Heinz Kohut, "Überlegungen zum Narzißmus und zur narzißtischen Wut," in Heinz Kohut, *Die Zukunft der Psychoanalyse,* op. cit., p. 228). The tendency of the victims of bullying to react with narcissistic rage can in fact be observed in the United States, where, for instance, the Columbine High School Shooting in April 1999 was an act of revenge by the victims against their bullies. In Japan the victims seem to acquiesce in their situation of shame.

11. Thomas Messias, "Hikikomori: la vie cloîtrée des ados en retrait," *Slate,* March 15, 2015. http://www.slate.fr/story/98961/hikikomori.

12. Hisao Ikeya, "Jungenprobleme im heutigen Japan—'Gewaltkultur' und soziale Exklusion in Schule und Familie," in Jürgen Budde and Ingelore Mammes (eds), *Jungenforschung empirisch—Zwischen Schule, männlichem Habitus und Peerkultur,* (Wiesbaden: VS Verlag für Sozialwissenschaften/GWV Fachverlage GmbH, 2009), p. 226.

13. Kato, T. A., Tateno, M., Shinfuku, N., et al., "Does the *hikikomori* syndrome of social withdrawal exist outside Japan? A preliminary international investigation,"

Social Psychiatry and Psychiatric Epidemiology, 47, 1061–1075 (2012). https://www.ncbi.nlm.nih.gov/pmc/articles/PMC4909153/.

14. Tuukka Toivonen, "Moral Panic versus Youth Problem Debates: Three Conceptual Insights from the Study of Japanese Youth," in Charles Krinsky (ed.), *The Ashgate Research Companion to Moral Panics,* (London and New York: Routledge, 2016), p. 275.

15. Drew Desilver, "Millions of young people in U.S. and EU are neither working nor learning," *Pew Research Center,* January 28, 2016. https://www.pewresearch.org/fact-tank/2016/01/28/us-eu-neet-population/.

16. "Young people not in education, employment or training (NEET), UK: May 2020," *Office for National Statistics,* May 28, 2020. https://www.ons.gov.uk/employmentandlabourmarket/peoplenotinwork/unemployment/bulletins/youngpeopl enotineducationemploymentortrainingneet/may2020.

17. Nora Stifter, "Hikikomori: Ein rein japanisches Phänomen?" *Goethe Institut Japan,* no date. https://www.goethe.de/ins/jp/de/kul/mag/20720273.html.

18. Andréas Saada with Sophie Vouteau, *En retrait du monde, je suis un hikikomori,* (Paris: Éditions Pygmalion, 2018).

19. Virginie Skrzyniarz, "Reclus et sans projet: qui sont les Hikikomori français?" *L'Express,* February 3, 2019. https://www.lexpress.fr/actualite/societe/reclus-et-sans-projet-qui-sont-les-hikikomori-francais_2050894.html.

20. Marcel Rufo and Marie Choquet, *regards croisés sur l'adolescence—son évolution, sa diversité,* (Paris: Éditions Anne Carrière, 2007), p. 349.

21. Marco Crepaldi, "Chi soni gli hikikomori?" *Hikikomori Italia.* https://www.hikikomoriitalia.it/p/chi-sono-gli-hikikomori.html.

22. "When it's not OK not to be OK—Victoria's invisible mental health and education crisis," School phobia / school refusal Australia—Submission to Victoria's Royal Commission into Mental Health Services, no date. https://s3.ap-southeast-2.amazonaws.com/hdp.au.prod.app.vic-rcvmhs.files/3015/7059/3251/School_Refusal_Australia.pdf.

23. Ibid.

24. Reddit. https://www.reddit.com/r/NEET/comments/7dlia1/is_it_possible_to_be_bullied_so_much_you_have_no/ (Accessed June 24, 2020).

25. Wendy H. Craig and Debra J. Pepler, "Observations of bullying and victimization in the school yard," *Canadian Journal of School Psychology,* Vol. 13, Issue 2, June 1, 1998. https://journals.sagepub.com/doi/abs/10.1177/082957359801300205.

26. E. D. Barker, L. Arseneault, M. Brendgen, N. Fontaine, and B. Maugham, "Joint Development of Bullying and Victimization in Adolescence: Relations to Delinquency and Self-Harm," *Journal of the American Academy of Child & Adolescence Psychiatry,* 47 (9), 2008. http://www.louise-arseneault.com/CMSUploads/2008-Joint-Develepment-of-Bullying-and-Victimisation.pdf.

27. "PISA 2015 Results (Volume III) *Students' Well-Being,* PISA, OECD Publishing, Paris, April 19, 2017, p. 135. https://read.oecd-ilibrary.org/education/pisa-2015-results-volume-iii_9789264273856-en.

28. Dan Olweus, Susan P. Limber, Kyrre Breivik, "Addressing Specific Forms of Bullying: A Long-Scale Evaluation of the Olweus Bullying Prevention Program,"

International Journal of Bullying Prevention, 1 (2019), March 11, 2019. https://link .springer.com/article/10.1007/s42380-019-00009-7#citeas.

29. Ibid.

30. "Youth Risk Behavior Surveillance—United States, 2017," *Centers for Disease Control and Prevention,* Surveillance Summaries, Vol. 67, No. 8, June 15, 2018. https://www.cdc.gov/healthyyouth/data/yrbs/pdf/2017/ss6708.pdf.

31. "The Annual Bullying Survey 2019," *Ditch the Label,* November 2019. https: //www.ditchthelabel.org/wp-content/uploads/2020/05/The-Annual-Bullying-Survey -2019-1-2.pdf.

32. "DAK-Gesundheit, Präventionsradar, Kinder-und Jugendgesundheit in Schulen, Erhebung Schuljahr 18/19," *Institut für Therapie-und Gesundheitsforschung IFT-Nord,* Kiel 2019, p. 26.

33. E. D. Barker, L. Arseneault, M. Brendgen, N. Fontaine, and B. Maugham, "Joint Development of Bullying and Victimization in Adolescence: Relations to Delinquency and Self-Harm," op. cit.

34. Susan Swearer and Shelley Hymel, "Understanding the Psychology of Bullying—Moving Toward a Social-Ecological Diathesis-Stress Model," *American Psychologist,* Vol. 70, No. 4, May-June 2015, p. 349. https://www.apa.org/pubs/ journals/releases/amp-a0038929.pdf.

35. E. D. Barker, L. Arseneault, M. Brendgen, N. Fontaine, and B. Maugham, "Joint Development of Bullying and Victimization in Adolescence: Relations to Delinquency and Self-Harm," op. cit.

36. John D. Haltigan and Tracy Vaillancourt, "Joint Trajectories of Bullying and Peer Victimization across Elementary and Middle School and Associations with Symptoms of Psychopathology," *Development Psychology,* 50 (11), November 2014. https://pubmed.ncbi.nlm.nih.gov/25313592/.

37. Wendy H. Craig and Debra J. Pepler, "Observations of bullying and victimization in the school yard," op. cit.

38. "Bullying: Fifth of young people in UK have been victims in past year-report," *BBC,* November 11, 2019. https://www.bbc.com/news/uk-50370667.

39. "Sharing and not caring," *The Economist,* March 28, 2020.

40. Ibid.

41. Jane Hanks, "Speak out! . . . and help stop bullying," *Connexion France,* November 9, 2017. https://www.connexionfrance.com/French-news/Speak-out!-and -help-stop-bullying.

42. Caroline Beyer, "Brigitte Macron mobilisée contre le harcèlement à l'école," *Le Figaro,* March 6, 2018.

43. Quoted in Mattea Battaglia and Mariama Darame, "120 propositions contre le harcèlement scolaire," *Le Monde,* October 14, 2020.

44. Ibid.

45. Ibid.

46. "Gewalt an Schulen," *Polizeiliche Kriminalprävention der Länder und des Bundes.* (no date). https://www.polizei-beratung.de/themen-und-tipps/ jugendkriminalitaet/gewalt-an-schulen/.

47. Michael Staton, "The largest study of bullying prevention in U.S. schools reveals positive impact," *Clemson World,* September 27, 2018. https://clemson.world /the-largest-study-of-bullying-prevention-in-u-s-schools-reveals-positive-impact/.

48. Georgia Wells, Jeff Horwitz, and Deepa Seetharaman, "Facebook Knows Instagram Is Toxic for Teen Girls, Its Research Shows," *Wall Street Journal,* September 15, 2021.

49. Ibid.

50. Ibid.

51. Ibid.

52. Micha Hilgers, *Scham—Gesichter eines Affekts,* (Göttingen: Vandenhoeck & Ruprecht, 1997), p. 36.

53. Dan Milmo, "Mark Zuckerberg hits back at Facebook whistleblower claims," *Guardian,* October 6, 2021.

54. Dan Milmo, "Facebook boss 'not willing to protect public from harm,'" *Guardian,* October 24, 2021.

55. Greg Bensinger, "Facebook's strategies to hook kids are dangerous," *New York Times,* October 5, 2021.

56. Kara Swisher, "Will Facebook finally pay for its toxic policies?" *New York Times,* October 7, 2021.

57. Ross Douthat, "Instagram should just be for adults," *New York Times,* September 29, 2021.

58. Misha Valencia, "Protecting your child from online hate," *New York Times,* September 21, 2021.

59. "Devious licks," *Economist,* October 23, 2021.

60. Ibid.

61. Ibid.

62. Tara Subramaniam, "The Facebook Papers—The big takeaways from the Facebook Papers," *CNN Business,* October 26, 2021.

63. Damien Leloup and Alexandre Piquard, "Chez Facebook, un algorithme qui échappe au contrôle de ses créateurs," *Le Monde,* October 27, 2021.

Conclusion

RESPECT: WHAT IS IT AND TO WHOM DO WE OWE IT?

In 1967 the African American singer Aretha Franklin sang a song, titled "Respect," which soon became an international top hit. The year 1967 was a crucial year in the civil rights movement which shook the United States. The singer, an African American woman, is singing about a woman who demands respect from her partner. However, it is not difficult to recognize the deeper message of the text: it is the African American community which is demanding respect from the white population.

SELF-ESTEEM AND SELF-RESPECT

The reverse of respect is contempt. Axel Honneth mentions three kinds of contempt. The first, and worst kind is a violation of a person's physical integrity. To this belong being raped, tortured, or being at the mercy of someone else. This is not only a question of physical pain, but also of psychological pain, caused by the feeling "of being defenseless . . . subjugated to the will of another subject."[1] The second kind is being excluded from certain rights: "this is not just the violent restriction of personal autonomy, but its connection with the sense of not possessing the status of a full-fledged, morally equal interaction partner."[2] The third kind is being the object of insults. African Americans have been the victims of all three kinds of contempt. Although in the twenty-first century the worst forms of discrimination and contempt have disappeared, the demand of African Americans to be respected has lost nothing of its urgency. But not only African Americans demand to be respected: *each* human being has the right to enjoy respect.

But what does it mean: being "respected"? Showing respect to someone is the opposite of shaming or humiliating someone. When you show respect you recognize a person's worth, his or her value as a person. This value has different aspects. In the first place there is the value the person has in his own eyes, compared with the value of others. This is commonly called *self-esteem*. In hierarchical, feudal societies this self-esteem is preordained by the class structure. Feudal lords, who are at the top of the social pyramid, have high self-esteem, while the serfs who are at the bottom, tend to have low self-esteem. Konstantin Levin, an aristocrat who is one of the main characters of Tolstoy's novel *Anna Karenina,* claims this aristocratic self-esteem with the following words:

> No, excuse me, but I consider myself and other people like me to be aristocrats who can point to three or four honest generations going back in their family, who are in the highest degree educated (talent and intelligence are another matter), who have never demeaned themselves before anyone and never depended on anyone for anything, which is how my father and my grandfather lived.[3]

The self-esteem of this nobleman is based on dynasty—the fact of being the representative and heir of an honorable bloodline. Konstantin Levin mentions also other characteristics of the aristocrat: his economic independence and his education, although he—rightly—doesn't claim that a good education is a guarantee for having talent or intellect. Note that this nobleman's self-esteem does not depend on work. In the 19th century Russian aristocratic society physical work is done by serfs. In our modern society the class structure has become more fluid. Self-esteem is no longer preordained by one's position in a fixed and immutable class system, but has become more flexible. Self-esteem is based on comparison with others and in a democratic society in which the citizens are political equals the competition for self-esteem is extremely fierce: one can boost one's own self-esteem not only by having a good opinion of oneself, but also by contempt for others.

Normally it is those who occupy positions of higher prestige who look down on those with lower social prestige. However, this is not always necessarily so. William Miller, for instance, draws attention to the phenomenon of "upward contempt," which, according to him, is "the contempt teenagers have for adults, women for men, servants for masters, workers for bosses, Jews for Christians, blacks for whites, the uneducated for the educated, and so on."[4] He gives the example of a builder whom he hired to do some work in his house. "He was a large beefy man," he writes, "with several tattoos of the conventional sort: dragons, Vikings, and other over-muscled comicbook-like figures. His jeans were worn low so that when he bent over his rear fissure . . . was exposed." Miller continues: "The mason said to my wife,

'He a teacher?' The failure of the 'is' to introduce that question captures only some of the contemptuousness of his tone."[5] "He and I each have no small amount of contempt for the other," wrote Miller.[6] It was *mutual* contempt: on the one hand the contempt of the worker for the unphysical, skinny, bespectacled, intellectual "egghead" and on the other hand the contempt of the intellectual for the vulgar, beefy, tattooed worker. Self-esteem is a question of competition, it has to do with keeping one's rank, "keeping up with the Joneses," and—if possible—outranking them.

A quite different way to assess one's worth, however, is *self-respect.* Self-respect is something that digs deeper into the self. It is no longer about one's rank in society's pecking order, but about one's deeper aspirations and deeper values and how far one's life reflects these aspirations and values. Unlike self-esteem, which is influenced by the esteem one receives from others, self-respect is not dependent on the judgment of other people. The principle of self-respect is: "I respect myself not with reference to other people but with reference to a standard."[7] This means that "the practice of respecting oneself isn't a competitive practice. Once we know what the norm is, we measure ourselves against that. . . . "[8] We, ourselves, are the sole judges and arbiters of our self-respect. Self-respect, therefore, has less to do with superficial attributes of property, beauty, rank, fame, and class, than with moral character, with being a *mensch:* being someone with an independent way of thinking who makes the right existential choices, eventually swimming against the tide if necessary. We may assume, for instance, that General De Gaulle, who certainly had high self-esteem, also had a high level of self-respect, which allowed him in June 1940 to ignore the French government's imminent decision to sign an armistice with Nazi Germany and to continue the war by organizing the Free French from London. Rosa Parks, the black woman, who, in 1955, in Montgomery, Alabama, refused to relinquish her seat on the bus to a white person and became an icon of the civil rights movement, is another example. But one doesn't need to be a hero to have self-respect. It is rather a question of integrity and dignity. Even an enslaved person can have self-respect, as Michael Walzer reminds us, writing that "the philosopher slave Epictetus measured himself by his conception of humanity and sustained his self-respect."[9] A snob, on the contrary, who is overly obsessed with his self-esteem and seeks at any price to be friends with celebrities, rich people, and people of high standing, looking down on anyone he considers inferior, is likely to be an opportunist with low real self-respect. Self-respect, therefore, is in principle a more "democratic" good than self-esteem: it is in principle available to everyone, independent of one's position on the social ladder.

APPRAISAL RESPECT: RESPECT FOR WHOM?

In the case of self-respect we are our own judge and jury. However it is different in the case of respect. Here it is others who are the judges. They are the ones who, in the way they treat us, express their opinion about our person. Stephen Darwall has emphasized rightly that there are two different kinds of respect: *appraisal respect* and *recognition respect*.[10] The first, an appraisal, is a positive assessment of the qualities of the other. The second is the basic respect that should be granted to all human beings without exception. Appraisal respect, unlike recognition respect, is very selective. One can ascribe to someone one or more qualities, while admitting that he or she lacks other qualities. An example of this is the judgment "He is an excellent tennis player and comes from a good family, but he was a dunce at school." In this sentence respect is paid to only some aspects of the person: the fact that he is an excellent tennis player and comes from a good family. One can respect a person for his personal qualities or for the position he occupies. Respect for the one does not have to coincide with the other. One can respect the position of a prime minister, while holding the person who occupies this position in contempt. Appraisal respect is a scarce good and it is always fragile, because it is others who decide whether one is worthy of it.

In his book *Respect in a World of Inequality* Richard Sennett tries to develop criteria for appraisal respect. He mentions three. In the first place the respect one earns through developing one's abilities and skills. "The highly intelligent person who wastes a talent does not command respect," he writes, "someone less gifted working to the limits of his or her ability does. Self-development becomes a source of social esteem. . . . "[11] The second source of respect lies in care of the self: "learning how to regulate the body's pleasures and pains" which facilitates "not becoming a burden upon others, so that the needy adult incurs shame, the self-sufficient person earns respect."[12] Finally, the third way to earn respect is "to give back to others."[13] Sennett calls this "the most universal, timeless, and deepest source of esteem for one's character," which he distinguishes from the second, because "the self-sufficient person is ultimately of no great consequence to other people, since he has no mutual connection, no necessary need of them."[14] What is interesting in Sennett's enumeration of sources of respect is the central place he attributes to effort and work. In the first case: "working to the limits of his or her ability," it is the *effort* one puts into one's work rather than the result which is the determining factor. In the second case: "learning to regulate the body's pleasures and pains," he seems to be referring to a moderate life style without excesses (food, drugs, alcohol), which is a precondition for "not becoming a burden upon others"—which means that one can find work and earn a living. One may ask whether these two sources of respect, mentioned by Sennett, are not a reflection of a protestant work ethic, which one can already find in the works of the philosopher Hegel (1770–1831), who spoke about the "workshy" rabble which "doesn't have the honor to secure subsistence through its work."[15] The English author William Somerset Maugham, however, has—interestingly—a quite different point of view.

> We hear much of the nobility of labour, but there is nothing noble in work in itself. Looking at early societies, we see that when warfare was rampant, work was despised and soldiering honoured. Now that the vast majority are workmen work is honoured. The fact is simply that men in their self-conceit look upon their particular activities as the noblest object of man. Work is lauded because it takes men out of themselves. Stupid persons are bored when they have nothing to do. Work with the majority is their only refuge from ennui; but it is comic to call it noble for that reason. It requires many talents and much cultivation to be idle, or a peculiarly constituted mind.[16]

One may interpret Maugham's plea in favor of idleness as a return to an aristocratic ethic which left physical work to the lower classes, but that would be too simple. Neither is it the disdain of the successful writer who considers his own activity not as work, but as a vocation. What about those who are condemned to a life of drudgery and monotonous, debilitating work? Do they deserve our respect only if they put all their effort into it? And what about those who are unemployed or unable to work? Don't they deserve our respect? The problem with Sennett's first two sources of respect is that they don't guarantee that a person with a disability, who is unable to work, is treated with respect. By emphasizing work as a legitimate basis for earning respect, the long term unemployed are implicitly also excluded from being "respectable people."[17] This is a problem. Sennett himself admits this and writes, for instance, that "ghetto adolescents are highly sensitive to being 'dissed,' that is, dis-respected. In places where resources are scarce and approval from the outside world is lacking, social honor is fragile; it needs to be asserted each day."[18]

RECOGNITION RESPECT: BACK TO IMMANUEL KANT

It is here that the second kind of respect, mentioned by Stephen Darwall: *recognition respect*, enters the picture. This kind of respect is completely different from appraisal respect, because recognition respect "is just this sort of respect which is said to be owed to all persons."[19] It is respect to which one is entitled *as a human being*. This respect is based on the idea of a fundamental equality. In the words of Max Scheler, "As a human being, as a living creature, the other has for you the same value as yourself; the other's existence is as true and real as yours; the value of the stranger is equivalent to your own value."[20] This means that this kind of respect is a form of respect to which everyone, without exception, is entitled. And, contrary to appraisal respect, it is also not a question of degree, of more or less: you have it or you don't have it. However, as a human being nobody has the right to deny it to you. In Toni Morrison's novel *The Bluest Eye* this recognition respect was denied to the black girl by the white shop owner: he didn't even look the black girl in the eyes. He did not respect her, because for him she was a non-person. Recognition respect was defended by Immanuel Kant (1724–1804) in his *Metaphysics of Morals*. "Showing respect for a human being as a moral being . . . ," wrote Kant, "is also a duty that others have toward him and a right to which he cannot renounce his claim."[21] Recognition respect establishes also a different relationship between subject and object. In the case of appraisal respect the subject evaluates the respectability of the other person according to his own criteria. In the case of recognition respect it is the other person, the object, who makes the moral claim to be treated with respect *as a human being.*

One might ask: is Kant's position not exaggerated? For instance, should this right to be treated with respect be accorded also to wicked people or criminals? The answer of the Somali-born Dutch-American activist and Islam critic Ayaan Hirsi Ali is a clear "no." "The thing to remember," she writes, "is that people, whether they are Muslims or not, only have the right to be respected if they themselves respect others. You can't deal with human rights and apply double standards."[22] In the same vein Thomas Hill writes that

> It is natural to wonder, *why* we should respect those who refuse to respect others, who blatantly disregard even the minimum standards of a morality of respect for persons. To be blunt, are not some people, as a former colleague would say, "moral garbage," mere "scum" that pollutes rather than enriches life for the rest of humanity? How can we respect such people in any meaningful sense? Why suppose that we are committed to respecting those who have done nothing to *earn* it?[23]

However, recognition respect is not a question of a *quid pro quo,* is not something to be *earned.* Kant's answer was clear: "I cannot deny all respect to even a vicious man as a human being, even though by his deeds he makes himself unworthy of it."[24] A similar position is taken by Martha Nussbaum, who wrote:

One religion that makes me cringe is an evangelical sect that requires its members to handle poisonous snakes . . . I find that one bizarre, I would never go near it, and I tend to find the actions involved disgusting. But that does not mean that I don't respect its followers as bearers of equal human rights and human dignity. Because they have equal human rights and human dignity, they get to carry on their religion unless there is some compelling government interest against it.[25]

BUILDING A DECENT, NONSHAMING SOCIETY

Paying recognition respect to other people seems to be the right approach—not only as an antidote in a society in which discrimination is rampant, but in *any* society whose citizens consider themselves civilized, decent, and humane. Does this mean that there is no place left for appraisal respect? This would be unrealistic. Rousseau had already remarked that mankind is characterized by *le désir de se distinguer*—the wish to stand out. "It is certain, therefore," he wrote, "that we seek our happiness less within ourselves than in the opinion of others."[26] Together with this wish to stand out, people have an urge to judge others. This urge has two sides. On the one hand people need heroes and role models to look up to. On the other hand people need people to look down on. This can take the form of outright contempt. This contempt can take pathological forms, as was the case with Adolf Hitler, who in *Mein Kampf* expressed his disgust vis-à-vis Jews, comparing them with maggots in a rotten body:

> The moral and other purity of this people was a case in point. One could immediately see from their outward appearance that they didn't like water, unfortunately very often the case, even with your eyes closed. Later the smell of this people in their caftans often made me feel sick. Add to this the unclean clothing and the ignoble appearance. All this already made it difficult for them to be in any way attractive; but one was really repelled, when, looking beyond the physical impurity, one suddenly discovered the moral stains of the chosen people. . . .
> If one cautiously probed with a knife into such an abscess, one found a little Jew, like a maggot in a rotting body, often completely dazzled by the sudden light.[27]

Hitler continues his long litany of hate, calling Jews a "spiritual pestilence, worse than the former black death, which once infected people."[28] He described them with terms such as "leech,"[29] and "swarm of rats."[30] Dehumanizing Jews, comparing them with disgusting and harmful insects was only the first step. It was followed by harassment, isolation, persecution, and—in the end—genocide.

Recognition respect will certainly not eradicate contempt, nor put an end to shaming practices. However, emphasizing the fundamental dignity of each human being can have the function of building a protective wall around the individual which impedes his being treated as subhuman. In a time in which the United States and other Western countries are showing a tendency to develop from guilt societies into shame societies the task of fighting shame and humiliation is more urgent than ever. In his book *The Decent Society* Avishai Margalit defined a decent society as "a society which does not humiliate."[31] He is right. "If a decent society is a nonhumiliating society," he asked, "does this mean it is also a nonshaming society?"[32] He replied in the affirmative to this question:

> The shame society has very little to do with the decent society, since the latter is not concerned with the social honor of persons but only with their self-respect. If this is the case, then decent societies can be found only among guilt societies and not among shame societies. Shame societies . . . cannot be decent societies in the sense of giving each person equal respect as a human being.[33]

Margalit emphasized rightly the moral superiority of a guilt society over a shame society. Building a decent society means building a nonhumiliating and nonshaming society in which everybody has an equal right and an equal claim to be respected.

WHAT CAN WE DO?

That said, the question is: what can we do? The development of the modern Western guilt society was not a planned project, it *just happened.* It was the result of a number of sometimes unrelated factors, such as the rise of individualism, Descartes' cogito, Luther's attack on the Roman Catholic Church, the capitalist bourgeoisie liberating themselves from feudal and absolutist rule, industrialization, urbanization, the individualist loner, the Romantic Movement and its cult of the creative individual, and so on. In an analogous way also the progressive transformation of our Western guilt society into a shame society wasn't a planned process, but it was, equally, the result of a number of unplanned events, such as demographic changes which led to smaller families which brought more permissive childrearing methods; the emergence of a new character type: the conformist "other-directed person"; the growth of narcissism; an increase in shaming and bullying at schools; the new phenomenon of cyberbullying; the role of the smartphone and the social media as new, powerful shaming devices; the emphasis on physical beauty; the search for authenticity; the happiness cult. . . . None of these things were planned: they *just happened.* However, this does not mean that we have no choice but to accept this development. When we come to the conclusion that a guilt society is a better place to live in than a shame society we can take concrete steps to diminish the influence of shame. How? Let us consider some examples.

1. In the first place one should avoid introducing public shaming sanctions, as has been the case in different American states. According to James Whitman "American criminal justice has seen the revival of two styles of punishment that had almost entirely vanished from the Western world: public shaming and public forced labor of an ostentatiously degrading kind."[34] Doing forced labor or driving around with a Drunken-Driver bumper sticker are not innocent events, because they stigmatize people. This is the reason, wrote Whitman, why "the Western European media regularly runs pieces expressing shock at the extreme severity of American punishment. Meanwhile, continental [European] justice systems have come to treat America as something close to a rogue state, hesitating to extradite offenders to the United States."[35]

2. Childrearing practices should avoid the Scylla and Charybdis of neglect and lack of warmth on the one hand, and idealization of the child by 'helicopter parents' on the other hand, setting it on a pedestal. Both extremes are liable to produce a narcissistic personality disorder in the child. Parents should adopt a reality-based approach, accepting the child as it is, with its virtues and vices, and not burden the child with their grandiose expectations. They should neither shame the child for its vices, nor treat it as a prodigy, but rather strengthen its capacity for experiencing guilt by explaining the child that its unpleasant or selfish behavior has negative consequences for others.

3. Schools should restrict—and even ban—the use of smartphones.

4. Schools should introduce effective anti-bullying programs.

5. Bullying should be made a criminal offense. A model is the so-called Brodie's Law, introduced in June 2011 by the government of Victoria, Australia, after the suicide of a woman, Brodie Panlock. The law makes serious bullying a crime punishable by up to ten years in jail. Brodie's Law applies to physical, psychological, verbal, and cyberbullying anywhere in the community: at workplaces, schools, sporting clubs, and on the Internet—including email and social media.[36] A similar law proposal was made in France in November 2021, when bullying leading to suicide or attempted suicide by the victim was made punishable by up to ten years in jail and a fine of €150,000.[37]

6. Providers of social media should no longer be permitted to accept anonymous accounts.

7. Providers of social media should improve their monitoring of cyber harassment—a practice which consists of repeated attacks against

an individual with the aim of doing harm; and of hate speech, which involves inciting discrimination or violence against a group. Governments should initiate laws in this respect.

8. Doxxing should be made illegal. This is the practice of publishing people's private information on the Internet (such as home addresses, phone numbers, medical files, photographs, credit card numbers, etcetera) with the aim of intimidating the victims, harassing them, invading their private sphere, or inviting aggression.

9. Hashtag movements, such as #MeToo, which use public shaming as a tool, should, rather than disseminating accusations without (enough) evidence, help the victims of sexual assault to file legal complaints in the courts.

10. Anti-discrimination policies to protect minorities should be more pro-actively pursued, in particular attacking the sources of more hidden, systemic discrimination.

11. So-called microagressions should be challenged making this a topic in school curriculums.

Of course, these recommendations will not guarantee that we will soon return to a guilt society, however they would certainly reduce "old shame" and hamper the emergence of "new shame."

NOTES

1. Axel Honneth, *Kampf um Anerkennung—Zur moralischen Grammatik sozialer Konflikte,* (Frankfurt am Main: Suhrkamp Verlag, 1994), p. 214.

2. Ibid., p. 216.

3. Leo Tolstoy, *Anna Karenina,* (Oxford: Oxford University Press, 2016), p. 175.

4. William Ian Miller, *The Anatomy of Disgust,* (Cambridge, Mass., and London: Harvard University Press, 1997), p. 207.

5. Ibid. pp. 207–208.

6. Ibid., p. 208.

7. Cf. Michael Walzer, *Spheres of Justice—A Defense of Pluralism and Equality,* (New York: Basic Books, Inc., 1983), p. 274.

8. Ibid., p. 275.

9. Ibid.

10. Stephen L. Darwall, "Two Kinds of Respect," *Ethics,* Vol. 88, No. 1 (October 1977).

11. Richard Sennett, *Respect in a World of Inequality,* (New York and London: W. W. Norton & Company, 2003), p. 63.

12. Ibid.

13. Ibid., pp. 63–64.

14. Ibid., p. 64.

15. G. W. F. Hegel, *Grundlinien der Philosophie des Rechts,* (Frankfurt am Main: Ullstein, 1972), § 244, Zusatz, p. 208.

16. W. Somerset Maugham, *A Writer's Notebook,* op. cit., p. 24.

17. According to Brian O'Connor, "one can conjecture that the genuinely idle would be spared the various forms of pain that are held in store even for those who try to make the most of the twinned institutions of work and social esteem." (Brian O' Connor, *Idleness—A Philosophical Essay,* op. cit., p. 3).

18. Richard Sennett, *Respect in a World of Inequality,* op. cit., p. 34. Interesting in this context is the position of John Rawls, who didn't emphasize the importance of work or effort *as such,* but of *meaningful* work. "The lack of . . . the opportunity for meaningful work and occupation," he wrote, "is destructive not only of citizens' self-respect, but of their sense that they are members of society and not simply caught in" (John Rawls, *The Law of Peoples,* [Cambridge, Mass., and London: Harvard University Press, 1999], p. 50). Note that Rawls considered meaningful work in the first place to be important for the *self*-respect of the person.

19. Stephen L. Darwall, "Two Kinds of Respect," op. cit., p. 38.

20. Max Scheler, *Wesen und Formen der Sympathie,* (Bern and Munich: Francke Verlag, 1974), p. 71.

21. Immanuel Kant, *The Metaphysics of Morals,* Edited by Lara Denis, (Cambridge: Cambridge University Press, 2017), p. 226.

22. Ayaan Hirsi Ali, *The Caged Virgin: An Emancipation Proclamation for Women and Islam,* (New York: Atria Books, 2015), p. 73.

23. Thomas E. Hill, Jr., *Respect, Pluralism, and Justice—Kantian Perspectives,* (Oxford and New York: Oxford University Press, 2000), p. 88.

24. Immanuel Kant, *The Metaphysics of Morals,* op. cit., p. 226.

25. Martha C. Nussbaum, *The New Religious Intolerance—Overcoming the Politics of Fear in an Anxious Age,* (Cambridge, Mass., and London: The Belknap Press of Harvard University Press, 2012), p. 119.

26. Jean-Jacques Rousseau, "De l'honneur et de la vertu," in Jean-Jacques Rousseau, *Œuvres Complètes,* Tome III, Du Contrat Social, Écrits Politiques, (Paris: Éditions Gallimard, 1964), p. 502.

27. Adolf Hitler, *Mein Kampf,* (Munich: Verlag Franz Eher Nachfolger, 1933), p. 61.

28. Ibid., p. 62.

29. Ibid., p. 339.

30. Ibid., p. 331.

31. Avishai Margalit, *The Decent Society,* (Cambridge, Mass., and London: Harvard University Press, 1998), p. x.

32. Ibid., p. 130.

33. Ibid., pp. 130–131.

34. James Q. Whitman, *Harsh Justice: Criminal Punishment and the Widening Divide Between America and Europe,* (Oxford and New York: Oxford University Press, 2003), p. 58.

35. Ibid., p. 4. There exists, indeed, a big difference between Europe and the United States in this respect. Saskia Sassen, for instance, stresses the fact that human rights law plays a greater role in Europe than in the United States: "This growing authority of human rights law is particularly evident in Europe. It was not until the 1980s that such law began to exert significant influence in the United States, where it still does not carry the weight it has in Europe." (Saskia Sassen, *Losing Control—Sovereignty in an Age of Globalization,* [New York and Chichester: Columbia University Press, 2001], p. 98).

36. "Bullying—Brodie's Law," Victoria State Government, no date. https://www .justice.vic.gov.au/safer-communities/crime-prevention/bullying-brodies-law.

37. "Proposition de loi (No. 4658) visant à combattre le harcèlement scolaire," *Assemblée Nationale,* November 5, 2021. https://www.assemblee-nationale.fr/dyn/15 /textes/l15b4658_proposition-loi.

Bibliography

André, Christophe, and Lelord, François, *L'estime de soi,* (Paris: Odile Jacob, 2019).

Arendt, Hannah, *The Human Condition,* (Chicago and London: The University of Chicago Press, 1958).

Arendt, Hannah, "The Crisis of Culture," in Hannah Arendt, *Between Past and Future—Eight Exercises in Political Thought,* with an Introduction by Jerome Kohn, (New York and London: Penguin Books, 2006).

Aristotle, *The Nicomachean Ethics,* Aristotle in Twenty-Three Volumes, XIX, Loeb Classical Library, with an English translation by H. Rackham, (Cambridge, MA: Harvard University Press, 1975).

Aurelius, Marcus, *Meditations,* (New York: Knopf Doubleday, 2009).

Baneke, Joost, *Waarom vrouwen zich meer schamen dan mannen—Over psychologie, criminaliteit en cultuur,* (Amsterdam: Uitgeverij Bert Bakker, 2009).

Barnes, Colin, and Mercer, Geof, "Disability: Emancipation, Community Participation and Disabled People," in Gary Craig and Marjorie Mayo (eds), *Community Empowerment,* (London and New Jersey: Zed Books, 2004).

Beck, Ulrich, *Gegengifte—Die organisierte Unverantwortlichkeit,* (Frankfurt am Main: Suhrkamp Verlag, 1988).

Bell, Daniel, *The Cultural Contradictions of Capitalism,* (London: Heinemann, 1979).

Bellah, Robert N.; Madsen, Richard; Sullivan, William M.; Swidler, Ann; Tipton, Steven M., *Habits of the Heart—Individualism and Commitment in American Life,* (Berkeley, Los Angeles, London: University of California Press, 1996).

Benedict, Ruth, *Patterns of Culture,* (Boston and New York: Houghton Mifflin Company, 1934).

Benedict, Ruth, *The Chrysanthemum and the Sword—Patterns of Japanese Culture,* with a new Foreword by Ian Buruma (Boston and New York: Houghton Mifflin Company, 2005).

Bentham, Jeremy, *The Principles of Morals and Legislation,* with an introduction by Laurence J. Lafleur, (New York and London: Haffner Press, 1973).

Berger, Peter L., "The Blueing of America," in Peter L. Berger, *Facing Up to Modernity—Excursions in Society, Politics, and Religion,* (Harmondsworth and New York: Penguin Books, 1979).

Blain, Keisha N., "Civil Rights International—The Fight Against Racism Has Always Been Global," *Foreign Affairs*, Volume 99, No. 5, September/October 2020.

Bloom, Allan, *The Closing of the American Mind*, (New York and London: Simon & Schuster, Inc., 1987).

Bok, Hilary, *Freedom and Responsibility*, (Princeton, NJ: Princeton University Press, 1998).

Breasted, James H., *The Dawn of Conscience*, (New York and London: Charles Scribner's Sons, 1934).

Brogaard, Berit, "Vulnerable vs Grandiose Narcissism: Which Is More Harmful?" *Psychology Today*, June 23, 2019.

Brontë, Charlotte, *Jane Eyre*, (Mineola, NY: Dover Publications, 2002).

Brummelman, Eddie; Thomaes, Sander; Nelemans, Stefanie A.; Orobio de Castro, Bram; Overbeek, Geertjan; and Bushman, Brad J., "Origins of narcissism in children," *Proceedings of the National Academy of Sciences of the United States of America* (PNAS), March 9, 2015.

Cabanas, Edgar, and Illouz, Eva, *Manufacturing Happy Citizens—How the Science and Industry of Happiness Control Our Lives*, (Cambridge: Polity Press, 2019).

Camus, Albert, *La chute*, (Paris: Gallimard, 1956).

Carnegie, Dale, *How to Win Friends and Influence People*, (London: Vermilion, 2006).

Castoriadis, Cornelius, "Psychanalyse et société II," in Cornelius Castoriadis, *Domaines de l'homme—Les carrefours du labyrinthe 2*, (Paris: Éditions du Seuil, 1986).

Cederström, Carl, *The Happiness Fantasy*, (Cambridge: Polity Press, 2018).

Clark, Kenneth B., and Clark Mamie P., "Racial Identification and Preference in Negro Children," 1947.

Cleaver, Eldridge, *Soul on Ice*, (New York: Delta Books, 1992).

Collier, Paul, and Kay, John, *Greed Is Dead—Politics After Individualism*, (London and New York: Allen Lane, 2020).

Cooper, James Fenimore, *The American Democrat*, with an introduction by H. L. Mencken, (Indianapolis: Liberty Fund Inc., 1981).

Darwall, Stephen L., "Two Kinds of Respect," *Ethics*, Vol. 88, No. 1 (October 1977).

De Funès, Julia, *Développement (im)personnel—Le succès d'une imposture*, (Paris, Éditions de l'Observatoire, 2019).

De Gaulejac, Vincent, *Les sources de la honte*, (Paris: Desclée de Brouwer, 1996).

Descartes, René, *Discours de la méthode*, (Paris: Livre de poche, 1970).

De Swaan, Abram, "Identificatie in uitdijende kring," in Abram de Swaan, *De draagbare De Swaan*, (Amsterdam: Prometheus, 1999).

De Swaan, Abram, "Uitgaansbeperking en uitgaansangst: over de verschuiving van bevelshuishouding naar onderhandelingshuishouding," in Abram de Swaan, *De Draagbare De Swaan*, (Amsterdam: Prometheus, 1999).

Du Bois, W. E. B., *The Philadelphia Negro—A Social Study*, Introduction by Elijah Anderson, (Philadelphia: University of Pennsylvania Press, 1996).

Du Bois, W. E. B., "On Being Ashamed of Oneself: An Essay on Race Pride," *The Crisis*, 1933.

Elias, Norbert, "Wandlungen der Wir-Ich-Balance," in Norbert Elias, *Die Gesellschaft der Individuen*, (Frankfurt am Main: Suhrkamp Verlag, 1991).

Elias, Norbert, *Etablierte und Außenseiter*, (Frankfurt am Main: Suhrkamp Verlag, 1993).

Emerson, Ralph Waldo, *Self-Reliance and Other Essays*, (Mineola, NY: Dover Publications, Inc., 2017).

Erikson, Erik H., *Young Man Luther—A Study in Psychoanalysis and History*, (New York: W. W. Norton & Company, Inc., 1962).

Erikson, Erik H., *Dimensions of a New Identity: The Jefferson Lectures in the Humanities*, (New York: W. W. Norton & Company, 1974).

Erikson, Erik H., *Identity and the Life Cycle*, (New York and London: W. W. Norton & Company, 1994).

Erikson, Erik H., *Childhood and Society*, (London: Vintage, 1995).

Etzioni, Amitai, *The Spirit of Community—Rights, Responsibilities and the Communitarian Agenda*, (London: Fontana Press, 1995).

Fanon, Frantz, *Peau noire, masques blancs*, (Paris: Éditions du Seuil, 1952).

Farrell, Amy Erdman, *Fat Shame: Stigma and the Fat Body in American Culture*, (New York and London: New York University Press, 2011).

Feist, Gregory J., "The Function of Personality in Creativity—The Nature and Nurture of the Creative Personality," in James C. Kaufman and Robert J. Sternberg, *The Cambridge Handbook of Creativity*, (Cambridge: Cambridge University Press, 2010).

Florin, Christiane, *Warum unsere Studenten so angepasst sind*, (Reinbek bei Hamburg: Rowohlt, 2014).

Freud, Sigmund, "Das Unbehagen in der Kultur," in Sigmund Freud, *Studienausgabe Band IX, Fragen der Gesellschaft, Ursprünge der Religion*, (Frankfurt am Main: S. Fischer Verlag, 1974).

Freud, Sigmund, "Massenpsychologie und Ichanalyse," in Sigmund Freud, *Studienausgabe Band IX, Fragen der Gesellschaft, Ursprünge der Religion*, (Frankfurt am Main: S. Fischer Verlag, 1974).

Galbraith, John Kenneth, *The Age of Uncertainty*, (London: British Broadcasting Corporation, 1977).

Gewirth, Alan, *Self-Fulfillment*, Princeton, NJ: Princeton University Press, 1998).

Giddens, Anthony, *Modernity and Self-Identity—Self and Society in the Late Modern Age*, (Stanford, CA: Stanford University Press, 1991).

Gide, André, *Journals*, Volume 3, 1928–1939, (Urbana and Chicago: University of Illinois Press, 2000).

Goffman, Erving, *Stigma—Notes on the Management of Spoiled Identity*, (Harmondsworth: Penguin Books, 1976).

Goffman, Erving, *The Presentation of Self in Everyday Life*, (London and New York: Penguin Books, 1990).

Goldberg, Jacques, *La culpabilité axiome de la psychanalyse*, (Paris: Presses Universitaires de France, 1985).

Goudsblom, J., "De functies van schaamte," *De Gids*, 158, No. 5, May 1995.

Graham, Carol, *Happiness around the world—The paradox of happy peasants and miserable millionaires,* (Oxford and New York: Oxford University Press, 2009).

Grayling, A. C., "Free Speech and Political Correctness—What Can We Say?" in A. C. Grayling, *Thinking of Answers—Questions in the Philosophy of Everyday Life* (London, Berlin, New York: Bloomsbury, 2010).

Grayling, A. C., "Plastic Surgery—When is it justified to be doubtful about the value of plastic surgery?" in A. C. Grayling, *Thinking of Answers—Questions in the Philosophy of Everyday Life,* (London, Berlin, New York: Bloomsbury, 2010).

Griffiths, John, "Review Essay: Village Justice in the Netherlands," *Journal of Legal Pluralism,* 22, 1984.

Habermas, Jürgen, "Lawrence Kohlberg und der Neoaristotelismus," in Jürgen Habermas, *Erläuterungen zur Diskursethik,* (Frankfurt am Main: Suhrkamp Verlag, 1991).

Haidt, Jonathan, *The Happiness Hypothesis—Putting Ancient Wisdom and Philosophy to the Test of Modern Science,* (London: Arrow Books, 2006).

Hamilton, Alexander; Madison, James; Jay, John, *The Federalist Papers,* (New York, Ontario, London: New American Library, 1961).

Hattori, Yuichi, "Social Withdrawal in Japanese Youth: A Case Study of Thirty-Five Clients," *Journal of Trauma Practice,* Vol. 4, 2006, Issue 3–4.

Hauser, Marc D., *Moral Minds—How Nature Designed Our Universal Sense of Right and Wrong,* (New York: HarperCollins, 2006).

Hayek, F. A., *Individualism and Economic Order,* (Chicago: University of Chicago Press, 1958).

Hegel, G. W. F., *Grundlinien der Philosophie des Rechts,* (Frankfurt am Main: Ullstein, 1972).

Heumann, Judith, with Kristen Joiner, *Being Heumann—An Unrepentant Memoir of a Disability Rights Activist,* (Boston: Beacon Press, 2020).

Hilgers, Micha, *Scham—Gesichter eines Affekts,* (Göttingen: Vandenhoeck & Ruprecht, 1997).

Hill, Thomas E., Jr., *Respect, Pluralism, and Justice—Kantian Perspectives,* (Oxford and New York: Oxford University Press, 2000).

Hirschman, Albert O., *Shifting Involvements—Private Interest and Public Action,* (Princeton, NJ: Princeton University Press, 1982).

Hirsi Ali, Ayaan, *The Caged Virgin: An Emancipation Proclamation for Women and Islam,* (New York: Atria Books, 2015).

Hitler, Adolf, *Mein Kampf,* (Munich: Verlag Franz Eher Nachfolger, 1933).

Hofstadter, Richard, *The American Political Tradition,* (New York: Vintage Books, 1948).

Hofstadter, Richard, *The Age of Reform—From Bryan to F.D.R.,* (New York: Vintage Books, 1955).

Honneth, Axel, *Kampf um Anerkennung—Zur moralischen Grammatik sozialer Konflikte,* (Frankfurt am Main: Suhrkamp Verlag, 1994).

Honneth, Axel, "Das Ich im Wir," in Axel Honneth, *Das Ich im Wir—Studien zur Anerkennungstheorie,* (Frankfurt am Main: Suhrkamp Verlag, 2010).

Hoover, Herbert, *American Individualism,* (New York: Doubleday, Page & Company, 1922).

Huntington, Samuel P., *Who Are We? The Challenges to America's National Identity,* (New York and London: Simon& Schuster, 2005).

Hwang, Harry S., and Spiegel, Jeffrey H., "The Effect of 'Single' vs 'Double' Eyelids on the Perceived Attractiveness of Chinese Women," *Aesthetic Surgery Journal,* 2014, Vol. 34 (3).

Ikeya, Hisao, "Jungenprobleme im heutigen Japan—'Gewaltkultur' und soziale Exklusion in Schule und Familie," in Jürgen Budde and Ingelore Mammes (eds), *Jungenforschung empirisch—Zwischen Schule, männlichem Habitus und Peerkultur,* (Wiesbaden: VS Verlag für Sozialwissenschaften / GWV Fachverlage GmbH, 2009).

Illouz, Eva, *Gefühle in Zeiten des Kapitalismus,* (Frankfurt am Main: Suhrkamp Verlag, 2006).

Inglehart, Ronald, *Modernization and Postmodernization—Cultural, Economic, and Political Change in 43 Societies* (Princeton, NJ: Princeton University Press, 1997).

Jacquet, Jennifer, *Is Shame Necessary? New Uses for an Old Tool,* (New York and London: Penguin Books, 2015).

James, William, *The Varieties of Religious Experience—A Study in Human Nature,* (New York and London: Penguin Books, 1985).

James, William, "What Makes a Life Significant," in William James, *Pragmatism and Other Writings,* (New York and London: Penguin Books, 2000).

Jankélévitsch, Vladimir, *La mauvaise conscience,* (Paris: Aubier-Montaigne, 1966).

Jauk, Emanuel, Weigle, Elena, Lehmann, Konrad, Benedek, Mathias, Neubauer, Aljoscha, "The Relationship between Grandiose and Vulnerable (Hypersensitive) Narcissism," *Frontiers in Psychology,* 8:1600, September 13, 2017.

Jonas, Hans, *Das Prinzip Verantwortung—Versuch einer Ethik für die technologische Zivilisation,* (Frankfurt am Main: Suhrkamp Verlag, 1984).

Kant, Immanuel, *The Metaphysics of Morals,* Edited by Lara Denis, (Cambridge: Cambridge University Press, 2017).

Kapteyn, Paul, "Het geweten is een modern product," *De Gids,* 141, No. 9/10, 1978.

Kato, Takahiro. A., Tateno, M., Shinfuku, N., et alii, "Does the *hikikomori* syndrome of social withdrawal exist outside Japan? A preliminary international investigation," *Social Psychiatry and Psychiatric Epidemiology,* 47, 1061–1075 (2012).

Kato, Takahiro A., Kanba, Shigenobu, Teo, Alan R., "Defining pathological social withdrawal: proposed diagnostic criteria for hikikomori," *World Psychiatry,* 19:1, February 2020.

Kaufman, Gershen, *Shame—The Power of Caring,* (Rochester, VT: Schenkman Books, Inc; 1985).

Kendi, Ibram X., *How To Be An Antiracist,* (London: The Bodley Head, 2019).

Kernberg, Otto F., *Borderline Conditions and Pathological Narcissism,* (New York: Jason Aronson, Inc., 1976).

Klein, Alan M., "Life's Too Short to Die Small—Steroid Use Among Male Bodybuilders," in Donald Sabo and David F. Gordon, (eds), *Men's Health and*

Illness—Gender, Power, and the Body, (Thousand Oaks, London, New Delhi: SAGE, 1995).

Kohut, Heinz, "Überlegungen zum Narzißmus und zur narzißtischen Wut," in Heinz Kohut, *Die Zukunft der Psychoanalyse,* (Frankfurt am Main: Suhrkamp Verlag, 1975).

Kołakowski, Leszek, "On Boredom," in Leszek Kołakowski, *Freedom, Fame, Lying and Betrayal—Essays on Everyday Life,* (London and New York: Penguin Books, 1999).

Lasch, Christopher, *The Culture of Narcissism—American Life in An Age of Diminishing Expectations,* (New York: Warner Books, 1979).

Lasch, Christopher, *Haven in a Heartless World—The Family Besieged,* (New York: Basic Books, Inc., 1979).

Lasch, Christopher, *The True and Only Heaven—Progress and Its Critics,* (New York and London: W. W. Norton & Company, 1991).

Lasch, Christopher, *The Revolt of the Elites and the Betrayal of Democracy,* (New York and London: W. W. Norton & Company, 1995).

Laurent, Alain, *De l'individualisme—Enquête sur le retour de l'individu,* (Paris: Presses Universitaires de France, 1985).

Lavelle, Kristen, and Feagin, Joe, "Hard Truth in the Big Easy: Race and Class in New Orleans, Pre-and Post-Katrina," in Michael D. Yates, (ed.), *More Unequal—Aspects of Class in the United States,* (New York: Monthly Review Press, 2007).

Layard, Richard, with George Ward, *Can We Be Happier? Evidence and Ethics,* (London: Pelican, 2020).

Leighton, Dorothea, and Kluckhohn, Clyde, *Children of the People: The Navaho Individual and His Development,* (Cambridge, MA: Harvard University Press, 1947).

Lewis, Helen B., *Shame and Guilt in Neurosis,* (New York: International Universities Press, 1971).

Locke, John, *Second Treatise of Government,* edited by C. B. Macpherson, (Indianapolis and Cambridge: Hacket Publishing Company, Inc., 1980).

Locke, John, *Selected Correspondence,* edited by Mark Goldie, (Oxford and New York: Oxford University Press, 2007).

Lukianoff, Greg, and Haidt, Jonathan, *The Coddling of the American Mind—How Good Intentions and Bad Ideas Are Setting Up a Generation for Failure,* (New York: Penguin, 2019).

Luther, Martin, "Ninety-Five Theses or Disputation on the Power and Efficacy of Indulgences," in *Selected Writings of Martin Luther, Volume I, 1517–1520,* edited by Theodore G. Tappert, (Minneapolis: Fortress Press, 2007).

Lynd, Helen Merrell, *On Shame and the Search for Identity,* (New York: Harcourt, Brace and Company, 1958).

Maassen, Marcel, and Oosterwijk, Frans, *Taboe—100 gevoelens waar Nederlanders zich voor schamen,* (Amsterdam: TNS NIPO/Uitgeverij Balans, 2006).

Macpherson, C. B., *The Political Theory of Possessive Individualism—Hobbes to Locke,* (London, Oxford, New York: Oxford University Press, 1972).

Maistre, Joseph de, "The Pope," in Joseph de Maistre, *The Works of Joseph de Maistre*, selected, translated, and introduced by Jack Lively, with a new foreword by Robert Nisbet, (New York: Schocken Books, 1971).

Marcuse, Herbert, *One-Dimensional Man—Studies in the Ideology of Advanced Industrial Society*, (London and New York: Routledge, 1991).

Margalit, Avishai, *The Decent Society*, (Cambridge, MA, and London: Harvard University Press, 1998).

Marx, Karl, *Das Kapital*, Volume I, (Berlin: Dietz Verlag, 1969).

Marzano, Michela, *Philosophie du corps*, (Paris: Presses Universitaires de France, 2007).

Maslow, A. H., *Motivation and Personality*, (New York: Harper & Row, 1970).

Maugham, W. Somerset, *A Writer's Notebook*, (London: William Heinemann Ltd., 1991).

McWhorter, John, *Woke Racism—How a New Religion Has Betrayed Black America*, (New York: Portfolio/Penguin, 2021).

Mead, Margaret, "Third Plenary Session on Collective Guilt," in J. C. Flugel (ed.), *Proceedings of the International Conference on Medical Psychotherapy, Volume III*, (London and New York: Columbia University Press, 1948).

Meyrowitz, Joshua, "Medium Theory: An Alternative to the Dominant Paradigm of Media Effects," in Robin L. Nabi and Mary Beth Oliver (eds), *The SAGE Handbook of Media Processes and Effects*, (Los Angeles and London: SAGE Publications, Inc., 2009).

Miegel, Meinhard, and Wahl, Stefanie, *Das Ende des Individualismus—Die Kultur des Westens zerstört sich selbst*, (Munich: Verlag Bonn Aktuell, 1993).

Miller, William Ian, *The Anatomy of Disgust*, (Cambridge, MA, and London: Harvard University Press, 1997).

Mitscherlich, Alexander, *Auf dem Weg zur vaterlosen Gesellschaft—Ideen zur Sozialpsychologie*, (Munich: Piper & Co. Verlag, 1980).

Molenaar, G., "Seneca's use of the term *conscientia*," *Mnemosyne*, Vol. 22, Fasc. 2 (1969).

Morris, Herbert, "Guilt and Shame," in Herbert Morris, *On Guilt and Innocence—Essays in Legal Philosophy and Moral Psychology*, (Berkeley, Los Angeles, London: University of California Press, 1979).

Morrison, Toni, *The Bluest Eye*, (London: Vintage, 2016).

Morrison, Toni, "Black Matter(s)," in Toni Morrison, *The Source of Self-Regard—Selected Essays, Speeches, and Meditations*, (New York: Alfred A. Knopf, 2019).

Nagel, Thomas, "Concealment and Exposure," *Philosophy & Public Affairs*, Vol. 27, No. 1, (Winter 1998).

Neiman, Susan, *Why Grow Up? Subversive Thoughts for an Infantile Age*, (London and New York: Penguin Books, 2016).

Nietzsche, Friedrich, "Zur Genealogie der Moral," in Friedrich Nietzsche, *Werke in Drei Bänden*, Volume 2, (Munich: Carl Hanser Verlag, 1977).

Nisbet, Robert A., "The Decline and Fall of Social Class," in Robert A. Nisbet, *Tradition and Revolt—Historical and Sociological Essays*, (New York: Vintage Books, 1970).

Nozick, Robert, *The Examined Life—Philosophical Meditations,* (New York: Touchstone, 1989).

Nussbaum, Martha C., *Hiding from Humanity—Disgust, Shame, and the Law,* (Princeton and Oxford: Princeton University Press, 2004).

Nussbaum, Martha C., *Upheavals of Thought—The Intelligence of Emotions,* (Cambridge and New York: Cambridge University Press, 2005).

Nussbaum, Martha C., *The New Religious Intolerance—Overcoming the Politics of Fear in an Anxious Age,* (Cambridge, MA, and London: The Belknap Press of Harvard University Press, 2012).

O'Connor, Brian, *Idleness—A Philosophical Essay,* (Princeton and Oxford: Princeton University Press, 2018).

Oelmüller, Willi, "Schwierigkeiten mit dem Schuldbegriff," in Hans Michael Baumgartner and Albin Eser (eds), *Schuld und Verantwortung—Philosophische und juristische Beiträge zur Zurechenbarkeit menschlichen Handelns,* (Tübingen: J. C. B. Mohr [Paul Siebeck], 1983).

Ogien, Ruwen, *La honte est-elle immorale?* (Paris: Bayard, 2002).

Posch, Waltraud, "Zwischen Schönheit und Schönheitswahn," in Peter Kemper and Ulrich Sonnenschein, (eds), *Globalisierung im Alltag,* (Frankfurt am Main: Suhrkamp Verlag, 2002).

Prendergast, Lara, "The New Narcissism," *The Spectator,* August 11, 2018.

Prinz, Jesse J., *Gut Reactions—A Perceptual Theory of Emotion,* (Oxford and New York: Oxford University Press).

Putnam, Robert D., *Bowling Alone—The Collapse and Revival of the American Community,* (New York and London: Simon & Schuster, 2000).

Putnam, Robert D., *Our Kids—The American Dream in Crisis,* (New York and London: Simon & Schuster, 2016).

Rand, Ayn (ed.), *Capitalism: The Unknown Ideal,* (New York: New American Library, 1967).

Rawls, John, *The Law of Peoples,* (Cambridge, MA, and London: Harvard University Press, 1999).

Reece, Robert L., "The Gender of Colorism: Understanding the Intersection of Skin Tone and Gender Inequality," *Journal of Economics, Race, and Policy,* (2020), March 11, 2020.

Ricoeur, Paul, "Le sentiment de culpabilité: sagesse ou névrose?" Dialogue avec Marie de Solemne, in Marie de Solemne, *Innocente culpabilité,* (Paris: Éditions Dervy, 1998).

Rieff, Philip, *The Triumph of the Therapeutic—Uses of Faith after Freud,* (Chicago and London: Chicago University Press, 1987).

Riesman, David, "Individualism Reconsidered," in David Riesman, *Individualism Reconsidered,* (New York: Doubleday Anchor Books, 1955).

Riesman, David, "Some Clinical and Cultural Aspects of the Aging Process," in David Riesman, *Individualism Reconsidered,* (New York: Doubleday & Company, Inc., 1955).

Riesman, David, "The Study of National Character: Some Observations on the American Case," in David Riesman, *Abundance for What? & Other Essays,* (Garden City, NY: Doubleday, 1964).

Riesman, David, *The Lonely Crowd—A Study of the Changing American Character,* with Nathan Glazer and Reuel Denney, (New Haven and London: Yale University Press, 1978).

Riesman, David, "Egocentrism—Is the American Character Changing?" *Encounter,* August-September 1980.

Ronson, Jon, *So You've Been Publicly Shamed,* (New York: Riverhead Books, 2015).

Rosa, Hartmut, *Resonanz—Eine Soziologie der Weltbeziehung,* (Berlin: Suhrkamp Verlag, 2016).

Rosanvallon, Pierre, *La société des égaux,* (Paris: Éditions du Seuil, 2011).

Rousseau, Jean-Jacques, "De l'honneur et de la vertu," in Jean-Jacques Rousseau, *Œuvres Complètes,* Volume III, (Paris: Éditions Gallimard, 1964).

Rousseau, Jean-Jacques, "Sur l'origine de l'inégalité," in Jean Jacques Rousseau, *Œuvres Complètes,* Volume III, (Paris: Éditions Gallimard, 1964).

Rufo, Marcel, and Choquet, Marie *Regards croisés sur l'adolescence—son évolution, sa diversité,* (Paris: Éditions Anne Carrière, 2007).

Sadin, Éric, *L'ère de l'individu tyran,* (Paris: Bernard Grasset, 2020).

Sandel, Michael J., *The Tyranny of Merit—What's Become of the Common Good?* (New York and London: Allen Lane, 2020).

Sartre, Jean-Paul Sartre, *L'Être et le néant—Essai d'ontologie phénoménologique,* (Paris: Gallimard, 1973).

Sartre, Jean-Paul, *Carnets de la drôle de guerre—Septembre 1939–mars 1940,* (Paris: Gallimard, 1995).

Sassen, Saskia, *Losing Control—Sovereignty in an Age of Globalization,* (New York and Chichester: Columbia University Press, 2001).

Scheler, Max, *Wesen und Formen der Sympathie,* (Bern and Munich: Francke Verlag, 1974).

Schlesinger, Arthur M., Jr., *The Disuniting of America—Reflections on a Multicultural Society,* (New York and London: W. W. Norton & Company, 1998).

Schlick, Moritz, *Fragen der Ethik,* (Frankfurt am Main: Suhrkamp Verlag, 1984).

Schneiderman, Stuart, *Saving Face—America and the Politics of Shame,* (New York: Alfred A. Knopf, 1995).

Schopenhauer, Arthur, "Die Welt als Wille und Vorstellung," Volume 2, in Arthur Schopenhauer, *Sämtliche Werke,* Volume 3, (Wiesbaden: F. A. Brockhaus, 1972).

Scitovsky, Tibor, *The Joyless Economy—A Inquiry into Human Satisfaction and Consumer Dissatisfaction,* (New York and London: Oxford University Press, 1976).

Seligman, Adam B., *Modernity's Wager—Authority, the Self, and Transcendance,* (Princeton and Oxford: Princeton University Press, 2000).

Seneca, "Aus den Briefen an Lucilius," in Seneca, *Vom Glückseligen Leben,* (Stuttgart: Alfred Kröner Verlag, 1978).

Sennett, Richard, *The Fall of Public Man—On the Social Psychology of Capitalism,* (New York: Vintage Books, 1978).

Sennett, Richard, *Flesh and Stone—The Body and the City in Western Civilization,* (New York and London: W. W. Norton & Company, 1996).

Sennett, Richard, *The Corrosion of Character—The Personal Consequences of Work in the New Capitalism,* (New York and London: W. W. Norton & Company, 1999).

Sennett, Richard, *Respect in a World of Inequality,* (New York and London: W. W. Norton & Company, 2003).

Sennett, Richard, *The Culture of the New Capitalism,* (New Haven and London: Yale University Press, 2006).

Shain, Barry Alan, *The Myth of American Individualism—The Protestant Origins of American Political Thought,* (Princeton: Princeton University Press, 1994).

Shils, Edward, *Tradition,* (Chicago: The University of Chicago Press, 1981).

Simmel, Georg, "Die beiden Formen des Individualismus," in Georg Simmel, *Aufsätze und Abhandlungen 1901–1908,* Volume I, (Frankfurt am Main: Suhrkamp Verlag, 1995).

Simmel, Georg, "Die Großstädte und das Geistesleben," in Georg Simmel, *Aufsätze und Abhandlungen 1901–1908,* Volume I, (Frankfurt am Main: Suhrkamp Verlag, 1995).

Sjöberg, Richard L.; Nilsson, Kent W.; and Leppert, Jerzy, "Obesity, Shame and Depression in School-Aged Children: a Population-Based Study," *Pediatrics,* 116(3), September 2005.

Sloterdijk, Peter, *Die Verachtung der Massen—Versuch über Kulturkämpfe in der modernen Gesellschaft,* (Frankfurt am Main: Suhrkamp Verlag, 2000).

Sloterdijk, Peter, *Zeilen und Tage—Notizen 2008–2011,* (Berlin: Suhrkamp Verlag, 2014).

Stanley-Jones, D., "The Biological Origin of Love and Hate," in Magda B. Arnold (ed.), *Feeelings and Emotions—The Loyola Symposium,* (New York and London: Elsevier, 1970).

Stearns, Peter N., "History of Emotions: Issues of Change and Impact," in Michael Lewis and Jeannette M. Haviland-Jones (eds), *Handbook of the Emotions,* (New York and London: The Guilford Press, 2000).

Stearns, Peter N., *Shame—A Brief History,* (Urbana, Chicago, and Springfield: University of Illinois Press, 2017).

Stirner, Max, *Der Einzige und sein Eigentum,* (Stuttgart: Philipp Reclam Jun., 1972).

Taylor, Charles, *The Ethics of Authenticity,* (Cambridge, MA, and London: Harvard University Press, 1991).

Taylor, Charles, *Sources of the Self—The Making of the Modern Identity,* (Cambridge: Cambridge University Press, 1992).

Taylor, Charles, *Das Unbehagen an der Moderne,* (Frankfurt am Main: Suhrkamp Verlag, 1995).

Taylor, Charles, *A Secular Age,* (Cambridge, MA, and London: The Belknap Press of Harvard University Press, 2007).

Tazegül, Ünsal, "Comparison of the Narcissism Level of the Bodybuilders before and after the Application of Anabolic Steroid Cure," *Universal Journal of Educational Research,* 6(6), 2018.

Tocqueville, Alexis de, *Democracy in America,* Volume II, (New York: Alfred Knopf, 1945).

Tocqueville, Alexis de, *Democracy in America,* Translation Henry Reeve, (Penn State Electronic Classics Series, 2002).

Tocqueville, Alexis de, *Lettres choisies, Souvenirs 1814–1859,* (Paris: Gallimard, 2003).

Toivonen, Tuukka, "Moral Panic versus Youth Problem Debates: Three Conceptual Insights from the Study of Japanese Youth," in Charles Krinsky (ed.), *The Ashgate Research Companion to Moral Panics,* (London and New York: Routledge, 2016).

Tolentino, Jia, "The Age of Instagram Face—How social media, FaceTune, and plastic surgery created a single, cyborgian look," *New Yorker,* December 12, 2019.

Tolstoy, Leo, *Anna Karenina,* (Oxford: Oxford University Press, 2016).

Troeltsch, Ernst, *Protestantism and Progress—A Historical Study of the Relation of Protestantism to the Modern World,* (Boston: Beacon Press, 1958).

Troeltsch, Ernst, "Die Soziallehren der christlichen Kirchen und Gruppen," in Ernst Troeltsch, *Gesammelte Schriften,* Volume I, (Tübingen: Scientia Verlag Aalen, 1965).

Trump, Donald, *How to Get Rich,* (New York: Ballantine Books, 2005).

Turner, Frederick Jackson, *The Frontier in American History,* (New York: Henry Holt and Company, 1921).

Twenge, Jean M., and Campbell, W. Keith, *The Narcissism Epidemic—Living in the Age of Entitlement,* (New York and London: Free Press, 2009).

Twenge, Jean M., *iGen: Why Today's Super-Connected Kids Are Growing Up Less Rebellious, More Tolerant, Less Happy—and Completely Unprepared for Adulthood. And What That Means for the Rest of Us,* (New York and London: Atria Books, 2017).

Twenge, J. M., et al, "Age, Period, and Cohort Trends in Mood Disorder Indicators and Suicide-Related Outcomes in a Nationally Representative Dataset, 2005–2017," *Journal of Abnormal Psychology,* 2019, Vol. 128, No. 3.

Van Herpen, Marcel H., "Paris May '68 and Provo Amsterdam '65—Trying to Understand Two Postmodern Youth Revolts," *Cicero Foundation,* May, 2008.

Van Herpen, Marcel H., *Putinism—The Slow Rise of a Radical Right Regime in Russia,* (Houndmills, Basingstoke and New York: Palgrave Macmillan, 2013).

Van Herpen, Marcel H., *Becoming Marx—How the Young Karl Marx Became a Marxist,* (Maastricht: Cicero Foundation Press, 2016).

Van Herpen, Marcel H., *Putin's Propaganda Machine—Soft Power and Russian Foreign Policy,* (Lanham, MD, and London: Rowman & Littlefield, 2016).

Van Herpen, Marcel H., "Early Liberals and Universal Suffrage—Their Fear of Populists and 'Dangerous' People," *Cicero Foundation Great Debate Paper,* No. 19/01, June 2019.

Van Herpen, Marcel H., *The End of Populism—Twenty Proposals to Defend Liberal Democracy,* (Manchester: Manchester University Press, 2021).

Veblen, Thorstein, *The Theory of the Leisure Class—An Economic Study of Institutions,* (New York: B. W. Huebsch, 1922).

Veenhoven, Ruut, *Conditions of Happiness,* (Dordrecht, Boston, Lancaster: D. Reidel Publishing Company, 1984).

Vincent, David, *A History of Solitude,* (London: Polity, 2020).

Walls, Stephanie M., *Individualism in the United States—A Transformation in American Political Thought,* (New York and London: Bloomsbury Academic, 2015).

Walzer, Michael, *Spheres of Justice—A Defense of Pluralism and Equality,* (New York: Basic Books, Inc., 1983).

Weber, Max, "Die sozialen Gründe des Untergangs der antiken Kultur," in Max Weber, *Schriften 1894–1922,* edited by Dirk Kaesler, (Stuttgart: Kröner Verlag, 2002).

Weber, Max, "'Kirchen' und 'Sekten,'" in Max Weber, *Schriften 1894–1922,* edited by Dirk Kaesler, (Stuttgart: Alfred Kröner Verlag, 2002).

Whitman, James Q., *Harsh Justice: Criminal Punishment and the Widening Divide Between America and Europe,* (Oxford and New York: Oxford University Press, 2003).

Whitman, Walt, *Song of Myself,* (New York: Dover Publications, Inc., 2001).

Wilde, Oscar, *The Soul of Man under Socialism and Selected Critical Prose,* (London and New York: Penguin, 2001).

Wolf, Naomi, *The Beauty Myth—How Images of Beauty Are Used Against Women,* (London: Vintage Books, 1991).

Wolfe, Tom, "The 'Me' Decade and the Third Great Awakening," *New York Magazine,* August 23, 1976.

Woolf, Greg, *The Life and Death of Ancient Cities: A Natural History,* (Oxford and New York: Oxford University Press, 2020).

Woolf, Virginia, "Emerson's Journals," in Virginia Woolf, *Books and Portraits,* (Frogmore, St Albans: Triad Panther Books, 1979).

Wurmser, Léon, *The Mask of Shame,* (Baltimore and London: The Johns Hopkins University Press, 1981).

Zeldin, Theodore, "On the Subject of Happiness," *The London Review of Books,* Vol. 10, No. 13, October 1988.

Zeldin, Theodore, "How some people have acquired an immunity to loneliness," in Theodore Zeldin, *An Intimate History of Humanity,* (London: Sinclair-Stevenson, 1994).

Index

About the Author

Marcel H. Van Herpen is a Dutch sociologist and political analyst. He is director of the Cicero Foundation, a think tank, and a collaborator of the US think tank "The National Interest." He is the author of seven books on political philosophy and foreign policy which have been translated in five languages. For a detailed curriculum vitae see http://www.marcelhvanherpen.com/.

OTHER BOOKS BY THE AUTHOR

Putinism—The Slow Rise of a Radical Right Regime in Russia
Putin's Wars—The Rise of Russia's New Imperialism
Putin's Propaganda Machine—Soft Power and Russian Foreign Policy
Becoming Marx—How the Young Karl Marx Became a Marxist
The End of Populism—Twenty Proposals to Defend Liberal Democracy

www.ingramcontent.com/pod-product-compliance
Lightning Source LLC
Chambersburg PA
CBHW022309280326
41932CB00010B/1041

9 781666 914702